WordPress Search Engine Optimization

Second Edition

A complete guide to dominating search engines with your WordPress site

Michael David

BIRMINGHAM - MUMBAI

WordPress Search Engine Optimization
Second Edition

First published: April 2011

Second Edition: October 2015

Production reference: 1231015

Published by Packt Publishing Ltd.
Livery Place
35 Livery Street
Birmingham B3 2PB, UK.

ISBN 978-1-78588-764-2

www.packtpub.com

Credits

Author

Michael David

Reviewers

Alex Bachuk

Marthe Bijman

Cyril Pierron

Ardian Yuli Setyanto

Commissioning Editor

Veena Pagare

Acquisition Editor

Tushar Gupta

Content Development Editor

Sumeet Sawant

Technical Editor

Bharat Patil

Copy Editor

Ulka Manjrekar

Project Coordinator

Shweta H Birwatkar

Proofreader

Safis Editing

Indexer

Mariammal Chettiyar

Graphics

Jason Monteiro

Production Coordinator

Arvindkumar Gupta

Cover Work

Arvindkumar Gupta

About the Author

Michael David is the author of *SEO for WordPress* and a veteran of the search engine optimization industry. He founded the Austin-based WordPress development and search engine optimization firm, TastyPlacement. He originally trained as a lawyer and pursued Internet marketing as a second career. He lives in Austin, Texas.

About the Reviewers

Alex Bachuk is a web developer with over 7 years of experience, specializing in custom JavaScript and WordPress web applications. Alex has been working with WordPress since version 2.5 and has worked on projects ranging from a single page website to interactive web applications and social platforms.

These days, Alex mostly works on single page web applications powered by Angular.js and full stack JavaScript applications using Meteor. His current projects include `http://classmate.io`—a web application for education and `http://timebooklet.com/`—a timesheet-focused reporting application.

Alex also organizes and talks at WordPress meetups throughout New England. He writes about technology on his blog, `http://alexbachuk.com/`.

> I would like to thanks my wife, Oksana, who is an SEO/SEM specialist, for helping with this book's review.

Marthe Bijman is a writer, literary critic, and communications expert, specializing in mining engineering. She has worked extensively in the mining and information technology industries. She holds a number of post graduate degrees, including an MA in applied linguistics and literary sciences. She is the president of Red Pennant Communications Corp. (`http://red-pennant-communications.com/`) She has nurtured a lifelong interest in language and literary analysis and is an astute and prolific reader and literature reviewer. She publishes her reviews on her blog and website, `http://sevencircumstances.com/`. She has been a reviewer on Packt publications such as *Prezi Hotshot* by *Hedwyg van Groenendaal*, *Prezi Cookbook* by *Charlotte Olsson* and *Christina Hoyer*, *Prezi Essentials* by *Domi Sinclair*, and *Mastering Prezi For Business (2nd ed.)* by *Russell Anderson-William* and *JJ. Sylvia IV*. South African-born, she now lives and works in Vancouver, Canada.

Cyril Pierron is a tech-savvy web addict and life-curious engineer. He started programming at the age of eight . He has been working in the field of telecommunications for 12 years and as a solution architect in the e-commerce sector since 2011. He is married and the father of a lovely girl.

Cyril has worked as a technical reviewer on *Wordpress 4.x Complete* by *Karol Król* as well as *jQuery 1.4 Animation Technique* by *Dan Wellman*.

About his experience in SEO, he says, "As a solution architect working in the e-commerce space, I regularly face customers and web agencies' SEO requirements. SEO is a concern for all players, whatever their size, and a subject that inevitably draws a lot of questions. A good understanding of SEO's impact is definitely knowledge that can help anyone involved in website development to improve in their practice and support their customers better. I really hope this book will help them on their path to mastering SEO."

I would like to thank Packt Publishing for giving me the opportunity to work on this book as a reviewer. I would also like to thank Michael David, who did a nice job writing it. Finally, I would like to thank my wife and daughter for their patience in allowing me the freedom to work on all the projects I always get involved in.

Ardian Yuli Setyanto, has played with programming since high school. He joined the national selection for Tim Olimpiade Komputer Indonesia (TOKI, Indonesian Computer Olympiad Team) twice, in 2002 and 2003, which persuaded him to study computer science at Gadjah Mada University (UGM), and he graduated in 2009—the first among his friends—with a score of 3.5/4. He also used WordPress as his essay for his bachelor's degree. Adrian developed his own plugin and combined it with a GSM phone to read and send SMS (text messages) instead of the usual e-mail to manage WordPress comments in his essay.

After graduating from university, he started working as a freelancer using WordPress and Prestashop. Now, he is working as a backend developer using PHP (Symfony2) and Ruby (Rails and Sinatra) at sTRADEtegy (stradetegy.com). Previously, he created a file-sharing website at `www.kajian.info` using Symfony2.

You can read his blog at `http://www.ardianys.com/`, which discusses programming and his beloved family, Niela, Dzulqarnain, Nusaibah, and Mazaya. If you have any technical questions about this book, you can contact him via Twitter at his handle, `@ardianys`.

Many, many thanks and kudos to Packt Publishing for selecting me as a technical reviewer. I enjoyed reading your unpublished e-book. Also, for my new baby, Mazaya, your smile would add new spirit to me.

www.PacktPub.com

Support files, eBooks, discount offers, and more

For support files and downloads related to your book, please visit www.PacktPub.com.

Did you know that Packt offers eBook versions of every book published, with PDF and ePub files available? You can upgrade to the eBook version at www.PacktPub.com and as a print book customer, you are entitled to a discount on the eBook copy. Get in touch with us at service@packtpub.com for more details.

At www.PacktPub.com, you can also read a collection of free technical articles, sign up for a range of free newsletters and receive exclusive discounts and offers on Packt books and eBooks.

https://www2.packtpub.com/books/subscription/packtlib

Do you need instant solutions to your IT questions? PacktLib is Packt's online digital book library. Here, you can search, access, and read Packt's entire library of books.

Why subscribe?

- Fully searchable across every book published by Packt
- Copy and paste, print, and bookmark content
- On demand and accessible via a web browser

Free access for Packt account holders

If you have an account with Packt at www.PacktPub.com, you can use this to access PacktLib today and view 9 entirely free books. Simply use your login credentials for immediate access.

Table of Contents

Preface

WordPress is a powerful and effective open source web publishing platform that enables anyone, regardless of computer skills, to create and maintain a world-class website. Millions of people worldwide have adopted WordPress, and its popularity continues to increase. In February 2011, WordPress.org reported over 32.5 million downloads of WordPress version 3.0. When you combine all the WordPress users that haven't yet upgraded, it's obvious that WordPress is firmly established as one of the most popular web publishing platforms.

Its popularity is well-deserved. WordPress is easy to use, fun, efficient, and, as we will learn in this book, creates search engine-friendly websites.

This book offers a practical, hands-on approach to installing, building, and optimizing a WordPress blog or website in a way that search engines will love. We'll unlock the hidden and not-so-hidden elements that search engines look for when they return search results for their visitors. We'll also look at a wide range of new ways to market your website or blog through secondary channels such as video sites and social media, and we'll learn that WordPress is particularly well-suited for extension into these other channels.

We'll learn about Google's recommended best practices and how to implement the best ranking strategies when planning and executing your web marketing plan. We'll learn to identify and safely avoid a host of forbidden *black hat* techniques that search engines frown upon.

We'll learn the full spectrum of search ranking factors and techniques: keyword research, title tag optimization, link building, site architecture, and more. Finally, we'll take everything we learn about search optimization and learn how to implement it on the WordPress platform.

With the tools in this book and the inherent power of WordPress, you have the opportunity to create a high-ranking website that can compete with any search engines in the market.

What this book covers

Chapter 1, Getting Started – SEO Basics, covers the basics of SEO from start to finish, introducing topics such as on-page ranking factors, how search engines work, and link building.

Chapter 2, Customizing WordPress for SEO, helps align your SEO strategy with the WordPress platform and solidify your plan. You'll need to set realistic goals and timelines for your business or website through educated investigation and analysis. Proper and thorough planning will ensure that you'll succeed even in competitive search markets.

Chapter 3, Researching and Working with Keywords, begins by building a keyword list based on what you have to offer consumers. We'll examine whether it's wiser to focus on a few high-value terms or to build a broader keyword list and rank for a wide variety of phrases. You'll learn how to group the keywords into manageable groups and how to leverage the grouped keywords for maximum SEO benefit.

Chapter 4, Understanding Technical Optimization, covers how to take what you've learned about keyword research and implement a ranking strategy. You'll learn how to build a *perfect web page*: a web page where all the elements work together to achieve maximum ranking power. You will also learn how to craft a domain name that is well-poised to rank for primary keywords. We will examine how to create an effective WordPress permalink structure.

Chapter 5, Creating Optimized and Engaging Content, shows you how to better engage visitors with your content. You'll learn how to write effective titles and headlines—how to grab readers' attention from the start.

Chapter 6, Link Building, covers some general topics in link building such as how and where to get links. You'll learn about PageRank, Google's trademarked and patented process to count the inbound *votes* that we receive as links from other websites.

Chapter 7, Using Social Media, shows you how to harness social media in order to promote your company or website and supplement your search strategy.

Chapter 8, Avoiding the Black Hat Techniques, takes you on a tour through the seedy side of SEOs. We'll examine a wide range of black and gray hat techniques—and why it is imperative that you avoid them.

Chapter 9, Avoiding SEO Mistakes, examines the errors in keyword research that can lead to ranking trouble in the future. We will look at the complex challenges surrounding site architecture and some common mistakes that webmasters make.

Chapter 10, Testing Your Site and Monitoring Your Progress, covers a range of tools with which you can monitor the quality of your website, learn how search spiders interact with your site, measure your rankings in search engines for various keywords, and analyze how your visitors behave when they are on your site.

Appendix A, WordPress SEO Plugins, discusses some of the most helpful and powerful plugins that can help you take your WordPress site to the next level.

Appendix B, Other SEO Resources, provides you with some resources that can help you stay on top of search engine optimization for your website.

What you need for this book

Some prior knowledge of WordPress is expected but no prior knowledge of search engine optimization is required to use this book. You'll need to begin with a working installation of the self-hosted version of WordPress.

Beyond that, you'll need little more than a web browser and your wits. All the tools in this book — including the installation of powerful WordPress plugins — can be accessed through your web browser.

Who this book is for

This book is written for anyone using WordPress, ranging from owners of business sites to website developers and blog owners. Any WordPress user who wants to sell products or services or send out a message to the world will find that getting better rankings in the search engines will help them reach their goal faster.

Conventions

In this book, you will find a number of styles of text that distinguish between different kinds of information. Here are some examples of these styles, and an explanation of their meaning.

Code words in text, database table names, folder names, filenames, file extensions, pathnames, dummy URLs, user input, and Twitter handles are shown as follows: "We can include other contexts through the use of the include directive."

A block of code is set as follows:

```
Disallow: /2006/
Disallow: /2007/
Disallow: /2008/
Disallow: /2009/
Disallow: /2010/
Disallow: /2011/
```

New terms and **important words** are shown in bold. Words that you see on the screen, in menus or dialog boxes for example, appear in the text like this: "You can submit your XML sitemap to Google Webmasters by navigating to **Crawl**, and then **Sitemaps**".

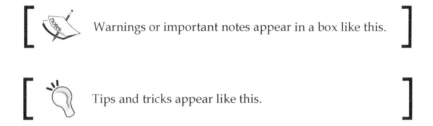

Warnings or important notes appear in a box like this.

Tips and tricks appear like this.

Reader feedback

Feedback from our readers is always welcome. Let us know what you think about this book—what you liked or may have disliked. Reader feedback is important for us to develop titles that you really get the most out of.

To send us general feedback, simply send an e-mail to feedback@packtpub.com, and mention the book title via the subject of your message.

If there is a topic that you have expertise in and you are interested in either writing or contributing to a book, see our author guide on www.packtpub.com/authors.

Customer support

Now that you are the proud owner of a Packt book, we have a number of things to help you to get the most from your purchase.

Downloading the color images of this book

We also provide you a PDF file that has color images of the screenshots/diagrams used in this book. The color images will help you better understand the changes in the output. You can download this file from `https://www.packtpub.com/sites/default/files/downloads/76420S_ColorImages.pdf`.

Errata

Although we have taken every care to ensure the accuracy of our content, mistakes do happen. If you find a mistake in one of our books—maybe a mistake in the text or the code—we would be grateful if you would report this to us. By doing so, you can save other readers from frustration and help us improve subsequent versions of this book. If you find any errata, please report them by visiting `http://www.packtpub.com/submit-errata`, selecting your book, clicking on the **errata submission form** link, and entering the details of your errata. Once your errata are verified, your submission will be accepted and the errata will be uploaded on our website, or added to any list of existing errata, under the Errata section of that title. Any existing errata can be viewed by selecting your title from `http://www.packtpub.com/support`.

Piracy

Piracy of copyright material on the Internet is an ongoing problem across all media. At Packt, we take the protection of our copyright and licenses very seriously. If you come across any illegal copies of our works, in any form, on the Internet, please provide us with the location address or website name immediately so that we can pursue a remedy.

Please contact us at `copyright@packtpub.com` with a link to the suspected pirated material.

We appreciate your help in protecting our authors, and our ability to bring you valuable content.

1
Getting Started – SEO Basics

Welcome to SEO for WordPress! This title is intended to take you through the steps required to make your blog or website rank in popular search engines such as Google, Yahoo, Bing, and more. If you've selected WordPress as the platform for your site, you have made a good choice. WordPress is both powerful and easy to use, and ideally suited for both large collaborative blogs and small business websites.

Even better, WordPress has innate characteristics that search engines love: simple navigation, SEO-friendly URL naming conventions, easy publishing, and more. With the tools in this book, you can take your WordPress blog or site to the next level. Whether you want to increase the reach and broadcasting power of your blog, or edge out the competition in search results for your small business, you'll find the tools and the guidance within these pages.

In this book, we will take an in-depth look into how to apply sound and tested search engine optimization techniques to the success of your WordPress website or blog.

So, let's get started.

In this first chapter, we will cover the basics of SEO from start to finish. This chapter is not intended as a complete search engine optimization guide; we simply won't have the opportunity to cover any individual topic with the depth that it requires. It's more important at this stage just to explore a general overview.

For some of you, these concepts will be a review while for others these concepts will represent the foundation upon which your more advanced knowledge of search engine optimization will be built.

Introducing SEO

Search Engine Optimization, or SEO, is the process and discipline of improving the quality and visibility of a website in order to increase its ranking in search engines, thereby increasing visitor traffic. That's a simple definition, but it captures the essence of SEO.

Webmasters started optimizing websites in the mid-90s soon after search engines began cataloguing the growing number of websites that were appearing on the internet. The term "search engine optimization" is believed to have come into use in 1997.

The roots of modern-day search optimization actually began decades earlier with the original database query technologies of the 1960s. The first search technologies were much simpler than today. A typical database query in the 1960s might search a few hundred thousand records for a specific term, such as, a city name or zip code. At the end of 2014, Google had indexed 30 trillion webpages using 920,000 servers.

SEO can be quite powerful: it can mean the difference between hundreds or thousands of engaged and relevant visitors to your website or nearly no visitors at all. In almost any marketplace for goods and services on the Internet, you can see businesses with top rankings enjoying financial prosperity.

The first 10 search results for a query – the first page of search results in nearly all search engines – is now universally seen as a highly desirable target placement. Indeed, statistics generally show that a very small number of search users ever look beyond the first page of search results; most studies reveal that only between 6 percent and 3 percent of all search engine queries result in a visit to the second page of search results – a meager portion.

SEO levels the playing field. Access to media such as, newspapers, magazines, and television used to be reserved for those willing to pay for the privilege. Nowadays, a small home-based business can compete for new business – sometimes quite effectively – with the largest Fortune 500 company.

Google doesn't care how big your office is, how many trucks your business uses in its distribution chain, or how many high-definition cameras you employ to produce your blog; Google has no way of knowing, and they probably wouldn't care. What Google can do, however, is apply its sophisticated algorithm to the content of your website's pages and the content of the sites that link to you.

There is a common joke about two campers in a forest that are approached by a bear. One camper reaches immediately for his running shoes. The other camper asks, *why are you putting on those running shoes, you can't outrun that bear?* The other camper replies, *I don't have to outrun the bear, I just have to outrun you.* That's how search placement works: you simply need to do a little bit more than the next guy. There is no minimum threshold for obtaining a search ranking other than the threshold established by your search competitors. Do a little bit more, be a little bit smarter, and your rankings will rise.

SEO has several close relatives. **SEM**, or **search engine marketing**, is a broader term that refers to SEO as well as paid search placement, contextual advertising, and paid inclusion advertising. It is also important to think of SEO as including *conversion optimization*—the study and practice of improving the conversion of visitors to customers after they visit your web page.

Always consider that a search engine's core purpose is to deliver relevant search results to a user entering a query.

Older readers will recall using the Lycos search engine at one time, but almost no one uses the service any more. Why not? Because the Lycos search engine didn't return very good results for users. Either the results were not relevant, or the results were diluted with ads. For whatever reason, Lycos was not as good as Google at delivering a relevant set of usable results in response to a query.

It's important to keep in mind the role of the search engine. Too often, webmasters think or say Google is *against* them because Google appears to rank lower-value sites in favor of their own. The truth is the exact opposite: Google wants you to rank—as long as your result serves the needs of its user base. You need to give Google what it's looking for (or Yahoo or Bing, as the case may be), and Google will rank your site higher.

Improving your rank on all search engines

While Google is the leading search engine in the Western Hemisphere, there are, of course, alternative search engines such as Yandex in Russia and Baidu in China. The fortunes of the various search engines ebb and flow, with Google maintaining a commanding lead. Comscore.com is a well-regarded analyst of search engine metrics and reports that in 2014, Google's share of US search queries at about 75 percent, Yahoo at about 10 percent, and Bing/Microsoft at about 10 percent. The remaining field is made up of a handful of 3rd-tier search engines like Ask.com (`http://www.ask.com/`), Blekko.com (`http://blekko.com/`), and hundreds of smaller search engines.

So, how does one rank for all search engines? The answer is easy: optimize for Google. Google's search algorithm is the most advanced, and is certainly the best at detecting disfavored optimization techniques such as keywords stuffing, paid link arrangements, and the like. Furthermore, Google's technology is so dominant that the other search engines imitate most of Google's innovations.

And so, if you rank well for Google, you'll certainly be well-positioned to rank well in the other search engines. Keep in mind, however, that Google is also the most responsive search engine. Google crawls (visits) your site more often, and indexes websites faster than the other search engines. So, as you work on optimization, you might see positive changes in Google rankings in a few weeks, whereas the other search engines might take months to respond.

Exploring the changing nature of search engines

Keep an open mind about what constitutes a search engine. The traditional definition of a search engine—a destination website into which desktop-based users enter typed search queries is already eroding. For several years, Google has been testing, tweaking, and improving its voice recognition system. It was clear early on that Google had already envisioned a day in the near future where search queries would be voiced rather than typed. Sure enough, the increasingly popular Android mobile device platform has voice recognition technology integrated into its architecture. The near future will bring further progress in the types of devices on which users perform searches as well as the input device into which these searches are made. Near term trending shows that we'll see growth in both mobile-based searches and voice-input searches. Staying ahead of trends in search can help you best your competitors in search rankings.

While the type of input device doesn't necessarily change the fundamental nature of search, the increasing variety of specialized search properties does. In recent years, an increasing number of specialized sites have emerged for special-purpose searches. Yelp.com is a destination site for people seeking highly recommended local businesses and hot spots. Dedicated apps like Restaurant Finder on popular mobile platforms help users find restaurants near their current location. Goby is a recent search engine specifically designed to help users find activities in a local area. This is a trend—the first search engines were either directories, single search boxes, or both. Now, there are thousands of individual properties employing hundreds of different approaches to search.

Understanding a search engine's inner workings

One of my favorite academic questions to ask people about search technology is, *when do you think internet searching was invented?* While the exact date is elusive, the answer is nearly always wrong—by several decades. Routinely, people reflect the common understanding that search technology was invented in the 1990s.

Actually, a search engine merely employs search query and indexing principles that were conceived and implemented decades before in a mainframe environment. Indexing, coupled with search queries, allowed early computer operators to quickly select relevant information from large databases in the infancy of the computer age. The Internet is simply a much larger database and a modern search engine is simply a much more robust and sophisticated search query tool.

Preparing the index

A search engine does not store your web pages, it stores an index of your web pages. For your page to appear in a search engine's index, first that search engine sends a search spider to visit your site and read your web pages' content. The spider returns the information to a document processor that processes your web pages into a format that the query processor understands. The document processor performs several formatting tasks—it might remove stop words, lower-value terms that bear little relation to the page's topic, such as *the, and, it,* and many more. The document processor will also perform term stemming, where suffixes like *-ing, -er, -es,* and *-ed* are stripped from search terms. In essence, a document processor trims the content to reveal the contextual elements of a web page and prepares the entry for indexing.

The index contains much of the information from your pages, along with other data that the search engine uses to evaluate and categorize your pages. As a highly simplified example, Google's index of your page will contain the text of your page on a date in the recent past when its spider last visited along with other data which are as follows:

- A table of terms in order of the frequency in which they appear on your page (called the inverted file)
- The page's PageRank
- A term weight assignment: a numerical value that reflects the frequency of appearance of particular terms on a page
- The page's meta tags
- The page's destination URL

This description is grossly simplified, but illustrates that what the search engine attempts to match is not your page itself, but a processed and analyzed version of your page.

Querying the index

Once the index is prepared, the page is available for querying. The query processor, along with a search and matching engine, performs the nuts and bolts of the search function—matching a user's query to stored entries in the search engine's index. The final element is a sound methodology for ranking the query results. If all works as planned, the search engine returns a sensibly ordered set of results to each user's query.

Peeking into the mechanics of search gives us a few guidelines to follow. One core principle that emerges is this—words are the food upon which search engines feed. Without relevant, contextual words on your pages, the search engines cannot accurately index your pages. The other important idea is that a search engine searches an index—it doesn't search your pages directly. So, if your pages aren't in the index, they aren't going to be found. These concepts will re-emerge as we work through the chapters in this book.

Exploring on-page search ranking factors

SEO professionals lump search engine optimization techniques and thought into three categories—on-page optimization, off-page optimization, and conversion. On-page optimization is concerned with all of the text, images, code, words, navigation, structure, and so on that appear on your website—all of the factors you control that appear *on-page*. Off-page optimization refers to all of the material on the Internet concerning or pointing to your website that does not appear *on-page*; for the most part, off-page optimization refers to inbound links on third-party websites. Conversion refers to how effective your website is at making users take actions, once they appear on your site. A high-performing website needs all three elements working together.

On-page factors include the following:

- The body content—the main text of the page
- Title and meta tags
- Heading tags (h1, h2, h3)
- The quality and complexity of the HTML and CSS code that generates the webpage
- The images, their filenames and alt tags

- Text attributes such as the use of bold and underline
- Outbound links—their number and the anchor text used in each
- The use of either dofollow or nofollow attributes on any of the links
- The internal navigation and link structure
- The size of your files and the speed at which your website loads
- The total number of pages on your website
- The rate at which you update or add content to your website

But how important are each of these factors? How do we know that one factor is more important than another? The software or programs that Google and the other search engines use to determine rankings are referred to as an *algorithm*. While the behavior of search engines can sometimes appear remarkably intuitive and almost human, the science underlying a search algorithm is ultimately reduced to complex mathematics.

Weighing search factors

Not all on-page elements are as important as others—search engines must assign particular importance or weight to various on-page factors. A webpage's title tag, for example, is widely considered to be a strong indicator of the subject matter of a webpage. As such, a title tag has a very strong influence on search rankings. Conversely, the filenames of the images on a webpage, such as `texas_web_marketing.jpg`, would not necessarily be a strong indicator of the subject matter of a webpage. So, search engines apply much less weight to image file names in their ranking algorithms. The basket of on-page factors that influence search engine rankings are afforded a wide variation in influence in search engine rankings—this variance is referred to by SEO professionals as *weight*. Title tags and heading tags are afforded greater weight, while image filenames, alt tags (text tags that accompany images), and bold text are given less weight. That is not to say that bold text and image filenames are not important. In fact, it's the use of these lower-weight attributes that can give a webpage the extra push to higher rankings. When all of the ranking factors are present and utilized effectively and combined with a sound program of developing inbound links, the effect is almost supernatural—the combined effect of all factors working together can develop tremendous ranking power.

Understanding the search algorithm

The details of Google's search algorithm are not disclosed to the public. Google's public statements, Webmaster guidelines, and patent filings give us some general insight into the overall approach of its search algorithm. But the details are closely guarded secrets. For example, how does Google's algorithm treat a title tag—how much weight is afforded to this important component of a webpage? Is it 30 percent? 20 percent? Even if we did know, Google's search algorithm is subject to constant tweaking and updating. So, we know that a webpage's title tag is important, but the actual numerical importance within the Google algorithm, we will never know.

So, if the relative importance of different ranking factors isn't publicly disclosed, how do we even know which ranking factors are more important? The answer lies a little bit with the search engines' public statements, a little bit with logic, a little bit with experience, and a little bit by the consensus developed by SEO professionals and hobbyists.

We will examine each of these ranking factors in turn.

Ranking factor – body content

Body content simply means the *words on the page*, actual ASCII text readable by a search engine. This important factor is too often ignored by webmasters. Some of the most egregious examples of webmasters that miss this important factor are sites with little or no text, sites that rely on image files to display text and messages, and flash-based sites. Search engines do not read the text in pictures or effectively read the text in flash files. So, if you are describing your service in an image file, JavaScript, or a flash file, your message will not be read, and you will not rank for those terms.

A search engine needs to be able to find text on a webpage in order to make an evaluation of what your page is about. The text on your pages should meet the following rules:

- **Size**: A webpage should have at least 250 words of readable ASCII text
- **Focus**: A webpage should be focused on a reasonably narrow set of keywords
- **Keyword Density**: A webpage should not have keywords repeated, so that the density of the keywords is too high in relation to the total number of words

A webpage should be of a reasonable length, at least 250 words. A page length of 400 or 500 words is better, but one can get by with shorter pages in some cases. In a more competitive search market, 250 words may not be enough and you'll need to increase your page length to rank effectively.

A webpage's body text should be focused—the page should speak to a narrow set of keyword phrases and not try to cover too much ground. If your webpages cover too many separate topics or keyword phrases in one page, you'll dilute the ranking power of each individual phrase and you'll rank for nothing.

You need to stay on-topic. If you are creating a page describing your expert IT services, don't fill the page up with 60 percent testimonials; those testimonials may have value to your readers—and testimonials certainly have a place and a role in creating websites where your target readers are potential customers—but testimonials will not necessarily contain the keywords for which you want to rank. So, keep your webpages' body text focused on the topic of that page.

Similarly, don't cover too many topics within your body text. For example, say you want to create an Amazon affiliate page on your website and try to rank for *WordPress books*, *Joomla books*, and *books on web design*. If you try to rank for all three keywords on one page, you'll have to divide your content among a discussion of these separate topics. You'll dilute your ranking power for the phrase *WordPress books* by repeating the terms *Joomla books* and *books on web design* within the body text of your page. The better approach is to build three separate pages, each with a focus on one related family of keywords. Conversely, if you wanted to rank for *WordPress books*, *books on WordPress*, and *best WordPress books*, you could create a single page to rank for all those terms because you can easily write body text which includes all those phrases. Your focused page will rank quite well.

Serious ranking power – title tags and meta tags

Title tags and meta tags are strings of text that are inserted in the head section of a webpage. These tags are inconspicuous to a user, although not entirely hidden. The title tag appears in the top bar of the user's browser window, but does not appear on the webpage itself. The meta tags do not appear to the user, they are intended for search engines to read. The principal meta tags for use in search optimization are meta keyword tags and meta description tags.

Title tags are the most important ranking factor on an individual webpage; they are highly weighted by the search engines.

Often, a simple change to a title tag alone can yield significant changes in rankings. Again, remember the role of a search engine to determine the topic of a webpage and return relevant results to its users. The title tag, logically, is perhaps the greatest signpost of what a page is actually about.

Title tags serve another important role, when a user enters a search query into a search engine, the first line of each entry on a search engine results pages are taken from each page's title tag. So, now your title tag presents an opportunity to attract searchers to click on your result out of a field of other websites on a search engine results page. Not only that, both Yahoo and Google bold the words used in the search query within the title tags that they display on the search engine results page. So, if you use keywords effectively in your title tag, Google will highlight your entry in the search engine results page and that can help increase the click-through rate to your website pages.

Making perfect title tags

Keep in mind, space on a search engine results page is limited, so Yahoo and Google don't show title tags longer than 56 to 60 characters. Try a search for almost anything and you'll see that if the title tag of the destination webpage is too long, the search engines truncate the title tag. Keep your title tags to 60 characters or less.

Also keep in mind that search engines measure keyword prominence in title tags. This means that the first word in a title tag is afforded greater weight than the last word in the title tag. Put into practice, this means you should put your company name as the last word in your title tag and save the valuable and more prominent area of your title tag (the first 30 to 40 characters) for keywords related to your business or industry.

Your business' name is not a high-competition keyword

Don't use your business' name or slogan in valuable on-page positions like the first five words of your title tag—you'll likely rank for your business' name even if that name doesn't appear in your title tag at all because there's little competition for your business' name as a search term. Save those key positions for high-volume, competitive search terms, and use your business' name in less important positions like in the body of your text or at the end of your title tag, after the keywords. For example, an ideal title tag for a pet grooming service would be *Pet Grooming & Pet Care, | New York | The Pampered Pooch.*

Meta keyword tags are the subject of some confusion and remain misused and even abused. Some uninformed webmasters erroneously believe that stuffing keywords into a keyword meta tag will help rank for those terms. That hasn't been true since about 2000 or 2001, yet the myth persists. In fact, Google and Bing are both on record as saying that their algorithms no longer takes into account meta keyword tags.

Similarly, meta description tags are no longer very relevant to search results. However, meta description tags, like title tags, are used by search engines when they display search engine results pages. On a Google search engine results page, the description tag comprises the second and third line of each standard four-line entry. This presents an opportunity for your description tag. Your description tag can serve as a hook to readers to invite them to click on your result in lieu of all the other search results.

Sell with your meta description

Meta descriptions are not merely repositories for keywords! Your meta description can *hook* customers and bring them to your site.

Because search engines display the meta tag in search results pages, that text may have quite a lot to do with whether a person clicks on your link, or one of the 20 or so other links on a search results page. Don't use tired, stale descriptions, give your meta tag life and fire. See the following image for an example of an expertly drafted meta tag.

Google will nearly always display some text on the second and third line of each entry on its results page. What does Google display on search engine results pages if no description tag is present? If Google finds no description tag present, its algorithm will select some text from the body of the page and insert it as the description on its search engine results pages. For obvious reasons, this result is not ideal.

The following screenshot of a Google search result demonstrates Internet company SEOMofo's expert drafting of its meta description tag, which even includes a message to Google employee Matt Cutts:

SEO Mofo » **World's Greatest SEO**
WWWWW__WWW____WWWW___WWW_
WWWWW_W_____W_____W___W
WWWWW__WWW____WWW___W___W_
WWWWW_____W_W_____W___W_
WWWWW__WWW____WWWW___WWW_.
Google SERP Snippet - Hey, Matt Cutts, I'm using JavaScript to - Pages
www.**seo**mofo.com/ - Cached - Similar

Using heading tags (h1, h2, h3)

The earliest specifications for HTML included provisions for document headings and subheadings, elements known as heading tags. Heading tag elements begin at h1 and progress to h6, each level is intended to represent an ordered and organized taxonomy. These tags serve multiple roles.

As mark-up tags, these elements conveniently format the text elements to which they are applied. For example, an h1 tag will generate large text, in a bold font, with margins above and below — much like the headline in a newspaper article.

As HTML standards matured and CSS formatting became available in browsers, many web designers abandoned heading tags in search of prettier formatting for their headings. True, you can make text big and bold with CSS mark-up or with HTML formatting; you can make any text look like a heading without utilizing heading tags. However, in the world of search that is a blunder because you will build almost no search engine ranking power from simply formatting text.

For search engines, heading tags serve a supplemental function beyond formatting. Heading tags serve as signposts, that help search engines determine the context and topic of a web page. Heading tags are certainly part of search algorithms, and are given moderate weight in determining search position.

The best methodology for employing heading tags is to do the following. First, your page should only employ an h1 tag once. The text of the h1 tag should describe the main topic of the web page upon which it appears and should include the high-value, high-volume keywords for which you want to rank. Next, at a minimum you should employ both h1 and h2 tags. Your h2 tags should repeat your important keywords — but with additional terms to give context to the section that the h2 tag covers. For example, if you are writing a page about air conditioning service and repair, you might employ h2 tags with text such as, *Your best choice for air conditioning service*, and *Licensed and insured air conditioning service*.

The h3 tags are optional, but can come in handy for organizing longer pages. The search engine ranking power of heading tags decreases as you progress from h1 down through the lower orders of heading tags. Thus, h1 tags are mandatory, h2 tags are highly recommended, and h3 tags are necessary only in the most competitive markets. Heading tags have a complementary effect when combined with an effective title tag, body text, and meta description — when these elements are in accord, a search engine can more comfortably determine the main context of a web page, and can more confidently reward that web page with higher rankings.

Remember also, that keyword prominence applies to heading tags, so greater weight is given to the words at the beginning of the tag.

Optimizing code quality and load speed

Code quality is an often overlooked element of search ranking. Because it's overlooked, it represents a great opportunity to edge out less alert or less informed competitors. Code quality refers to the quality, amount, and load speed of the code and image sizes underline your website. Search engines like quality code and fast loading times; poor quality code and slow loading times mean a poor user experience for searchers.

HTML is an open source family of mark-up languages designed with fairly strict specifications set forth by the **World Wide Web Consortium (W3C)**. These standards are updated every few years and result in new versions of HTML, such as the upgrade from HTML 4 to HTML 5.

When the code quality underlying a website does not meet the specifications of the HTML standard, the website may not display properly in all browsers. If the code is filled with errors or lacks proper elements such as an HTML doctype declaration, then that website may actually perform poorly in search engines. To test your code for validation, visit the W3C's free validator at `https://validator.w3.org/`.

The amount of code underlying the website can affect its load speed. The proper use of CSS can help a website reduce mindless repetition of attribute statements like font-size and color. Users of WordPress can worry less about code quality. Assuming that the WordPress template employed by a website does not contain coding errors, WordPress generally delivers very lean code that validates perfectly. You can test your website's CSS code by using W3C's free CSS validator at `https://jigsaw.w3.org/css-validator/`.

Image size can also affect load speed. Always be sure you are using a compressed image format whenever possible. For example, use the JPEG format for photographs with an appropriate amount of compression. The faster the images load, the faster your webpages will load.

Menus, internal navigation, and link structure

Link architecture refers to the way a website's menus and navigation links are constructed. Link architecture can be very powerful and it's also one of the hardest topics in search to truly master.

The anchor text (the blue underlined text) of a website link is a ranking factor whether that link is from a site linking into your site, or is simply a link on your own site leading to another page within your site. For that reason, you have an opportunity to rank for certain terms by carefully selecting the anchor text that you use in your navigation menus. The most perfect example of the misuse of this principle in practice is the common employment of the term *Home* as the anchor text in navigation menus to point to a website's home page. A website's homepage has more ranking potential than any interior page on a website. For that reason, the anchor text pointing to the home page should be carefully selected. For example, instead of *Home*, consider employing keyword-rich phrases such as *Austin's Best Carpet Cleaning* or *VW Repair* as the navigation anchor text.

Another common mistake in site architecture and site structure is the use of image buttons for links. A link comprised solely of an image has no anchor text. It's a missed opportunity to include a keyword in a text link and send a signal to the search engines about what the topic of the destination page is. It's curious to see that this practice is still employed so often.

Other issues arise in link architecture when the navigation menus are written in JavaScript or Flash—search engines don't read those languages effectively. The safest approach to constructing navigation menus is with HTML. If you require active navigation—dropdown or flyout sub-menus—make sure they are constructed with search-friendly code such as CSS. Or, the problem of *shifting navigation*, where the navigation menus change as the user moves through a site. A good rule to follow is that if navigation is confusing for users, it's probably confusing for search engine spiders as well.

When securing inbound links from other websites, you would never want high number/high proportion links that all use the exact anchor text—you'll likely trip a search engine filter if you do. Google wants to see natural linking patterns. A website with hundreds of links that all have the same anchor text (that is, *New York Dentist*) does not look natural to a search engine, so a ranking filter would likely be imposed by the search engine to knock that listing down a few pages. The anchor text you choose for your site-wide navigation serves as an opportunity to use anchor text in higher numbers and in higher proportion that you wouldn't use for external links. The search engines have no anchor text penalty for your internal links, you can point 100 percent of your internal links to your front page with any anchor text you like.

Finally, the great opportunity with link architecture is simply to make sure the number and quality of links are pointing in greater numbers to the high-value pages such as your home page and product pages, and are pointing in lower numbers to your low value pages such as your privacy policy, your contact form, and your return policy. An easy way to accomplish this, is to simply have your standard navigation either horizontally at the top of your website, or on a left or right sidebar; then, to send extra link power to your most important pages, create a footer with links to your home page and a few other high-value pages. Additionally, you can always create extra link power by creating text links to your key pages within the body of text throughout your site.

WordPress handles link architecture well. WordPress presents very simple site-wide navigation menus by default. In fact, many have criticized WordPress for not offering users as much control over navigation menus as they would like. With WordPress releases beginning with 3.0, however, WordPress users enjoy the ability to customize navigation menus with the new menu feature, available under the appearance tab in the WordPress dashboard.

For users less experienced with SEO, we recommend sticking with WordPress' reliable default navigation.

The customizable navigation is flexible and powerful—but that flexibility and power in inexperienced hands can yield poor search ranking results.

Image filenames and alt tags

Image names and image alt tags are an example of a ranking factor that is afforded lower weight in search rankings, that is, `wordpress-expert.jpg` as a filename in an attempt to rank for *WordPress expert*. Certainly, image names alone will never make anyone rank for any term or phrase that is highly competitive. However, image names and alt tags can be effective as supplemental weight for search terms when the more important elements such as title tags and heading tags are highly focused and in accord.

Text attributes – bold, italics, and underline

Emphasizing text with the use of bold and underline has long been known to have a marginal effect on ranking. Search algorithms follow predictable logic—do the elements of a web page serve to reliably indicate the subject of the web page, and if so, to what degree? Text attributes do tend to indicate the subject and context of a page but rarely to a great degree. Rightfully, text attributes are not given much weight. Again, this technique is best used as a supplement to other stronger ranking factors.

This technique is commonly misused by inexperienced webmasters. While the effect of the technique is slight, overzealous designers often employ the technique on dozens of phrases on a web page. This technique will yield little to no effect, and will almost certainly undercut your user experience.

The best practice is to employ text attributes for a maximum of two phrases per web page—your primary keywords only.

Ranking factor – high page count

There is a general rule that larger sites outrank smaller sites in search engine results. Consider the collective effect of a large website: larger sites cover more topic areas, and therefore more keywords and garner broader traffic. The broader traffic yields larger numbers of inbound links from broader classes of other websites. In turn, the site earns trust with search engines more quickly. Meanwhile, each individual page within a site generates a small thimble of PageRank that can ultimately contribute to the overall site PageRank. The collective effect of a large website can bring tremendous ranking power.

The power of this simple device is available to everyone. You need not be an expert at SEO—you simply need to start writing.

As a webmaster, you should always aspire to create a site that covers broad topic areas. That does not mean have a blog about soccer, baseball, guitar greats, and web design all jumbled together. It means that if your blog is about web design you would have a range of topics discussed within that discipline, such as sound coding practices, logo design, navigation tools, and web design trends. To a small business owner employing WordPress as a **Content Management System** (**CMS**), that means building a page for each city in which you offer services as well as offering free tips and tools within the WordPress blog section.

In my web design and SEO business, I employ WordPress as both a CMS and a blogging platform. I maintain pages for the main areas of interest to potential clients: one page each for my service offerings (the pages are intentionally separated for ranking purposes: SEO, web design, WordPress development, social media marketing, call tracking, PPC management, and more), a page for a design gallery, a page for SEO case studies, a page for testimonials, and some service and contact pages. However, I utilize WordPress' blogging functionality to write (hopefully) helpful and valuable tips on SEO, such as *How Does Google Local Order Its Search Results*, and *Top Android Apps for SEO*. Each month, I take the time to write about three or four such posts. My site ranks highly, but more important to me is the high number of search phrases for which my site ranks.

Anyone can rank for one search phrase. The truly exceptional sites, however, are the sites that have broadness—the sites that rank for wider classes of keywords.

When your site has broadness, other benefits follow. First, you'll garner greater numbers of inbound links—and you'll earn them from a greater variety of sources more quickly than you normally would. Say you've are a web designer and you write a blog post about an innovative CSS trick that you invented. Your blog post will be of interest to other web designers and bloggers. With WordPress' innate tagging functionality, your post will be easy for other webmasters to find. Those other bloggers and designers might mention your post on their site with a link back to you. Congratulations, you just earned a link to an interior page (links to interior pages are usually harder to get than links to your front page) from a website within the same niche as you (links from same niche sites carry more power). You just earned a link that you otherwise would not have had.

Consider also the PageRank effect of that single page. PageRank is part of Google's search algorithm; Google assigns a numerical value to each indexed page on the Web. When an indexed page hyperlinks to another page on the Web (including your own pages), a portion of that numerical value is passed from the linking page to the target page, thereby increasing the target page's PageRank. Inbound links increase your PageRank and in turn, your search rankings. The amount of PageRank generated by a single page is admittedly slight—but it adds up quickly.

One of WordPress' most singular advantages as a search-friendly platform is that it offers simple and speedy publishing of new content. If you have 15 minutes and a good idea, you can create a decent page of new content. If you have 3 hours and a great idea, you can create a great page of new content.

Fodder for search engines – fresh content

Search engines respond to fresh, original content. Even more, search engines love a steady stream of fresh, original content.

I am sure we have all heard people talk about the website they are about to launch, saying *I am having a website built and it is almost finished*. When I hear that exact phrase—and I hear it a lot—I cringe just a bit and feel like responding, *Really? Well, my website will never be finished*. That's because a website should be alive and constantly changing. The old way of thinking about websites is that when a website was finished, it would sit frozen and immovable until the next redesign. Even the word *site* implies something fixed in the ground, not something constantly in motion.

A search engine sees a website for what it is. If a website has static content that never changes, the search engine knows it. Over time, the search engine spiders will come less often. Why send a search spider for content that doesn't change? The site will not be seen by search engines as high-value to its users. On the other hand, publish regular content to your site and the search engines will know it. In fact, search engines are moving toward real-time search results, although this technology isn't yet fully developed. The search engines will send spiders to your site more often looking for both new content and changes to old content. Your site will rise in the rankings. And, if that wasn't enough, new content will get a fresh content bump.

The fresh content bump refers to a supplemental boost in ranking power that search engines assign to fresh content served up from blogging platforms like WordPress for the first few weeks after the published date.

WordPress began as a pure blogging platform and the search engines see new WordPress posts as timely, topical, and potentially newsworthy items. The search engines reward new posts with a little boost in position. As time passes, the posts will settle down in the rankings. You can use the fresh content bump to cleverly schedule prime rankings for matters of seasonal interest to readers. For example, you would write a post titled "Spring Activities in South Florida, 2016" where you deftly advertise your scuba diving service along with other activities. If you time it right, you'll get a boost in rankings right when the last tourists are having their vacations.

Your fresh content need not be entirely free give-aways with no benefit to you. Your new content can be a post or page about how you now serve a new area; put the name of the new town in the page as a keyword, and you'll rank for searches in which that town name appears. Or, how about a page announcing a summer sale? Google likes new content—but it doesn't have to be completely fantastic content every time.

Another benefit: new content is great when it is new, but new content is also pretty great when it is old. A site with continually fresh content becomes a very large site very quickly. We discussed the benefits of a large site in the previous section.

If you are reading this book, you likely have a WordPress site or are considering a WordPress site. With WordPress, your ease and speed of publishing is unmatched — you'll create new and better content faster than other webmasters, your site will be alive with regularly fresh content and your site will grow up quickly.

Using the subtle power of outbound links

You can also gain ranking power by making outbound links from your site to other sites. The theory goes something like the following. You have a website for your gardening business and you want to rank for the phrase "gardening service San Diego." If you have an outbound link to other sites about gardening services and the anchor text of that outbound link is "gardening service", then that link can serve as a signpost to search engines that your site is about gardening services.

This technique has a potential disadvantage (there's disagreement within the SEO community about this point that remains unresolved): by linking to other sites, you are directing valuable PageRank away from your page to the page to which you are linking. So, you lose some PageRank, but gain ranking power for the keyword. You may not want to overdo it — maybe just a few outbound links on a few pages, and always to reputable websites. This is a technique that requires some finesse, so you might employ some testing to see where outbound linking can be most effective.

Understanding off-page ranking factors

Off-page ranking factors can be summarized with one phrase: inbound links. Inbound links from other websites are the real power that makes sites rank. In the competitive search markets, links might comprise 80 to 90 percent of the work that goes into a website.

Links are the power

The best way to think of the relationship between on-page factors an off-page factors is this: on-page factors are like tuning up a car for a race to make sure all the parts run reliably and strongly, off-page factors are the fuel.

So, if your car isn't running right, all the fuel in the world isn't going to make it go. Similarly, if you don't have any fuel, even the most highly-tuned car will go nowhere. In the world of search optimization, you need both.

Creating natural links

Google, more than any other search engine, was the great innovator with respect to measuring inbound linking power and then adjusting search results in favor of sites that enjoy high numbers of inbound links. The reasoning is sound: sites with high numbers of inbound links are most likely superior websites, to those that have low numbers of inbound links. This innovation that links between websites are *votes* for the quality of the destination site, is now employed by all major search engines. And, for the most part, the principle does ensure superior search results when users search for information through a search engine.

What Google wants, ideally, is for inbound links to be natural links, not artificially generated links. If a website owner earns inbound links through paid link-building schemes, then the methodology is skewed — the lower value site that has paid for inbound links now enjoys higher ranking power than a superior site with fewer links. That result is not what is intended by the inbound link component of the search algorithms.

The search engines know that in the real world, not all linking between websites will be natural. They are fully aware that webmasters attempt to game the system through a variety of linking practices that range from relatively innocent reciprocal linking to more sinister practices, like automated forum spamming and hidden links. Google forbids *link schemes* in its webmaster guidelines, and penalties are common.

The task for the legitimate webmaster is to secure links naturally. Natural linking will ensure that your site will never suffer a penalty, and links that you obtain naturally will carry much more power than links obtained through any schemes or artificial means. We cover specific line building methods in *Chapter 6, Link Building*.

Avoiding over-optimization

Over-optimization occurs when a website's elements are present in too high a proportion or too high in power for a given keyword phrase. Over-optimization yields poor search performance. An example of over-optimization would be the incessant use of keywords on your website, so that your keywords represent 50 percent of the total density of words on the page. Another example would be a website with 100 inbound links, all with the same exact anchor text. First-time SEO hobbyists tend to be ensnared by over-optimization as they zealously pursue the new elements of SEO that they learn; they stuff keywords into title tags, meta tags, body text, and secure links all with the same anchor text.

Over-optimization is difficult to quantify, and can be difficult to detect and repair. The best way to think about over-optimization is that websites should never be *too perfect*. Remember, a search engine ultimately must employ mathematics to its ranking criteria. It's easy for a search engine to mathematically determine that a page with a keyword density — keywords as a percentage of total words on the page — exceeding 8 percent is attempting to game the algorithm and therefore should not be ranked.

Thinking about over-optimization in this way, repetition is often the main culprit. To avoid over-optimization you'll need to be vigilant to watch for excessive repetition of terms in the main elements of a website and in inbound links. In other words, just do good writing and the rest will follow naturally. You wouldn't keep repeating yourself in good writing.

Converting visitors to customers – the third spoke of SEO

Too often, people think of SEO solely in terms of ranking position. They forget that if your website cannot turn that casual visitor into a customer — your ranking did nothing for you except send a visitor to your site for a moment.

Conversion science is the discipline of making sure the visitors to your site take some action to bring them closer to being a customer. Successful websites have specific and effective calls to action. A call to action is a phrase, graphic, or a section of your website that urges the visitor to take some tangible step toward becoming a customer or user of your product or website. The call to action can be a box that says *Call Now for Immediate Service*, *Shop Now!*, or *Subscribe for Free! Get Updates by RSS*.

A call to action doesn't necessarily mean that visitors purchase something right there, but that they take steps toward becoming a purchaser.

Your call to action will differ based on the space in which you compete. If you are a blogger and want to expand the reach of your blog, you'll want users to sign up to your RSS feed, or follow you on Twitter. In more traditional business environments, like retail and home services, you'll want people to call or e-mail to make an appointment. In a full e-commerce environment, you'll want to immediately drive people to make purchases.

The following screenshot shows an aggressive call to action in the home services (pool construction) niche:

For your calls to action to be effective, you need to keep them prominent, above the fold (on the upper part of your web pages that are visible before scrolling down is required), and persuasive. *Above the fold* is a term from the newspaper industry, meaning above the halfway point where a newspaper was folded.

Another rule of conversions is to have fallback positions, a second best option. In other words, if your users don't purchase something today maybe they'll sign up for your Twitter feed, which lets you keep them updated to new products. Perhaps later, these new contacts will eventually become customers.

Creating conversion-based websites

Each competitive space is different. However, conversion science does teach a few absolute principles that can help you create highly effective conversion-based websites:

- Don't hide contact information. About 30 percent of all websites do not display contact information prominently. In a business environment, this mistake is pure suicide. Put that phone number and e-mail up top where users can find it.

- Put the meat where the eyes are. Use the "above the fold" portions your header and sidebars for conversion tools and messages. Studies show that user's eyes typically scan the top and sidebar areas for information. Don't expect users to scroll to hunt for your phone number.

- Mix it up. Some users like to call, others like to e-mail. Give users more than one choice.

- Don't frustrate your users by directing them to non-functioning elements. For example, don't use *Chat now* buttons that lead to dead ends, that is, *Chat is not available right now*. If you utilize a call to action, make absolutely sure the action is available, even if it's a voice mail, that is still better than wasting a customer's time.

- Don't broadcast your poor service. Don't say *To reach sales, call between 1pm and 5pm*. That's just begging your customers to go elsewhere. If you must be out of the office (all of us must leave work sometimes) just send folks to a friendly voicemail and return the call later.

- Give fewer choices. Don't confuse readers with too many selections. If your viewers get confused or overwhelmed, they might slip into *choice paralysis*.

- Always give the next step. Don't lose your customers along the way. If they don't buy, get them to sign up for your newsletter. If you convert them to watch your video, make the next step an invitation to purchase.

- Sell benefits, not features. *Your car will run faster!* will convert better than *Our fuel additives are the most powerful in the industry.*

- Use testimonials. Tell your customers what other users say about your service.

- Guide their eyes and attention. You can literally point users to your desired action with arrows and buttons.

The following screenshot of Google's Cloud Print service shows several elements of expert conversion science at work. The user is guided visually to the call to action with a clear and simple button in a contrasting color. The benefit, *Print anywhere, from any device*, is short and clear. The page is uncluttered, which enables a clearer path to action for the user. The placement of the conversion tool is above the fold:

Truly effective calls to action are going to differ widely depending on the space in which you participate. You'll want to try different approaches and measure your results. In *Chapter 10, Testing Your Site and Monitoring Your Progress*, we'll cover how to measure the performance of your website.

Summary

We covered a wide range of material in this first chapter. We covered all the major disciplines within on-page optimization: body content, title tags, meta tags, heading tags, and code quality and load speed. We examined lower-weight SEO factors such as image filenames, alt tags, text attributes such as bold and underline, outbound links, and discussed the benefits of larger websites with regularly freshened content. Finally, we examined over-optimization and how to avoid it, and delved into the fundamental principles of conversion science.

Now, we are ready to put these core concepts into practice, as we learn to take WordPress' innate functionality to the next level.

2
Optimizing WordPress for SEO

In this chapter, we'll align your SEO strategy with the WordPress platform and help you solidify your plan. You'll need to set realistic goals and timelines for your business or website through educated investigation and analysis. Proper and thorough planning is needed to ensure that you succeed in the competitive search markets.

We will begin by setting up the goals for your Internet presence and determining how to best leverage WordPress' flexibility and power for maximum benefit. We'll examine how to best determine and reach out to the specific audience for your goods or services. Different Internet models require different strategies. For example, if your goal is instant e-commerce sales, you strategize differently than if your goal is a broad-based branding campaign. We'll also examine how to determine how competitive the existing search market is, and how to develop a plan to penetrate that market.

It's important to leverage WordPress' strengths. WordPress can effortlessly help you build large, broad-based sites. It can also improve the speed and ease with which you publish new content. It serves up simple, text-based navigation menus that search engines crawl and index easily. WordPress' tagging, pingback, and trackBack features help other blogs and websites find and connect with your content. For these reasons, and quite a few more, WordPress is search ready. In this chapter, we will look at what WordPress already does for your SEO.

Of course, WordPress is designed as a blogging platform and a content management platform—not as a platform purely for ranking. We'll look at what WordPress doesn't accomplish innately and how to address that.

Finally, we'll look at how WordPress communicates with search engines and blog update services. Following this chapter, we'll know how to plan out a new site or improve an existing one, how to gauge WordPress' innate strengths and supplant its weaknesses, and learn how WordPress sites get found by search engines and blog engines.

Setting goals for your business and website and getting inspiration

A dizzying variety of websites run on the WordPress platform, everything from The Wall Street Journal's blog to the photo sharing comedy site PeopleofWalMart. com (`http://www.peopleofwalmart.com/`). Not every reader will have purely commercial intent in creating his or her web presence. However, nearly all webmasters want more traffic and more visibility for their sites. With that in mind, to increase the reach, visibility, and ranking of your website, you'll want to develop your website plan based on the type of audience you are trying to reach, the type of business you run, and what your business goals are.

Analyzing your audience

You will obviously want to analyze the nature of your audience. Your website's content, its design, its features, and even the pixel width of the viewable area will depend on your audience. Is your audience in the 65+ age group? If so, your design will need to incorporate large fonts and you will want to keep your design to a pixel width of 800 or less. Senior citizens can have difficulty reading small text and many use older computers with 800 pixel monitors. And you can forget about the integrated Twitter and Facebook feeds; most seniors aren't as tuned into those technologies as young people. You might simply alienate your target users by including features that aren't a fit for your audience.

Does your audience include purchasers of web design services? If so, be prepared to dazzle them with up-to-date design and features. Similarly, if you intend to rely on building up your user base by developing viral content, you will want to incorporate social media sharing into your design. Give some thought to the type of users you want to reach, and design your site for your audience. This exercise will go a long way in helping you build a successful site.

Analyzing your visitors' screen sizes

Have you ever wondered about the monitor sizes of the viewers of your own site? Google Analytics (`http://www.google.com/analytics/`), the ubiquitous free analytics tool offered by Google, offers this capability.

To use it, log on to your Google Analytics account (or sign up if you don't have one) and select the website whose statistics you wish to examine. On the left menu, select and expand **Audience**, navigate to **Technology**, then **Browser & OS**. Then just under the graph, select **Screen Resolution**. Google Analytics will offer up a table and chart of all the monitor resolutions used by your viewers.

Determining the goal of your website

The design, style, and features of your website should be dictated by your goal. If your site is to be a destination site for instant sales or sign-ups, you want a website design more in the style of a single-purpose landing page that focuses principally on conversions. A landing page is a special-purpose, conversion-focused page that appears when a potential customer clicks on an advertisement or enters through a search query. The page should display the sales copy that is a logical extension of the advertisement or link, and should employ a very shallow conversion funnel. A conversion funnel tracks the series of steps that a user must undertake to get from the entry point on a website to the satisfaction of a purchase or other conversion event. Shallow conversion funnels have fewer steps and deeper conversion funnels have more steps.

When designing conversion-focused landing pages, consider if you want to eliminate navigation choices entirely on the landing page. Logically, if you are trying to get a user to make an immediate purchase, what benefit is served by giving the user easier choices to click onto the other pages? Individualized page-by-page navigation can get clunky with WordPress; you might want to ensure that your WordPress template can easily handle these demands. Let's have a look at the following screenshot:

The previous screenshot shows the expert landing page for Netflix's Video on demand service. Note the absence of navigational choices. There are other sophisticated conversion tools as well: clear explanation of benefits, free trial, arrows, and a color to guide the reader to the conversion event.

If you sell a technical product or high-end consulting services, you rely heavily on the creation of content and the organization and presentation of that content on your WordPress site. Creating a large amount of content covering broad topics in your niche will establish thought leadership that will help you draw in and maintain new customers. In sites with large amounts of educational content, you'll want to make absolutely sure that your content is well organized and has an easy-to-follow navigation.

If you will be relying on social media and other forms of viral marketing to build up your user base, you'd want to integrate social media plugins and widgets into your site. Plugins and widgets are third-party software tools that you install on your WordPress site to contribute to a new functionality. A popular sports site integrates the TweetMeme and Facebook connect widgets. When users retweet or share the article, it means links, traffic, and sales. When compounded with a large amount of content, the effect can be very powerful.

Following the leaders

Once you have determined the essential framework and niche for your site, look for best-in-class websites for your inspiration. Trends in design and features are changing constantly. Aim for up-to-the-minute design and features: enlightened design sells more products and services, and sophisticated features will help you convert and engage your visitors more. Likewise, ease of functionality will keep visitors on your website longer and keep them coming back.

For design inspiration, you can visit any one of the hundreds of website design gallery sites. These gallery sites showcase great designs in all website niches. The following design gallery sites feature the latest and greatest trends in web design and features (note that all of these sites run on WordPress):

- **Urban Trash** (`http://www.urbantrash.net/cssgallery/`): This gallery is truly one of the best and should be the first stop when seeking design inspiration.
- **CSS Elite** (`http://csselite.com/`): Another truly high-end CSS galleries. Many fine sites are featured here.
1. **CSSDrive** (`http://www.cssdrive.com/`): CSSDrive is one of the elite classes of directories, and CSSDrive has many other design-related features as well.

For general inspiration on everything from website design to more specialized discussion of the best design for website elements, such as sign-up boxes and footers, head to Smashing Magazine, especially its *inspiration* category (`http://www.smashingmagazine.com/category/inspiration/`).

Ready-made WordPress designs by leading designers are available for purchase off-the-shelf at `http://themeforest.net/`. These templates are resold to others, so they won't be exclusive to your site. A head's up: these top-end themes are full of advanced custom features. They might require a little effort to get them to display exactly as you want.

For landing pages, get inspiration from retail monoliths in competitive search markets. DishNetwork and Netflix have excellent landing pages. Sears' home improvement division serves up sophisticated landing pages for services such as vinyl siding and replacement windows. With thousands of hits per day, you can bet these retail giants are testing and retesting their landing pages periodically. You can save yourself the trouble and budget of your early-stage testing by employing the lessons that these giants have already put into practice.

For navigation, usability, and site layout clues for large content-based sites, look for the blogging super-sites, such as `http://blogs.wsj.com/`, `http://www.politico.com/`, `http://www.huffingtonpost.in/`, and `http://wikipedia.com`.

Gauging competition in the search market

Ideally, before you launch your site, you want to gauge the competitive marketplace. On the web, you have two spheres of competition:

- One sphere is traditional business competition: the competition for price, quality, and service in the consumer marketplace
- The other sphere of competition is search competition; competition for clicks, page views, conversions, user sign-ups, new visitors, returning visitors, search placement, and all the other metrics than help drive a web-based business

While this book is concerned with the search competition, you'll naturally want to consider both as you grow your business.

The obvious way to get started gauging the search marketplace is to run some sample searches on the terms you believe your future customers might use when seeking out your products or services. The search leaders in your marketplace will be easy to spot, they will be in the first six positions in a Google search.

While aiming for the first six positions, don't think in terms of the first page of a Google search. Studies show that the first five or six positions in a Google search yield 80 to 90 percent of the click-throughs. The first page of Google is a good milestone, but the highest positions on a search results page will yield significantly higher traffic than the bottom three positions on a search results page.

Once you've identified the five or six websites that are highly competitive, you want to analyze what they're doing right and what you'll need to do to compete with them. Here's how to gauge the competition:

- Don't focus on the website in terms of the number one position for a given search. That may be too lofty a goal for the short term. Look at the sites in positions four, five and six. These positions will be your initial goal. You'll need to match or outdo these websites to earn those positions.

- First, you want to determine the Google PageRank of your competitor's sites. PageRank is a generalized, but helpful indicator of the quality and number of inbound links that your competitor websites have earned. Install a browser plug-in that shows the PageRank of any site to which you browse. For Firefox, try the SearchStatus plug-in (available at `http://www.quirk. biz/searchstatus/`). For Chrome, use SEO Site Tools by Sitexy (available through the Google Chrome Extensions gallery at `https://chrome.google. com/extensions`). Both of these tools are free, and they'll display a wide array of important SEO factors for any site you visit.

- How old are the domains of your competitor websites? Older sites tend to outrank newer sites. If you are launching a new domain, you will most likely need to outpace your older competitors in other ways, such as building more links or employing more advanced on-page optimization. Site age is a factor that can't be overcome with brains or hard work (although you can purchase an older, existing domain in the after market).

- Look at the size and scale of competing websites. You'll need to at least approach the size of the smallest of your competitors to place well.

- You will want to inspect your competitors' inbound links. Where are they getting their links from and how many links have they accumulated? To obtain a list of backlinks for any website, visit the Open Link Profiler at `http://openlinkprofiler.org`. This free tool displays up to 1,000 links for any site. If you want to see more than 1,000 links, you'll need to purchase inbound link analysis software like SEO Spyglass from `http://link-assistant.com`. For most purposes, 1,000 links will give you a clear picture of where a site's links are coming from. Don't worry about high link counts because low-value links in large numbers are easy to overcome; high-value links like `.edu` links, and links from high PageRank sites will take more effort to surmount.

- You will want to examine the site's on-page optimization. Are the webmasters utilizing effective title tags and meta tags? Are they using heading tags and is their on-page text keyword-focused? If they aren't, you may be able to best beat your competitors through more effective on-page optimization.

- Don't forget to look at conversion. Is your competitor's site well-designed to convert his or her visitors into customers? If not, you might edge out your competition with better conversion techniques.

When you analyze your competition, you are determining the standard you will need to meet or beat to earn competitive search placement. Don't be discouraged by well-placed competitors. Around 99 percent of all websites are not well optimized. As you learn more, you'll be surprised how many webmasters are not employing effective optimization. Your goal as you develop or improve your website will be to do just a little bit more than your competition. Google and the other search engines will be happy to return your content in search results in favor of others if you meet a higher standard.

Knowing what WordPress already does for your SEO

Now, we will turn to what WordPress accomplishes naturally for your SEO efforts. Luckily, WordPress handles much—but not all of the nuts and bolts of search engine optimization naturally. WordPress has an innate economical architecture that generates lean and fast-loading code that search engines love. It enjoys respect and familiarity among search engines, which aids in search spidering. It is a speedy platform that lets you build bigger and better sites in less time. RSS feeds are built in, so you can reach more readers quite easily. WordPress automatically builds keyword-rich URL strings for further SEO benefit. And WordPress effortlessly builds reliable text-based navigation. We'll handle each of these elements in turn and learn how to harness these strengths for maximum benefit.

Understanding WordPress' economical architecture

WordPress employs sound economical architecture to display pages reliably and quickly. In the early days of HTML, each display element on a web page was displayed through the use of markup tags such as `<font face="verdana" color="green">This is some text!</font>` to display a string of green text in the `verdana` font style. One of the inherent weaknesses of this approach was that it led to the incessant repetition of markup tags. **WYSIWYG** editors (**what you see is what you get**) compounded the problem by tending towards excessive repetition of markup tags: a web page with 20 paragraphs might have 20 font declarations, one for each paragraph. Repeating markup code makes websites display more reliably, but it makes them far less efficient because they take longer to load and longer for the browser to process the markup.

There is another inherent problem. If you wanted to change the text on your website from green to black, you would have to edit each individual font color declaration throughout your site.

With the advent of CSS (cascading style sheets), the declarations for every element on a web page could be made either at the head of the page, or ideally in an off-page text file called a **stylesheet**. This answered the issue of both the uneconomical repetition of the markup, as well as giving webmasters the ability to change a single element sitewide by changing one declaration. With well-crafted CSS, pages display more quickly and hence rank better.

WordPress' internal architecture is entirely CSS-based. Unless the WordPress template is poorly coded, WordPress uses off-page CSS stylesheets to define elements. A WordPress page might display with 180 lines of code, where the equivalent page created by a static WYSIWYG editor might display 350 lines of code. Pages load faster, so the search engines respond with good rankings and users enjoy a good experience while visiting your site.

WordPress' inherent economy doesn't end there. WordPress pages are generated quickly and neatly by a simple and quick processing engine. WordPress sites generate proper, valid HTML code that search engines love, although a poorly-crafted WordPress template can undermine code quality.

Building large sites quickly with WordPress

WordPress began its history as a blogging/publishing platform. Even as WordPress has matured into a capable content management platform, it has retained the features that make it adapt as a speedy and agile publishing tool. WordPress will enable you to create content more quickly than other platforms and certainly more quickly than with static HTML pages.

Search engine optimization relies on content. The more content that appears on your site, the more opportunities you will have to rank for the wider families of keyword phrases. Also, each page of content on your website contributes to the whole. Remember, all indexed web pages generate PageRank. So, even a minor page on your website generates a small thimble of PageRank, which contributes to the overall ranking power of your site.

Earning respect with search engines

WordPress enjoys both respect and familiarity from search engines. When a search engine encounters a website with unusual or non-standard navigation, the search engine must do its best to follow the navigation to the deepest files within the website's organizational structure. If the search spider cannot reliably and confidently follow a website's navigation to discover the deepest pages within a website, then those pages are unlikely to be indexed. Because of WordPress' reliability and familiarity to search engines, spidering errors almost never occur.

Because of the sheer number of installations worldwide, search engines crawl and index content on WordPress sites with ease. Faster and more thorough crawling and indexing means that more of your content will be placed in the search engine indexes.

Leveraging WordPress' blogging capabilities

This capability almost goes without saying, because blogging is the historically core purpose of WordPress. WordPress has retained many of the features of a pure blogging platform, such as the presentation of articles in reverse chronological order as its default setting and built-in RSS feed capabilities. The great power of WordPress comes into effect when its inherent blogging capabilities are employed within a commercial site.

Understanding Pages and Posts

WordPress publishes two separate classes of documents, namely, Pages and Posts. Posts are traditional blog entries that are displayed in reverse chronological order and are assigned to categories and tags. Pages are static documents, not listed by date, and do not employ categories or tags. A business' website will typically use WordPress Pages for static company information, such as a Contact page, About us page, Home page, and will use Posts for blog entries and updates.

A sound and standard approach to a commercial site on the WordPress platform is to have the main services pages for a business published on the front page and in the **Pages** section of WordPress, while the educational articles, product updates, general blog posts, and commentary are published to the **Posts** section. The **Posts** section of WordPress is traditionally where blog posts appear. With this dual capability, a website owner can outpace competitors that aren't employing a blog.

Displaying RSS feeds

RSS feeds come standard with all WordPress installations. RSS stands for **really simple syndication**, and refers to a family of formatting standards that allow for the timely publication of freshly-updated web content to other websites and devices. In a practical sense, the RSS feeds of your site can be utilized by users to follow your content in an RSS reader such as a Google Reader (now as a Chrome Extension) or an RSS reader app without necessarily visiting your site. When a user *subscribes* to your RSS feed, they'll receive regular updates of all new content you generate. RSS represents another avenue by which users can remain engaged with you and your content.

You need not do anything to set up your WordPress feed—it's already there. However, you may wish to take a few steps to ensure that users can find your feed. You do this by using a link, which in common practice, is represented visually with the familiar orange RSS icon.

Finding your RSS feed

If you need to submit your feed to the search engines or feed engines, you can use any of the following four standard feed locations. Each one represents a different feed standard, but they all accomplish the same thing and search engines can read all of them:

```
http://yourDomain.com/?feed=rss
```

```
http://yourDomain.com/?feed=rss2
```

```
http://yourDomain.com/?feed=rdf
```

```
http://yourDomain.com/?feed=atom
```

Promoting your RSS feed

Many webmasters make the mistake of not promoting their feed. The single best way to promote your feed is to make sure you have clearly visible RSS icon, with a link to your feed visible throughout your site. If the RSS feeds fit within your strategy, put your RSS icon prominently in the header or sidebar. You can also submit your RSS feed to special search blog-only search engines; we'll learn later how to submit your blog to blog engines.

Automatically creating descriptive URLs with WordPress permalinks

WordPress seamlessly and automatically handles the creation of URLs through its permalink feature. A permalink is simply WordPress' way of describing the URL for a particular page. Because keywords in the URL of a page are a ranking factor, if you want to rank for *WordPress Development* then this URL `mysite.com/wordpress-development` will perform better in search than `mysite.com/index.php?page=5`. WordPress' permalink functionality gives you the descriptive URL strings for search engines to follow, with no effort at all.

First, you'll need to turn on permalinks within the WordPress dashboard — permalinks are not activated in a default installation. To turn on permalinks, log in to the dashboard and follow the left side navigation to **Settings | Permalinks**. At the **Permalink Settings** page, in the section titled **Common Settings**, click on the radio button for **Post name** or **Custom Structure**, and enter `/%postname%/`. This permalink structure will automatically generate URLs from your Page and Post titles — but you'll still be able to manually change them if necessary.

Because the titles of your Posts and Pages are relevant to the topic of your content, the permalinks based on your titles will be relevant as well.

With the adjusted permalink setting, the WordPress page editor will automatically construct a well-formatted permalink from your Page title. This feature aids in search rankings. The permalink can be customized if you desire a custom URL.

Creating reliable and text-based navigation

WordPress automatically generates simple, text-based navigation that works well for both users and search spiders. Site visitors employ your website's navigation to browse your site and find content. Search engines use your navigation in a similar way, with a twist. Search engines follow the links in your navigation to find and index your pages. In addition, search engines use the text in your navigational links to reliably determine the topic of the destination page. In other words, the text you use in your navigation is a search engine ranking factor.

> **Avoiding image links in navigation**
>
> It is possible to create a navigation menu that employs images instead of text. However, when a search engine spider encounters an image link with no anchor text, the search engine has no text to define that element for the destination page. So, for search optimization, it's clearly better to use text links rather than image links in navigation.

Luckily, WordPress generates text-based navigation menus based on your Post and Page titles. WordPress accomplishes this automatically. For the most part, this is an effective approach to search optimization. There was some criticism for earlier versions of WordPress because the navigation menus that WordPress generated were difficult to customize—they were truly automated, in the sense that they were very difficult to adjust manually. For example, if you wrote a page with a 30-word title, WordPress would display the entire 30-word title in the navigation. For some users, the better approach would be to allow customization of the navigation entries.

In response to this limitation, a host of third-party plugins such as *Exclude Pages*, and *My Page Order* emerged to give webmasters more control over menus. With the release of WordPress 3.0 and continued in WordPress 4.0, a complete menu control area is now fully integrated into the dashboard. With WordPress 3.0 menus, you can now control the following:

- The title of the Page need not be the text of the navigation link; you can enter custom text for the navigation.

- You can create custom links to other websites or pages and include them within your navigation.

- You can place entire Post categories within your Page navigation. This wasn't possible with WordPress versions before 3.0.

There is one limitation with WordPress 4.0 menus. The full functionality is available for Pages, but not for Posts. However, there is a slightly clunky workaround. To make a post appear in the custom menu, grab the full URL of the post and enter it into your custom menu as a *custom link*. That way, you can mix your Posts within your Page navigation, as well as create custom text for the navigation links.

One warning goes along with using custom menus: when you are using a custom menu for navigation, new Posts and Pages won't automatically appear in your custom navigation as they would in traditional WordPress menus — you need to remember to enable the new content in the custom menu for the Pages or Posts to appear.

Engaging visitors with built-in collaboration, contribution, and community building

WordPress is ready-made for collaboration, contribution, and community building — the 3 Cs that can transform a stale, static website into a vibrant web-based community. Two key collaborative features, User Roles and the Commenting System, keep both new and returning visitors engaged with your website.

When thinking about search optimization, it is tempting to focus only on the competitive grind of search ranking positions, and not focus on user retention and user loyalty. A strong position in search results will certainly bring new customers, but always think of ways to keep your visitors engaged to your website, and hence to your products and services. A first-time user of your website is a visitor, but on their second visit they become a potential customer.

WordPress incorporates several collaborative and community features that can help you engage your visitors, interact with your customers, and even procure free content.

Employing user roles to get your team involved

The first feature is User Roles. User Roles are simply the system by which you can approve new users and set their administrative level. Higher administrative levels mean that the users have more authority and power on the site. Here is a summary of the available User Roles in WordPress:

User Role	Description
Administrator	Full access to all the administration features. By default, one administrator is created when WordPress is installed, and that user cannot be deleted. Keep in mind that an **Administrator** has the authority to upload and delete plugins and themes. An inexperienced **Administrator** can damage a website.
Editor	Editors can publish pages and modify pages created by others. Editors do not have access to full administrative functions, so they cannot change themes or install plugins.
Author	Authors can publish and manage their own posts, but cannot modify posts published by others.
Contributor	Contributors can write and manage posts, but can't publish content.
Subscriber	Subscribers can only manage their profile, but can't publish posts.

With User Roles, you can easily and safely open your website up to all the members of your organization. More writers mean more content. Collaborative websites grow larger and quicker with more interesting content.

Improving ranking with user comments

Here's where WordPress really starts to leave static websites in the dust: the commenting system. WordPress' commenting system is simply a feature that let's any visitor to your website leave comments (good or bad) about your Pages and Posts. You get the final say on whether a comment gets approved or deleted, and you can turn commenting on or off for individual Posts/Pages.

The commenting system brings your website's visitors into the dialog. You can learn a lot from the comments that users leave on your website. Some customers might point out a design flaw in one of your products, or pose a question that benefits all your visitors.

Page/Post comments are great for SEO; your users are now generating content for you. When your users comment on a page they create new content with almost no intervention from you, except to click on the **Approve** button in the WordPress dashboard.

When the search engines visit your site, they'll find the new comments and index your new *content*—the search engines have no idea if you wrote it or not, and they wouldn't care anyway. When a search engine discovers periodic fresh content on your website, your site now gets treated differently. As a site with regular new content, you get more visits from search spiders, faster indexing, and higher ranking.

An extreme example of faster indexing through the creation of fresh content is Craigslist. Craigslist is the ultimate content site: millions of new, original pages are created each week. Google knows that Craigslist is constantly updated by its users, so they send multiple search spiders to Craigslist to constantly index this flood of new content. That's why while ordinary websites might wait 12 days for a new page to be indexed by Google, a new page on Craigslist might show up in the Google index in 15 minutes.

Commenting is a powerful device that you should keep implemented on all your Posts. Commenting on Pages doesn't always work as well, because Pages have a different character (your Home page, your Contact Us page—sometimes commenting on such pages isn't a fit). If you do turn commenting on, be prepared to moderate some spam comments.

WordPress' commenting system at work makes good pages into great pages. A popular blog post that offered a WordPress tutorial generated user comments, with suggestions for additions to the list. We periodically add suggestions from the comments to the Post itself. It's a win-win scenario; the Post gets free content from our visitors, and the visitors feel engaged and empowered. Let's have a look at the following screenshot:

Using update services

The final element that WordPress contributes to your SEO efforts is the Update Services. Update Services are tools you can use to let other people know you've updated your website. WordPress automatically notifies popular Update Services that you have published new content on your site by sending an XML-RPC ping each time you create or update a Page or Post. Then, the Update Services process your ping and index your new content. Users on sites like Technorati or Weblogs can discover your new content. This means more traffic for your site.

WordPress is set up by default to ping only Ping-O-Matic's server at `http://rpc.pingomatic.com/`, but you can manually add other ping services by navigating in your dashboard to **Settings** and then **Writing**, and enter ping services in the field labeled **Update Services**.

Understanding what WordPress doesn't do for your SEO

Now, we will turn to some ways in which WordPress does not automatically further your SEO efforts, and some ways in which it can potentially undermine your efforts. Note the term *automatically* — because WordPress can be made to do anything with a little bit of effort.

The best way to think of where WordPress fits within the universe of the major open source platforms like Joomla! or Drupal is the following: WordPress is easier to use and more automated than Joomla! or Drupal, but with that simplicity and automation comes restrictions in the ease with which it can be customized. Both WordPress' strengths and its weaknesses as a search platform flow from its simplicity. WordPress doesn't easily offer a lot of page-by-page customization, either in the body of the document or in the navigation menus, WordPress generally wants to generate one style of page and one menu structure for an entire site. Also, in its default setup, it does generate duplicate content that can confuse search engines. We'll examine each of these limitations in turn, and discuss a few clever workarounds.

Tackling duplicate content within WordPress

In the default setup, WordPress will generate some duplicate content. Duplicate content within a site undermines SEO efforts because it confuses search engines (which page of the duplicates is the page that should be indexed), and it may make your site appear low-value to search engines.

Here's how duplicate content is generated in a typical WordPress setup. Say you or another webmaster creates a Post titled `Great Ways to Save Money on Beer`, selects two categories (`beer` and `money`) for the Post and one Tag for the Post (`saving money`). When the Post is published, WordPress then does the following:

1. The Post is published as `mysite.com/great-ways-to-save-money-on-beer`.

2. Category pages are created. An entry for the Post containing its title, a link to the Post, and a 55-word excerpt (called the excerpt in WordPress parlance) is created on two category pages here at `mysite.com/category/beer` and `mysite.com/category/money`.

3. A **Tag** page is created. Another duplicate entry of the Post with a title, link, and 55-word excerpt is created on a **Tag** page here at `mysite.com/tags/saving-money`.

4. If that wasn't enough repetition, WordPress also creates yearly and monthly archives that contain another copy of the title, a link to the Post, and the excerpt. The archives display in this format `mysite.com/2010` and `mysite.com/2010/07`.

We don't want to disable these pages because they help users find content—but we have to find a way to control duplicate content to maximize our SEO efforts. There is one other wrinkle at work in this scenario. The 55-word excerpt that WordPress generates automatically for each Post (unless we create an excerpt manually for each Post), is generated from the first 55 words of the Post! So, the excerpt itself is a partial duplicate of the actual content! So, we have two problems:

- The excerpt is a partial duplicate of existing content
- Multiple archive pages with duplicate content

If this duplicate content isn't controlled, a search engine might index your Tag index page instead of the content on the Post page itself—not an ideal scenario.

The answer is simple and solves the problem completely: a custom `robots.txt` file. Our custom `robots.txt` file will tell search engines not to index our category archive pages, our tag archive pages, and year and month archive pages. In the next chapter, we'll create the ultimate WordPress `robots.txt` file. With our `robots.txt` file, you'll solve these duplicate content issues and secure sensitive areas of your site.

We address the duplicate content in the excerpt by going the extra mile and taking the time to write excerpts for all Posts. To write an excerpt for a Post, simply scroll down from the main edit window when composing a Post and find the box titled **Excerpt**.

Overcoming landing page customization limitations

WordPress does not offer a simple and elegant way to create custom landing pages. It's helpful to understand the nuts and bolts of how WordPress creates pages. When a user browses your site, WordPress generates a few different sections to compose the page. With 99 percent of all WordPress sites, this works as follows: WordPress generates the header, then the content area (the actual content, such as your blog post or contact page), followed by the sidebar, and finally the footer.

In some cases, a WordPress site will have two sidebars instead of one, or an additional element such as a fancy slider under the header, but the method remains the same. Generally, only the content area changes from page to page, the other elements remain the same regardless of what page is requested.

Increasingly, with more advanced frameworks and templates that have emerged in recent years, the WordPress admin area will offer the ability to rearrange and edit individual sections. Your template or framework may offer increased capabilities. Essentially, the decision to use an advanced framework for your WordPress site will boil down to the following: more powerful frameworks deliver more features, but have a higher learning curve.

WordPress ships with a default template, and this default template changes every year. For the year 2015, WordPress shipped with the Twenty Fifteen template. It's a good idea to play with this default template on a sandbox installation (a throw-away, temporary installation) to learn about how to manage a WordPress installation.

With Joomla!, by comparison, pages are constructed with a far more flexible and complex system based on modules. This module-based system means that webmasters can create and utilize different components within modules on different pages. For example, a Joomla! sidebar can have, say, a newsletter sign up box only on particular pages—the webmaster designates the pages on which the sidebar will appear. WordPress' approach is simpler, but less flexible.

WordPress obviously allows you to change the appearance of the content area page-by-page. Page-by-page changes in the other elements of your website, the header, footer, and sidebar, are possible but require the coding of custom templates, or the use of an advanced framework or template.

This limitation can limit your ability to easily and quickly create fully customized, highly graphical landing pages.

Understanding the limitations of page-by-page navigation

In addition, WordPress limits the flexibility with which you can create page-by-page navigation. You may have noticed this effect when browsing WordPress sites: the navigation menus remain fixed and constant as you browse throughout the site. Generally, WordPress will call your sidebar when it generates a page. That sidebar is defined by the choice of sidebar widgets you make, within the appearance section (from your WordPress dashboard, select **Appearance**, then **Widgets**). Furthermore, the use of the nofollow attribute is generally not possible with WordPress' dynamically-generated navigation menus. Multiple variations of sidebars are certainly possible, but require that either custom templates to be coded or a framework/template with drag-and-drop capability be employed. There is no menu selection that can accomplish this.

There is a hidden benefit to these limitations, you can't mess up what you can't customize.

Tinkering with a website's navigation can be dangerous: you are tinkering with the pathways by which search engines find and assign a relative value to your content.

That said, with experience, customizing your navigation can bring great optimization benefits. The goal with navigation architecture is to sculpt the flow of PageRank to increase the flow to your highest value pages, and to restrict the flow of PageRank to low-value pages like your privacy policy and contact pages. In larger sites, dead zones can develop, areas where search spiders have difficulty crawling and indexing. While this doesn't occur often in WordPress sites, customized adjustments in navigation will generally fix the problem.

Some users will find the restrictions in customization inconvenient, others will never notice.

Summary

While WordPress does have a handful of limitations, it's generally a superb platform for search optimization. But that's all it is, a platform. No platform is going to write good content, contact other webmasters and ask for links, do your keyword research, or gauge the relative strength of your competitors. But, what WordPress does is economize the presentation of content so that you can focus on the day-to-day tasks of building your website into a vibrant destination.

In this chapter, we learned how to plan your website strategy in a manner by which you can harness the power of the WordPress platform. We learned how to gauge the search competitiveness of competing websites, and adjust your plan to participate in the search market. We discovered ways through which you can gain inspiration for your site and discussed resources where the freshest and most advanced design ideas are presented.

We discussed WordPress' strengths: its inherently economical architecture, its blogging capabilities, and its ability to build up large sites quickly. We learned about RSS feeds and how to harness them for greater visibility. We covered WordPress' built-in collaborative capabilities.

We also covered a few areas where WordPress won't instinctively assist your SEO and learned a few workarounds for these limitations. In the next chapter, we'll dig deeper into the nuts and bolts of technical optimization by looking at the role of keywords.

3
Researching and Working with Keywords

Keywords are the currency of search optimization, and hence the currency of the new business environment. They are the words and phrases that millions of Internet users employ to find goods and services they need. They are the signposts that search engines use to store and retrieve web pages for search users. The search engines run on words. Success in a search environment depends greatly on sound keyword research and skills. Capturing search queries for the right phrases can bring phenomenal success. Likewise, capturing the wrong search terms might yield only lukewarm success.

Keywords are the foundation upon which the house (your website) is built.

In this chapter, we'll cover the following topics:

- We'll begin by building a keyword list based on what you have to offer consumers. What keywords and keyphrases will purchasers use to identify your products or services?

- We'll examine whether it's wiser to focus on a few high-value terms, or to build out a broad keyword list and rank for a wide variety of phrases.

- We'll look at some keyword qualifiers such as *best* and *expert* that can help boost traffic and edge out competitors.

- We'll learn how to group keywords into manageable groups and how to leverage grouped keywords for maximum SEO benefit.

- We'll look at popular keyword tools that can show you what phrases are being searched in high volumes, and how to spot regional and seasonally-based trends.

- Finally, we'll learn how to expand your keyword empire.

The goal of this chapter is simple: find high-value and high-volume relevant terms for your business so that you'll ultimately secure that search traffic with superior rankings.

Building your site's foundation with keyword research

Your keyword strategy is the foundation of everything you'll do in search optimization. Your page titles, navigation menus, content, even your domain name itself will all be dictated by your keyword strategy. Just like a building's foundation, if your keyword strategy is flawed, the house that sits upon the foundation will be flawed.

In the world of Internet search, the term keyword can refer to single words, or word phrases. Word phrases are also sometimes called keyphrases, keyword strings, or keyword phrases. In this book, we'll use all these terms interchangeably—regardless of how many individual words comprise a keyword. When implementing your keyword strategy, the family of keywords you incorporate into your strategy will likely be a mix of single terms and multi-word terms. Keep in mind that single word keyphrases are nearly always more competitive than multiple-word keyphrases—that's because single word searches are generally searched for in higher volumes than longer strings.

One core principle in keyword strategy is this: when you rank well for high-volume keywords, you may expect that ranking to generate a high number of visits to your website. That's not the whole story, but it's obviously a major part of it.

But will ranking for single word terms bring instant success? Not necessarily, single word phrases have relevancy problems for nearly all websites. For example, the term *coffee* is searched nearly 19,000 times daily throughout the world on Google alone. But is a web user in London searching for *coffee* necessarily a perfect customer for a coffee shop in Los Angeles? Of course not! Keywords must be relevant in order to be useful to you. Search volume alone is not enough. You need to find the right blend of high-search volume and relevance to your product or service.

Understanding relevance and the effect of short tail and long tail keywords

It's important to understand the distinction between short tail keywords and long tail keywords. The difference is simple: a short tail keyword is a short, one or two-word search phrase. A long tail keyword is a three, four, five-word, or longer keyphrase. An example of a short tail keyword would be *Dallas restaurant*, where an example of a long tail keyword would be *Top-rated West Dallas pizza*. As you might suspect, long tail keywords are almost always searched in much lower volumes than their short tail counterparts. However, long tail keywords possess important and valuable advantages over short tail keywords, as we will learn.

Examining user intent through keywords

To understand the value of long tail keywords, we need to think about how a chosen keyword reflects the intent, as well as the motivation of a web user. Let us examine a typical customer awareness cycle. First, a customer becomes aware of a product, or expresses interest in a product. Next, the customer seeks information about that product. In the final stages before a purchase decision, a consumer will evaluate choices and make a buying decision. That typical awareness cycle brings a customer closer to a purchase decision as they progress.

Ideally, you'll employ keywords that capture a customer when they are closest to a buying decision. Imagine two potential customers; one who searches for *Top-rated West Dallas pizza* and one who searches for *Dallas Restaurant*. The long tail searcher has expressed a greater degree of commercial intent and motivation than the short tail searcher. This user has most likely decided that he or she would like pizza. The user has also decided that he or she would like to eat in West Dallas, rather than some other part of the city. Finally, the user has tried to qualify his or her search even further by searching for *Top-rated* pizza. This customer is farther along in the customer awareness/purchase cycle, and is overwhelmingly more likely to buy quality pizza in West Dallas than a person searching simply for *Dallas Restaurant*.

The graph below illustrates long tail keywords at work; short tail keywords are searched more often, but long tail keywords enjoy a higher conversion rate:

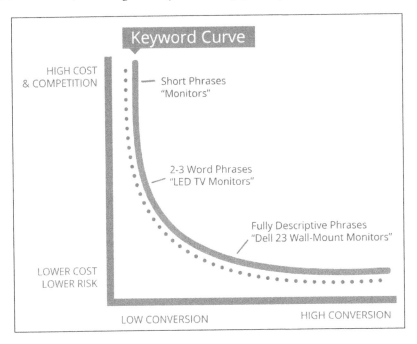

And so, the power of the long tail search comes into focus. The Internet searcher in the previous example, is pure gold to a business owner. The long tail search expresses motivation, intent, and specificity. Sure, the search volumes will be lower, but it'll be much easier to convert a higher number of long tail search users into customers. Now, here comes the bonus: most of your competitors are not going to do the extra work to capture long tail searches. While the competition is focused on the high-volume terms, you have the opportunity to secure high rankings for high value, easy-to-convert long tail searchers. Generally, the deeper you go in pursuit of long tail searches, the less search competition you'll encounter, both in natural search and pay per click. You'll need to know where to stop though; if you pursue search phrases that are too rare, you'll have no search traffic at all.

Developing a powerful long tail search strategy

Here are some tips and rules to follow to develop and maximize the power of long tail searches:

- Geographic locations are great qualifiers that turn general keywords into long tail searches. All the towns near your business location that fall within your service area can make great long tail search terms. In Dallas, for example, smaller communities like Plano and Carrollton can become *air conditioning service Plano*, and *air conditioning repair Carrollton*.

- Manufacturer names can make great long tail searches, for example, *Volvo repair Fairfax VA* and *Honda motorcycle parts Fairfax VA*.

- Don't get too specific in your long tail strategy or you'll rank for keywords with no search volume. Monitor your web analytics to see if the search phrases you are chasing are too esoteric.

- Additional qualifiers like *Top-rated* and *Best* can help form effective long tail searches.

Researching keyword search volume with online keyword tools

As we've worked through learning about how to build a keyword strategy, one central tenet always emerges: the overwhelming importance of keyword search volume. If keywords are the foundation of your entire web strategy, then keyword search volume data comprises the bricks that make up that foundation. Find the high-volume keywords and rank for those keywords and the customers will come.

Keyword research is done primarily with free and paid online tools that maintain databases of keyword search volume. In the following sections, we'll cover three popular and effective free tools: Google's search-based keyword tool, Google Trends, and Google Suggest.

Google's Adwords Keyword Planner

The Google Adwords Keyword Planner, formerly the SKtool, is designed to help you determine the best keywords to target in your Google AdWords campaigns. This is the grand-daddy of all keyword tools, and should be the place you start. If you only use one keyword tool, this is it.

You'll need to sign up for a Google Adwords account and create a basic campaign, before using the tool. Google Adwords is Google's paid advertising system, whereby business owners can bid to have their ads show up concurrently with search results. If you aren't ready to start spending big money in Adwords, that's ok, simply enter a daily budget of one dollar for your initial campaign, and one cent bids on any keywords you store in the campaign.

To get started, point your browser to `https://adwords.google.com/ KeywordPlanner`. You'll need to log in to your Google account to use the tool. If the site you are trying to find keywords for is not being advertised in AdWords, this tool may not return any results based on your actual website content.

You'll be greeted with two choices, **Find new keywords and get search volume data** and **Plan your budget and get forecasts**. Start with the former for a simple and easy-to-understand first look at keyword volumes.

With **Find new keywords**, select **Search for new keywords using a phrase, website or category**. Now you are ready to run the tool. You can enter one phrase or several; the tool will expand your list to related phrases which you can then evaluate. This screenshot shows where you'll try your first query:

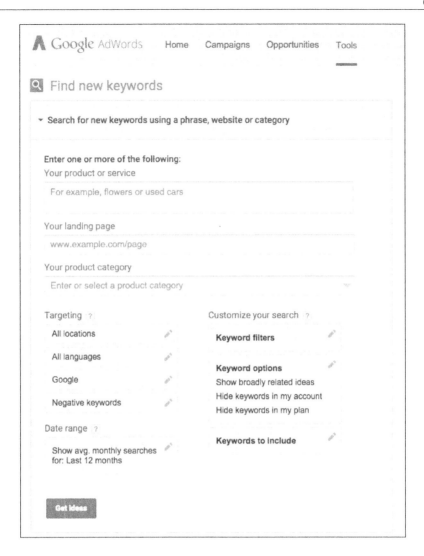

Note that you can set your geographic targeting by selecting the edit icon next to All locations below the query fields. You can ignore this for now; you want to gather large swaths of data and then drill down into what's specifically relevant to your business or goal.

The query results page will show a graph with tabular keyword data below, as shown in the following screenshot:

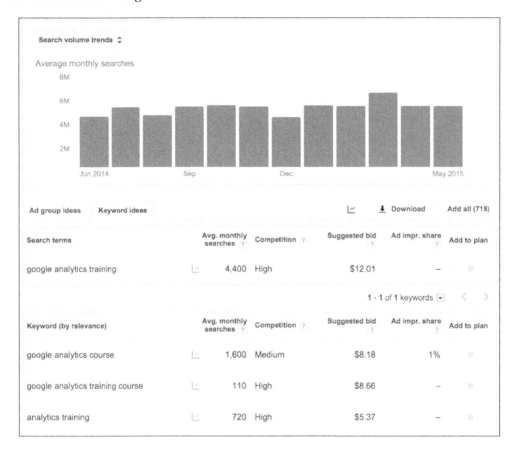

Let us break down these results. The graph at the top simply represents changes in the keyword volume for each of the last 12 months. Pay attention, because the tables below show average monthly query volume, but seasonal terms spike in particular times of the year.

Below the graph you'll want to make sure you've selected the Keyword Ideas tab to get to the display shown above. We entered a single search term, `google analytics training`, and we can see in the first table average monthly searches of 4,400 queries. The graph above shows some monthly variation, but a relatively steady volume. The second table shows us more—these are queries that Google has suggested as close variants of the query we entered. Our screenshot only shows the first few entries, but Google typically replies with dozens. This feature lets us discover new keyphrases.

Understand the purpose for which Google provides this tool to help customers build keyword lists and ad groups for its Adwords product. So, you will note that the tool's purpose is you entice you to add keywords to a paid Adwords campaign. You can simply ignore the **Suggested bid** and **Add to plan** features within the tool and use the **Download** button to export your keywords to a spreadsheet. Of course, if you are running an Adwords campaign in parallel to a search strategy, your keywords data serves both purposes.

Google's dominance in search, and the thoroughness and effectiveness of its Keyword Planner tool, makes it hard to suggest other tools for basic keyword research. However, we do want to cover a few specialty search tools that extend and supplement the Keyword Planner.

Spotting keyword popularity patterns with Google Trends

Google Trends is a useful tool when trying to determine the timing of a marketing campaign and setting long-range goals. It can also give you a bigger picture than just looking at the traffic for the most recent month or monthly average, which could help you avoid seasonal keywords that have had a high traffic volume recently, but may be getting ready to drop significantly in the near future. You can also avoid keywords that are fading in popularity over time. You can find the tool at `https://www.google.com/trends/`.

Some keywords are obviously seasonal, such as *Christmas recipes* and *Super Bowl party tips*. However, not all seasonal keywords are so obvious. Typing a keyword into Google Trends allows you to view a graph that shows the spikes in search volume for a given term over the past ten years. With such a huge amount of data available, it is easy to see whether the search volume spikes at the same time each year.

Let us take a look at a keyword that has both a seasonal variance, as well as a long-term downward trend in popularity; the keyword is **plasma tv**. Now, if you think about it, it's easy to see why this keyword is seasonal. A lot of people formerly bought these expensive televisions as a Christmas present for the family, so it makes sense that there is a huge spike in search volume for this keyword at the end of every year. Let us examine a screenshot of Google Trends for the keyword **plasma tv**:

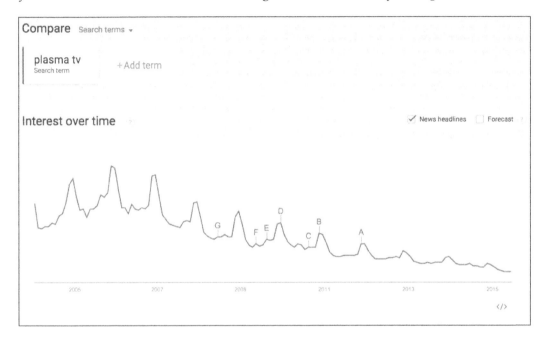

Two clear trends emerge. First is the confirmation of the end-of-year spike in keyword popularity. Second is the waning popularity of this search term. Plasma TVs, once the rage, were ultimately beaten out in the market by the emergence of LED TVs. **plasma tv** is a dying keyword. Would 2016 be a good time to launch a blog featuring reviews of Plasma TVs based on the data that Google Trends shows? Probably not. Google Trends is a powerful tool to see seasonal trends and make measured predictions of the future popularity of keywords.

If you want to narrow down the trends even more, you can filter the results in Google Trends by geographic region. You can also view data for each year separately, instead of viewing everything at once. Google Trends also gives links to the top related news stories and charts the location for each on the graph, so you can see what effect these events may have had on the search volume.

Keyword discovery with Google Suggest and Ubersuggest

We've all searched using Google, and we have all noticed that Google.com shows us a waterfall of suggested search terms that attempt to complete our query. This screenshot shows this popular feature:

Google Suggest is a specific feature of the Google search service, but you'll have to use it manually as shown above; there is no web-based interface for the service like with the Keyword Planner tool. The Google Suggest results are delivered in order of popularity, so it is a valuable tool for keyword discovery. Keyword discovery is simply the process of expanding your universe of potential keywords.

A more powerful variant of Google Suggest is Ubersuggest, which you'll find at `http://ubersuggest.org/`. Ubersuggest simply compiles Google Suggest data and then delivers it in a web-based format, with a range of additional features. Ubersuggest makes it faster and easier to leverage to the keyword discovery potential of Google Suggest. Remember that Ubersuggest is a keyword discovery tool that displays the relative popularity of terms, but doesn't tell you the exact numbers of search queries for each term. For search query volume data, you simply return to Google's Keyword Planner.

[Placing your keywords and corresponding search volumes into a spreadsheet makes it easier to sort keywords according to which terms garner the most traffic.]

Identifying and developing your initial keyword profile

Because keywords play such an important foundational role in the development of your search strategy, you will obviously want to spend a good deal of thought and effort developing a sound initial keyword profile. Keep in mind, though, your initial keyword research is merely a foundation. You'll work and rework your keyword profile throughout your campaign.

Developing your keyword list has several phases:

1. **Collection**: In the initial collection phase, you will simply collect large numbers of keywords and dump them on to a list.

2. **Analysis**: In the analysis phase, you will attach relative weight to terms and cull undesirable terms. For example, you'll undoubtedly collect terms for services and goods you don't sell. You'll obviously not want to put effort into ranking for such terms.

3. **Expansion**: The expansion phase will take place after your campaigns have been running for a while—this phase is a reaction to what you learn from the performance of your campaign, and from competitors in the marketplace.

Creating your keyword matrix

As you progress with your keyword research, you will want to develop a keyword matrix. A keyword matrix is a simple data set based on all the keywords you think might have value. Your keyword matrix is your front-line tool in analyzing your keywords.

[Spreadsheet software is particularly well suited to developing a keyword matrix.]

Your keyword matrix should be organized as follows: you should have a row entry for each potential keyword, with the keyword in the left column. In the next row, you will record the reported monthly or daily search volume for that specific keyword. We learned earlier how to pull data on keyword search volumes from the Google's Keyword Planner tool. In the following column, you will assign a relevance score to the keyword between 0 and 100. The relevance score is a numerical measurement of how valuable that keyword phrase will be to your business. We'll discuss relevance scores in the paragraphs that follow. The following screenshot shows a simple keyword matrix built around terms related to WordPress SEO books:

	A	B	C	D
	Keyword	Monthly Searches	Relevance %	Weighted Value
1				
2	wordpress books	720	15	108
3	wordpress seo book	220	100	220
4	wordpress seo plugin	3600	0	0
5	wordpress seo guide	140	80	112
6	wordpress and seo	170	70	119
7	wordpress seo tips	720	40	288
8	best wordpress seo	260	10	26

Calculating relevance scores for keywords

Let us examine how relevance scores are calculated. A high-relevance search term is a search term for which the commercial intent of the searcher is a sure match for your products or services. Let us examine the figure above showing a keyword matrix, to illustrate how to come up with a relevance score.

The keyword **wordpress seo book** is assigned a relevance score of 100. For a writer of WordPress SEO books, that search phrase is perfectly relevant to the goods offered. However, the relevance score for **wordpress books** is **15** percent only. That is because this key term is much less desirable and only about 15 percent of those Internet searchers would be potential customers. The other 85 percent are looking for something else; someone searching for **wordpress books** might be looking for a beginning book on WordPress, not necessarily an SEO book.

Likewise, an Internet user searching for **wordpress seo plugins** is not searching for a book at all, they are obviously looking for a WordPress plugin. That searcher has no relevance to what we offer, so we assign a relevance score of **0**. The relevance score should reflect your best estimate of what percentage of the search volume represents actual potential customers.

We then use the relevance score to arrive at a weighted value for a given search term. The weighted value for a search term is the search volume for a given term multiplied by the relevance percentage to arrive at an adjusted number of monthly searches. This adjusted number represents the real value of the search term. And so, in our example, the search phrase **wordpress books** has a strong search volume: **720** monthly searches. However, at such a low relevance score of **15** percent (which might even be generous), this phrase has a weighted value of only **108** searches. On the other hand, the phrase **wordpress seo book** is perfectly relevant and yields a weighted value of **220** searches. And so, you can use a keyword matrix to analyze your keyword list, to prioritize the truly valuable keywords.

Gathering keywords – thinking about your customer's (imperfect) intent

Now that we have our keyword matrix in place, and an emerging understanding of how to approach our keyword strategy, we will want to continue to build out our keyword list.

Collecting keywords is relatively easy, just throw everything into the pot. We'll continually expand and narrow our keyword list throughout the life of our campaign. To build out your keyword list, you want to think about the services and products you offer and think of every possible word and combination of words that people might use to find what you sell.

It's important to think of not what words you use to describe your product, but what words your potential customers use.

Your customers might not use the same terms that you use; they might use derogatory terms, abbreviated terms, misspelled terms, or lingo terms. One illustrative example is cosmetic surgeon/plastic surgeon. Doctors who work in that field refer to themselves as *cosmetic surgeons*. The term *Plastic surgeon* does not enjoy the same prestige—but in search volume, *Plastic surgeon* is far more commonly employed as a search query, and so, the family of phrases including *plastic*, rather than *cosmetic* will be the better performing family of keywords. Even if it's not a term you would use, if any potential customer would use it, you should put that term on your keyword matrix.

Building keyword lists with common qualifiers

When you build out your keyword list, you should also build variations of the popular terms with common keyword qualifiers. A keyword qualifier is simply an additional term, usually an adjective, that the search users employ to further narrow their search. For example, some Internet users might search for *Expert plumbing repair*, rather than *Plumbing repair*. Qualifiers might not always represent desirable searches; qualifiers like *Free* and *Research* tend to indicate folks looking for a do-it-yourself or free solution to a problem. The most popular qualifiers generally fall into one of the few categories. Some common categories and corresponding search qualifiers are the following:

- Price qualifiers indicate searchers looking for a low price: cheap, free, discount, sale, bargain, and so forth. Although you should consider whether bargain hunters are the customers you want in the first place

- Quality/Experience qualifiers indicate searchers looking for *Best in class* providers. These searchers can make great customers because they might be prepared to pay a premium: best, expert, experienced, professional, licensed, bonded, and certified

- Informational qualifiers might indicate searchers that do not have commercial intent: research, info, how to, DIY, help, and so on

- Time qualifiers indicate searchers looking for businesses open outside of normal business hours: 24 hour, all night, express, late night, and so on

- Intent qualifiers are employed by searchers that expressly want to see commercial sites: buy, shop, store, online, and so on

- Category qualifiers could mean any type of product variation: green (that is, *Green furniture*), natural, energy-efficient, recycled, eco-friendly, and so on

Employing the human touch in keyword research

With all keyword research, you'll need to apply a *Human touch*. Keyword research is not an entire objective undertaken purely based on statistics. You will need to follow your instincts as you build and hone your keyword list and strategy.

Analyzing customer's search behavior

It's important to think about how users search for the products and services that they seek online. There has been a wealth of research undertaken on the subject, and our own patterns and techniques as search users can teach us much about how others use search.

Most of the research on user search patterns leads to a few basic conclusions. First, new users seeking information online tend to enter either longer search strings or shorter search strings than experienced users. A new user might enter a query such as `The hospital nearest to Oldham Road in Oklahoma City`. If you ever have the opportunity to observe an inexperienced user make use of a search engine for the first time, it can be a fascinating exercise.

As these new search users become more accustomed to search engines, they *learn* how to enter more economical queries — and research indicates quite strongly that this education happens nearly immediately. Users quickly distill their search patterns to the shortest possible phrase that will return what they are seeking.

The other mistake that new search users make is that they enter queries that are too short. An example would be a search user entering the query `Pool clean`, when seeking a local pool cleaning company. Such a search is far too broad to yield relevant local results: it will yield some educational content, a few national manufacturers of pool cleaning equipment, and some national online pool supply stores. And so, users very quickly learn that phrases that are too broad will not yield focused and relevant results. The searcher tries again, this time searching for `pool cleaning in Las Vegas` and the search engine returns a list of solely local pool cleaning companies — exactly what the searcher intended.

We are all users of search, and we have all passed through our informal education on how to use a search engine. Because all search users become accustomed to using search engines very quickly, as website owners, we can depend on a certain reliability in the way search users utilize search strings to find what they seek.

Building keyword lists with location names

If you are in a local market catering to a local clientele, then location names are going to be big money keywords for you. Internet users seeking products and services near their home or business quickly learn that a search phrase with a location name returns more relevant results than a search without a location, just like the Dallas pizza restaurant example earlier.

Learning how customers engage in local search

Search volume statistics demonstrate very reliable and common search patterns for locally-based searches. In nearly every niche, from medicine to lawn mowing, the high volume, big opportunity local search keywords follow the following patterns:

- Product/service description followed by city name (Dermatologist Jacksonville)

- City name followed by product/service description (Jacksonville dermatologist)

Sometimes, but not always, searchers include the full state name or state abbreviation (dermatologist Jacksonville FL). Let's take a look at some actual search volumes that illustrate these principles.

Daily Search Volumes for Dallas Dermatologists:

Keyword	Search Volume
dermatologist Dallas	390
dermatologist in Dallas Texas	40
Dallas dermatologist	590

The city-product pattern (Dallas dermatologist) enjoys the highest-search volume followed by the product-city pattern (dermatologist Dallas). Finally, the long tail pattern enjoys a lesser, but still respectable, amount of traffic. This is a generally reliable standard for local search queries. Naturally, we will measure specific search volumes before fully implementing a keyword strategy.

Applying long tail theory to local search

Bearing in mind what we have learned about local search usage, a great opportunity presents itself to the WordPress webmaster: long tail searches in local markets. This is an underutilized approach that can reward aggressive and diligent website owners. Experienced webmasters and SEO professionals use this approach and earn big gains. Here's how to do it.

In both major cities and local markets, there are always surrounding communities and towns that represent both customer opportunities and keyword opportunities. In the city of San Diego, for example, there are dozens of surrounding towns (Del Mar, National City, Chula Vista, Imperial Beach, Solana Beach, Encinitas, and so on) as well as neighborhoods (Pacific Beach, Old Town, Mission Bay, Bird Rock, La Mesa, Clairemont, and many others).

To a business owner, these additional geo-markets are all great keyword opportunities, especially for WordPress site owners. Long tail theory applies to smaller communities: because the communities have smaller populations, the search volumes in those areas will be light. However, the conversion rate in a smaller community will be higher, because the keyword is more closely focused on the searcher's location.

And, with WordPress, you can quickly and easily build out extra pages to capture this extra traffic. Finally, the icing on the cake: most other business owners won't or don't bother with optimization for smaller communities. Either they are too busy, too uniformed, or their website platform is too unaccommodating to easily modify or build out the extra content to capture this low-hanging fruit. If you cover enough towns and neighborhoods, your ultimate reward can be to completely dominate an entire region.

There's a wrong way to go about this, however. Some webmasters and less sophisticated SEO *professionals* will simply stuff a list of cities into the bottom of a page. That's wrong for two reasons. First, it's clearly keyword stuffing: the intentional inclusion of keywords in batches without regard to content, solely for the purpose of infecting keyword results. Keyword stuffing is against Google's webmaster guidelines. Second, it's just not effective. You need more than one or two words at the bottom of a page to rank for anything meaningful. The superior approach is to build out pages for each geo-market. With this approach, you can use the town's name in the title tag, body text, and other HTML elements—with this extra power, you'll rank soundly for searches that include that town name. Also, the individual pages you create will speak more directly to members of that community, so you'll out-convert competitors as well.

Building local pages the right way

You should avoid creating *thin* content pages to match each local keyword variant. An example of thin content pages would be if you created 20 content pages for 20 different small towns, but each page was a duplicate of all the others except for the city name. That technique worked wonders years ago, before Google's duplicate content capabilities grew more sophisticated. This technique is sometimes referred to as Mad Libs pages, based on the popular children's fill in the blank books.

There's a great example of the practice of building local pages by a company in Texas called Dawson Foundation Repair. Dawson has created individual content pages for about 100 individual cities. Each of these pages performs very well in search results for queries that include a town name, like `New Braunfels Foundation Repair`.

If we try that query and find `Dawson Foundation Repair` in search results, we see that Dawson's local page for New Braunfels is entirely unique content that is focused on the proper keyword popularity. Dawson has even gone as far as to discuss the soil characteristics in each town. Dawson has created unique and meaningful local pages for many cities and have performed well in search for years.

Following the people, following the money

When building your keyword list, you'll always want to return to the question *Who is my customer?* If you are a deck builder, pool builder, or plastic surgeon, your customer is a homeowner (in the case of home services), and a person of financial means (in the case of home services or plastic surgery). It's obviously helpful to know where the people with the money live. If the residents of a town or neighborhood aren't able to afford your product, you'll obviously not want to market there. Similarly, you'll prefer to put your efforts into high-population areas over low-population areas. This same approach can apply to other demographics that might impact your bottom line: *Where are the families with children? Where do the senior citizens live?* These inquiries are basic demographic questions that you can use to focus your keyword strategy.

For most, you'll have a sense of your own community: *where the population centers are?, where the wealthier people with disposable income live?*. There may be other variations: areas with new home construction under way are a gold mine for home services like window blinds, alarm companies, and pool builders.

If you don't have a true encyclopedic understanding of the demographics of your region, or you simply want to deepen your understanding of the local marketplace, there is a great web-based tool that can help you *follow the money*. The tool is Webfoot Maps and can be found at `http://maps.webfoot.com/`. Webfoot has created a collection of demographics-based Google Maps mashups that visually represent demographic data like the population density and household income as an overlay over a standard Google Map. With this tool, you can zoom into your town and see where the population centers are, and where the high-income folks are living. Webfoot Maps are currently only available for North America and Australia. The site offers a tremendous amount of data and it can be very helpful in crafting a keyword strategy. The census data upon which the site relies is from 2000, but it will likely be updated soon when the new 2010 census data becomes available. To use the tool, browse to `http://maps.webfoot.com/` and follow the link for **US 2000 Census**. From there, you can select any of the following demographic criteria:

- Median Household Income
- Population density
- Median Owner-occupied home value
- Median age
- Median home value/median income
- Percent White
- Percent Black
- Percent Hispanic
- Percent Asian
- Percent Native
- Percent Female
- Percent Male
- Percent of owner-occupied housing units
- Percent of renter-occupied housing units
- Percent of vacant housing units
- Average household size
- Average family size
- Percent with college degree
- 2008 Unemployment Rate (county)
- 2007 Unemployment Rate (county)
- Unemployment Rate Change 2008-7

Webfoot Maps present sensible graphical data for each default selection, but you can adjust the **Value** parameter to display, for example, you can display only areas with incomes above $100,000 per year.

Here's how Webfoot's demographic Google Maps mashup works at displaying household income in the geo-markets including and surrounding Dallas/Fort Worth. Darker areas indicate higher income levels. Areas with higher incomes can present excellent web marketing opportunities for some businesses, as shown in the following screenshot:

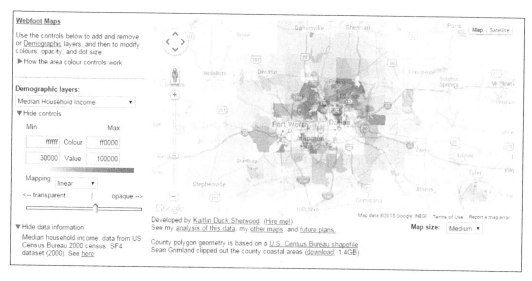

Tuning and honing your keyword list

In the beginning of this chapter, we introduced the three phases of keyword strategy: collection, analysis, and expansion. We have learned how to gather and collect keywords, and now we'll move on to the analysis phase: how to tune and hone your keyword list for maximum effectiveness, how to prioritize keywords, how to group keywords into families, how to account for seasonal variations in keyword traffic, and finally how to introduce negative keywords to avoid useless traffic.

Prioritizing keywords

Be realistic about the breadth of your keyword profile: if you are just starting out in a competitive market, you may not realistically rank for all your desired keywords. Even experienced SEO professionals with tremendous link building power at their disposal will prioritize certain keywords for an initial launch and then introduce other keywords and keyword families in phases once rankings have been established.

It makes sense to work in phases, preferably in 90-day increments. Choose keywords that present a realistic and attainable goal of competitive rankings in three months. Once you meet your ranking goals for the first set of keywords, move on to the next set of keywords.

Building first, second, and third tier keywords

So, which keywords should you work on first? Generally, your first tier keywords should get attention first. First tier keywords are your primary, high-volume and high-relevance terms. First tier keywords are generally more competitive, but they're likely where you'll get the lion's share of your traffic. For example, if you sell medical supplies in Chicago, your first tier keywords would include the following:

- Medical supplies Chicago
- Medical supplier Chicago
- Chicago medical supplier
- Chicago medical supplies

Next, you'll work on your second tier keywords. Second tier keywords are lower-volume category-based terms. This family of keywords will be larger than your first tier keywords, and search competition will be lighter. Some examples (again from the medical supply niche) of second tier keywords would include:

- Wheelchair supply Chicago
- Orthopedic supply Chicago
- Respiratory products Chicago

Finally, you will prioritize your third tier keywords. Your third tier keywords are your lowest volume: true long tail keywords. Third tier keywords describe specific products or services, and specific model names and numbers. Again, some keyword examples would include:

- 9000 XT wheelchair Chicago
- Electric powered wheelchair Chicago
- Blood glucose test meter Chicago

Obviously, it makes more sense to endeavor to rank for the first tier keywords before ranking for more specific and low-volume second and third tier keywords. Prioritizing high-volume terms first will help bring great numbers of visitors sooner. There is one important exception to that rule: if your first tier keywords are too competitive, you may take too long to rank for those terms and you may wish to consider inverting your plan and prioritizing your second or third tier keywords first. Your goal is to get traffic quickly when you start up. Starting with lower tier keywords where the competition is lighter can help bring traffic more quickly.

Accounting for seasonal trends

Seasonal trends effect keyword volumes in varying degrees. In some industries, there is almost no seasonal variation in keyword volume. Examples of such industries include staple products like groceries, telephone services, family medicine, auto repair — the things that all folks need pretty much all the time. Then on the other end of the spectrum are those products that are acutely seasonal. The most pronounced examples would be Santa dolls around Christmas time, pool building services in spring and summer, air conditioning repair in summertime in the Southern U.S., weight-loss programs just after New Year's and in the spring.

The truth is that nearly all keywords are seasonal to some degree — just perhaps not enough to worry about. Sure, family medicine business will drop off during summer while folks are away on vacation. But if you are a family practitioner, small dips in seasonal volume won't affect your strategy enough to warrant major changes in your approach. Seasonal variations in keyword volume will matter more to people in truly seasonally-based industries.

So, how would an air conditioning repair business work around seasonal changes in keyword traffic for *Air conditioning* terms? Surely the keyword traffic would drop off in cold weather (believe me, it does). The answer is to prioritize air conditioning terms in the spring and summer and then prioritize heating and heating repair terms in the late summer and fall to capture shifts in seasonal traffic.

Tuning your list – negative keywords

Negative keywords are words for which you do not want to capture search traffic. Put another way, negative keywords are words that when they appear in a search query, represent an intent that makes the searcher undesirable as a customer. For example, the term **do-it-yourself** (DIY) is a term typically employed by ambitious homeowners who want to find information to fix broken items themselves, rather than pay a service. Here's another example: if you offer window replacement for residential homes, you want to avoid traffic for *Car window repair*. You can use the negative keywords *Auto* and *Car* to avoid those searches.

The well-known SEO speaker Dan Thies once commented, when asked about a list of effective negative keywords that folks should exclude from their keyword campaigns, *I can give you a list of good negative matches: free. That's the list.* That's a helpful suggestion, but it's not that simple. If you offer free shipping, you'll hardly want to turn away people looking for *diamond rings free shipping*.

Negative keywords are most important in a pay per click environment where an irrelevant click might cost $3 — the *danger* of garnering an irrelevant click simply isn't present in natural search. Adding negative keywords to a Google AdWords campaign is easy, and can be done in two ways:

- You can add a negative keyword as you would with any other keyword — simply put a negative sign (-) before the negative term when you are populating your keyword list.

- You can also add negative keywords at the campaign level (which will apply the negative term to all your ad groups), by selecting the campaign, then selecting the **Keywords** tab, and scrolling down to the section titled **Negative keywords**.

Grouping keywords into families

You'll want to group your keywords into families of related terms. There are several benefits. Your keyword families form the genesis of sections, categories, and pages on your website. Also, your keyword families can serve as highly organized ad groups for pay per click marketing.

Let us examine, how to divide keywords into families based around common terms, and how to implement the families into your keyword strategy. First, group your keywords around popular terms, as shown in the following section.

Keywords organized into families in the niche of house painting

General terms:

- House painting
- House painter
- Painting company
- Painting contractor

Interior painting terms:

- Interior painting
- Interior painter
- Interior painting company

Exterior painting terms:

- Exterior painting
- Exterior painter
- Exterior painting company

Faux finishing terms:

- Faux finishing
- Faux painting

The preceding section is hyper-simplified, but illustrates a sensible way to categorize painting-related keywords. The *Interior Painting Terms* family is all based around the term *Interior* while the *Exterior Painting Terms* family is based around the term *Exterior*. It takes no great leap of logic to figure that it would also be sensible to structure sections and/or pages of your website around these families. For example, a well-written web page about interior painting services with pictures of interior painting projects, can serve as a landing page that ranks for (and converts) customers searching for interior painting services. Conversely, it would be more difficult to create a page that would rank for two families of terms, both *Interior* and *Exterior* terms. As all the terms in the Interior Painting Terms family contain the term *interior*, you need only one destination web page to rank for the entire family of terms. Naturally, the words *Interior painting* and *Interior painter* will be the primary keywords that you'll use in the core elements of the interior painting landing page.

These families of keywords can also serve as well-organized ad groups in pay per click campaigns. Both Google and Yahoo's pay per click services utilize a format where advertisers combine their keywords into groups. When pay per click keywords are organized into groups, the campaigns are more effective than single-group campaigns. The text ads served by group can be focused more relevantly on the topic of the group yielding higher click-through rates and higher quality scores. Then you can employ individual landing pages based on each keyword group, which will increase conversions over a general page.

Finding new keywords

You will always want to be alert to the new keyword opportunities. This is the *expansion* phase of your keyword development. New products and product model numbers will become new keywords as they are released to the market. New technologies create new keyword opportunities at an ever-increasing pace. New laws create new keyword opportunities as they are passed. Stay on top of these keyword trends and you'll further edge out your competitors.

Eyeing the competition

One way to find new keywords is to keep an eye on your competition. What keywords are your competitors utilizing for the important pages of their website? Is your competition advertising new products and services? If so, it may mean that they've found a micro-niche within their market that you can harness as well.

You can also use one of several keyword spying websites. The website Spyfu (`http://www.spyfu.com`) touts itself as a resource that empowers you to *spot new SEM/SEO opportunities and outsmart your competitors*. That's a fitting description. Spyfu gathers pay per click data on millions of websites and let's you discover what keywords your competition is employing in their pay per click campaigns. While the free version offers a peek, the paid version offers more data and more depth of features. As an alternative, the service SEMRush offers the same capability. Another great spying tool is Google Alerts. Google Alerts is a free tool with which you can *monitor the web for interesting new content*. Here's how it works: you enter a query term. When Google discovers new content that includes that query term, you receive an e-mail. This free service is great for monitoring your competition: simply enter the name of a competitor's website, and you'll receive an e-mail each time they publish new content on their website or issue a press release. The keyword tools we've described earlier in this chapter, Google Suggest and Ubersuggest, both present variants of keywords when you employ them. Use these tools to continually expand your keyword lists.

Finding new keywords with Google AdWords

A powerful keyword expansion tool is one that we discussed above: Google AdWords. Google AdWords, Google's popular pay per click advertising program, has a supplemental benefit: it's a powerful keyword research tool.

SEO professionals know that running a pay per click program in the Google AdWords program can generate two big benefits in the early stages of an SEO campaign: you'll get AdWords keyword suggestions, and you'll also supplement your clicks while you are working to rise up in the natural rankings.

Google AdWords is a prolific storehouse of keyword analytics. Besides the formidable keyword research capabilities discussed near the start of this chapter, Google AdWords automatically generates new keyword ideas for you in the keyword entry panel and in the **Opportunities** section of the interface.

To see suggested keywords in the Adwords keyword entry panel, begin by logging in and browsing to an active campaign. Again, when using Adwords as a keyword research tool you'll need an account and at least one active campaign. Select the **Keywords** tab at the top of the edit window. Then click the red **+ Keywords** button at the top of the table that opens up. Then simply add one or more keywords in the box to the left. In the example below, we've entered a term, `retargeting agency`. Google automatically makes keyword suggestions, which can be seen in the box to the right indicated by the red arrow. As always, you'll need to evaluate whether the suggestions are appropriate for you business, as shown in the following screenshot:

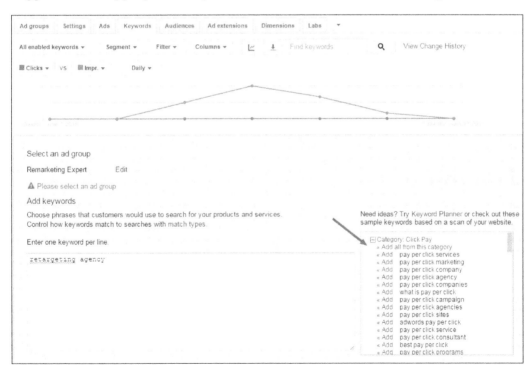

To see suggested keywords in the Adwords Opportunity too, log in to your Adwords account and browse to a campaign. You'll need to have an active campaign covering your principal keywords to see relevant keyword suggestions. Click **Opportunities** in the top menu bar.

You might see a variety of campaign opportunities such as **Raise your budgets** and **Use phrase or broad match**, but what you are looking for is **Add new keywords**, as shown in the following screenshot:

Click the **View opportunities** button, and you'll see Google's suggested keywords conveniently organized into keyword families. Click the **View** button to see the keywords. While AdWords is focused on encouraging you to increase the scope and budget of your pay per click campaign, these supplemental keywords can help you build out your main keyword list as well. From here, you'll apply your relevance analysis to see if you want to add keywords to your keyword profile, as shown in the following screenshot:

Summary

In this chapter, we learned how to build the foundation of your web empire: your keyword strategy. We learned how to harness the difference between long tail and short tail searches. We learned how to research and develop an initial list of keywords and employ a keyword matrix spreadsheet to begin to fine tune your keyword list.

We covered the use of several popular and effective keyword-suggestion tools: Google Suggest, Ubersuggest, and Google AdWords. We learned how to build out and harness the long tail with effective keyword qualifiers and location names. We learned how to employ demographic data to further the power and relevance of your keyword profile.

We learned how to hone and categorize your keyword list into tiers, and how to effectively prioritize for seasonal changes in search traffic. Finally, we learned a little bit of competitive espionage: how to monitor your competitors for new keyword opportunities.

With the tools in this chapter, you will have the ability to compete strongly against even professional SEO firms. In the next chapter, we'll dig deep into the technical nuts and bolts of search engine optimization where we'll put your keyword strategy into effect.

4
Understanding Technical Optimization

We now turn to the heart of this book, and the heart of natural search rankings: technical optimization. Technical optimization provides the nuts and bolts of on-page optimization: the subtle craft of organizing your content, link structure, title and headings, meta tags, images, and so on, to achieve high placement for your pages.

In this chapter, we will cover how to take what we've learned about keyword research and implement a ranking strategy. We'll build a *perfect web page*, a web page where all the elements work together to achieve maximum ranking power. We will learn how to craft a domain name that is well-poised to rank for primary keywords. We will examine how to create an effective WordPress permalink structure.

We will dig deep into page titles, title tags, navigation anchor text, and meta tags. We will learn sound strategies for crafting body content and how to control, analyze, and tweak keyword density. We will discover some expert techniques for WordPress theme/template optimization.

We will uncover the secrets of a sure-fire `robots.txt` file to control and harness WordPress' innate power. Finally, we will turn to two powerful tools that can aid in spider penetration and help troubleshoot crawling errors: XML sitemaps and the Google Webmaster Tool.

Remember that on-page optimization is only half the battle or one-third of the battle, really! Much of the power of ranking comes from link building, which we'll cover in the later chapters. Don't forget the analogy: on-page optimization is like tuning a car and getting it ready to race. The fuel that makes the car run at top speed is link building. If you follow the dictates of this chapter for all your pages, you'll build a solid foundation upon which your link building efforts will fuel your placement to new heights.

Choosing a keyword-rich domain name

We learned in the last chapter how keywords are the foundation of your optimization efforts. So, we begin with the keyword matrix we developed in the last chapter and employ it to map out your on-page strategy.

Almost all websites will rely on primary keywords on core pages, such as the front page. If your keyword research teaches you that one phrase or a very small group of related phrases represents your high-volume, high-relevance primary keywords, then you'll want to consider using those key phrases in a keyword-rich domain name. For some, this won't be possible or desirable: perhaps the domain name has already been chosen, or the business' marketing strategy revolves principally around a customized brand name. However, if you have the opportunity to choose a keyword-rich domain name, you'll benefit from a little extra power in your ranking efforts down the road. You may have noticed that often a competitive search market is populated with websites that have keywords in their domain name. This is particularly true for results that appear in the Bing search engine. This is no accident: key terms in the domain name are a ranking factor and experienced webmasters know it.

Choose your domain name wisely; if you ever need to change your domain name, it'll take a lot of work and you'll lose both incoming links and existing customers.

Follow the 80 percent rule

SEO professionals know that you don't always have—and won't always need—every SEO element (domain age, keyword-rich domain name, expert title tags, thousands of inbound links, and so on) to rank well. When you consider all the elements together that make a site rank well, you want to make sure you have 80 percent of the elements present—but don't fret if a few elements are out of your control.

Domain names are certainly an element that search engines consider as a ranking factor, although the weight that Google applies to domain names has been dialed back in recent years. Remember a search engine's core purpose: to deliver relevant search results to a user entering a query. Certainly, a domain name that includes a few of the searcher's query terms would tend to be relevant for that query. The weight afforded by search engines to keywords in domain names is moderate. In competitive markets, a keyword-rich domain name can provide some extra push to pass tough competitors. This can be frustrating in a market where every conceivable variant of a domain name has been snatched up.

Also, keep in mind that keyword prominence applies to keywords in domain names. This means that the first words in a domain name are afforded greater weight by the search engines than the last words in a domain name. You will also want to mirror the word order of popular search phrases whenever possible, and keep your important terms first in the domain name.

To craft a domain name, begin with your primary keywords. We'll use some real keyword data and search volumes surrounding the key phrase `Denver homes` as an example:

Keyword	Monthly Search Volume
Denver homes for sale	1,000
Denver homes	1,000
Denver homes for rent	280
New homes Denver	280

The preceding table demonstrates a few important points:

- `Denver` is the first word in both of the highest volume key phrases
- `Denver` appears in all four of the keyword variations
- `Homes` appears in all four of the keyword variations

In this example, the terms `new` and `for rent` aren't the valuable terms—unless, of course, your website is concerned with rental homes and apartments in Denver, in which case, the `Denver homes for rent` key phrase is the only relevant one on which to base your domain name. With `Denver` in the first position for the majority of searches, you will want to maintain that word order.

You should also consider **keyword overlap** in crafting domain names. Keyword overlap exists when one key phrase or keyword is incorporated either partially or fully within another—and you can use it to your benefit. In our example, `Denver homes` is fully overlapping with `Denver homes for sale`. When you see overlap like that with a robust search volume for both phrases, the longer key phrase becomes even more attractive as a primary keyword for your domain name. "New homes Denver" has only a partial overlap, and even that's a stretch because the word order is reversed.

And so, in our example, the path is clear: `Denver homes for sale` is a highly desirable high-volume phrase to use as the basis for a domain name. But what should you do if `denverhomesforsale.com` is already taken? You have two options:

- Buy an existing or dropped domain, play with hyphens
- Consider the plural version of key terms or create a clever variation with extra words

Buying/acquiring domain names

You can always buy a domain name from its owner or wait for an existing domain to expire (so-called *dropped* domains). For dropped domains, there are a host of online services that, for a fee, will help you navigate the increasingly complex world of expired domains. This approach will yield some inevitable frustrations: the system is dominated by experts that have mastered its subtleties. As a newcomer, you'll likely have to endure a learning curve. Also, an owner of an expired domain is entitled to a redemption period during which, you'll have to wait if you want to snatch up a choice domain. For most SEO pros, the extra time and risk isn't worth it—especially when you can overcome a less-than perfect domain name with sound on-page optimization and some extra linking power.

You can also buy a domain in the aftermarket from an existing domain owner. Dangers to watch out for with this approach are that some domain owners make it impossible to be found, and when you do find them, they have a completely deluded sense of the domain's value. Services like Sedo.com and Domainbrokers. com maintain ostensibly active listings of domains for sale. Domain registrars like GoDaddy.com offer domain *buying services*, where you select a desired domain name and they attempt to secure it for you.

In the domain resale market, asking prices for domains are typically astronomical. Overall, the domain resale market is riddled with complexities, dead ends, and punitive pricing. If you do undertake to purchase a domain, either by resale or following expiration, be prepared for a hunt. Smart SEO professionals don't overpay for domains, and they certainly don't endure unreasonable delays to launch their next project.

Hyphens and extra characters in domain names

It's true, all the easy domain names are taken. However, you still have an opportunity to fashion a keyword-rich domain name with a little creativity. All domain names must follow these technical rules:

- Domains can include letters (x, y, z)

- Domains can include numbers (1, 2, 3)

- Domains can include dashes/hyphens and can be repeated in sequence (-, --, ---)

- Domains cannot include spaces

- Capitalization of letters is ignored

- Domains can't begin or end with a dash

Hyphens present a good opportunity. In our example, we might consider checking for the availability of `denver-homes-for-sale.com`. This domain keeps the keywords in order, maintains keyword prominence, and the hyphens have two benefits: they certainly make the domain easier for humans to read and can help search engines distinguish the words (that is, `Kitchenspot` versus `Kitchen spot`). The drawback of hyphens—and it is worth consideration—is that hyphenated domains are awkward and unmemorable and can appear trashy. Visitors are unlikely to remember your specific combination of words and hyphens. It can also be inconvenient to express your e-mail address repeatedly as `Peter at Denver homes for sale, dot com, with hyphens between all four words`. That said, in a pure search environment where you are going solely for keyword-based traffic, you can worry less about memorability. You'll be getting your visitors solely from search and not requiring repeat visitors.

Hyphenated domains have a fairly deserved reputation as being a bit trashy; many link farms and thin content sites employ hyphens in their domain names.

A helpful variant of this technique is to simply apply a suffix to the domain, such as `denverhomesforsalenow.com` or `denverhomesforsale303.com` (`303` is an area code in Denver). Get creative: think of a term that adds value to your domain. The terms `express` and `pros` have positive connotations. `Express` suggests speedy, high-value service. `Pros` suggests someone licensed with experience. Find an appropriate suffix for your domain and you will have a keyword-rich domain without the hassle and expense of purchasing in the domain aftermarket.

As a final word on domains, make sure you use a reputable domain registrar. Some disreputable registrars may make it difficult for you to transfer your domain away later.

 Don't park your domains, put up content! Domain registrars like GoDaddy offer domain parking services. This isn't a service at all—it's a way for GoDaddy to squeeze a few pennies in pay per click ads out of your domain. The better approach is to put up even just a few paragraphs on your domain just to get the search engines indexing the page and building up some site age. Parked domains don't earn site age.

Creating an effective WordPress permalink structure

Our discussion of domain names dovetails nicely into our next topic: permalinks. Pages created in WordPress do not have filenames as we typically think of them, but they can have an ostensible filename that works exactly the same way, and that is a permalink. Because words in the URL string (both domain names and words in filenames) are ranking factors, we will want to do our best to employ keywords into our permalinks.

In the default setting, WordPress generates very SEO-unfriendly and unmemorable URL strings, like this: `http://www.TastyPlacement.com/?p=123`. The permalinks feature converts WordPress Page and Post titles into keyword-rich strings like `http://www.TastyPlacement.com/wordpress-book`.

Activating permalinks on your WordPress site takes only a minute. To access the permalinks menu, log in to your WordPress dashboard and look into the **Settings** menu. The screenshot below offers a view of the WordPress permalinks menu, showing the simple, but effective, `/%postname%` custom permalink:

Permalink Settings

Common Settings

○ Default   `https://www.TastyPlacement.com/?p=123`

○ Day and name   `https://www.TastyPlacement.com/2015/06/14/sample-post/`

○ Month and name   `https://www.TastyPlacement.com/2015/06/sample-post/`

○ Numeric   `https://www.TastyPlacement.com/archives/123`

○ Post name   `https://www.TastyPlacement.com/sample-post/`

◉ Custom Structure   `https://www.TastyPlacement.com`   `/%postname%`

It's worth mentioning that there is very little difference between the last two selections in the preceding screenshot. The **Post name** selection will yield the same permalinks as **Custom Structure**, with one small difference: the **Post name** selection will have a trailing **/** symbol at the end of each URL/permalink. There is no difference in ranking power between the two.

You have choices with permalinks. The most important rule is simply to use some form of permalink with WordPress. Never use the default setting, there is simply no reason to have your Pages and Posts identified by `?p=123`.

The permalinks menu offers you a few pre-designed options: **Default**, **Day and name**, **Month and name**, **Numeric**, a **Post name**, and **Custom structure**. For SEO reasons, the numeric option is really not better than the default setting. The **Day and name** and **Month and name** settings build URL strings with numbers representing years, months, and days, as the case may be, followed by the web page title separated with hyphens.

The pre-selection options are curious. What's been absent from the selections is the simple, effective, and often-employed permalink: the postname—but this was added with WordPress 4. To employ just the post name, which is the simplest, quickest, and most SEO friendly, just select **Post name** for your permalinks.

If you insist on displaying URLs without the trailing /, simply enter a **Custom structure** as in the preceding illustration. The presence or absence of the trailing / will appear in your final permalinks, the choice is up to you. The **Post name** permalink will take your Page or Post titled Best Golf in Texas and make a permalink http://yoursite.com/best-golf-in-texas/. That's going to be a fairly effective URL string for most purposes. Also, keep this in mind: when you designate a **Post name** or custom permalink, you still retain the ability to manually change the permalink in the edit window. The **Post name** permalink simply supplies a convenient initial URL-friendly version of your **Post name** in an editable box.

Highly customized permalinks

If you desire highly-customized permalinks, there are several shortcodes that you can input into the **Custom structure** edit window in the permalinks menu. A complete list of shortcodes for permalinks is as follows:

- %year%: This supplies the year that the Page or Post was created in four digits, that is, 2008.

- %monthnum%: This supplies the month that the Page or Post was created in two digits, that is, 09.

- %day%: This supplies the date that the Page or Post was created, that is, 31.

- %hour%: This supplies the hour that the Page or Post was created.

- %minute%: This supplies the minute that the Page or Post was created.

- %second%: This supplies the second that the Page or Post was created.

- %postname%: As discussed, this supplies a simplified, URL-friendly (no spaces, no capital letters, and no prohibited punctuation) version of the title of the Post or Page. For performance reasons, you must always use %postname% at the end of your string, and not followed by other shortcodes like day, month, year, and so on.

- %post_id%: This supplies the unique ID number of this Post or Page.

- %category%: This supplies the category name for Posts (Pages do not have categories).

- %tag%: This supplies a simplified version of the tag name.

- %author%: This supplies a simplified version of the author's name.

What's the best approach for permalinks? Should you select the year and month-based permalinks that WordPress offers?

The reason that WordPress offers the date-based options is that it brings a small performance benefit. If you use the `%postname%` structure shown above without any numeric field, such as the year or month or Post ID, it takes more time for WordPress to distinguish between Post URLs and Page URLs. To compensate, WordPress stores a lot of extra information in its database. As the page count gets high, some sites can experience problems. Sites under 1,000 pages need not worry about this performance issue.

If performance is not a concern for you, you can use the simple `%postname%` custom structure shown in the preceding screenshot. If you want peak server performance, use `%post_id%/%postname%/` or `%year%/%postname%/` as your permalink structure. And remember, if you change your permalink structure after your site is already indexed by search engines, the URLs will change, which will force search engines to re-crawl your entire site. This can be detrimental to the rankings; you need to pick one permalink structure early in your design and stick with it—this is vital. Never change the URL structure of a website without consulting a professional. If you are ever forced to move the location of your Pages or Posts within WordPress, you can accomplish it with a redirection plugin with either the Redirect plugin or the Redirection plugin. Both plugins allow you to designate a new location for pages that you have moved.

Optimizing your Page/Post titles and title tags

Now, we turn to a crucial pair of elements: Post/Page titles and title tags. We need to make a distinction between a WordPress Page title and a Page's title tag because in a default configuration, WordPress generates the title tag automatically from the Post title, but in an advanced SEO configuration (which we will employ through the use of plugins), we will generate meta title tags manually.

Page/Post title processing in WordPress

The WordPress Page/Post title is the upper-most element that you create when you create a Page or Post. WordPress then employs this Post/Page title in a few ways, depending on your setup:

- The Post/Page title is employed as the anchor text in internal WordPress navigation menus

- The Post/Page title serves as both the title, as well as, the anchor text when a Post is represented on category or archive pages

- Depending on the template, the Post/Page title will be employed automatically as an h1 or h2 heading tag on the Post or Page itself (although we'll challenge this standard approach later in this chapter under Template/Theme Optimization with some recommendations)

- If no SEO plugin is present, the Post/Page title will be employed automatically as the HTML title tag

Looking at the previous list, one might be struck by a few limitations. First, there is a danger of over-optimization when so many important on-page elements are in perfect concurrence. The other notable limitation is that what works for anchor text might not work for a title tag, especially in a long tail environment. Some webmasters prefer to keep their internal navigation neat and concise, but a longer title tag can work great to squeeze a few extra keywords in.

The following screenshot shows the Post creation window (the Page creation window appears exactly the same, but is titled **Add New Page**) with different on-page elements identified: Post/Page title, body text, as well as meta title tag, meta description, and meta keywords tag. Note that the WordPress SEO by Yoast plugin allows inclusion of the title tags and meta tags:

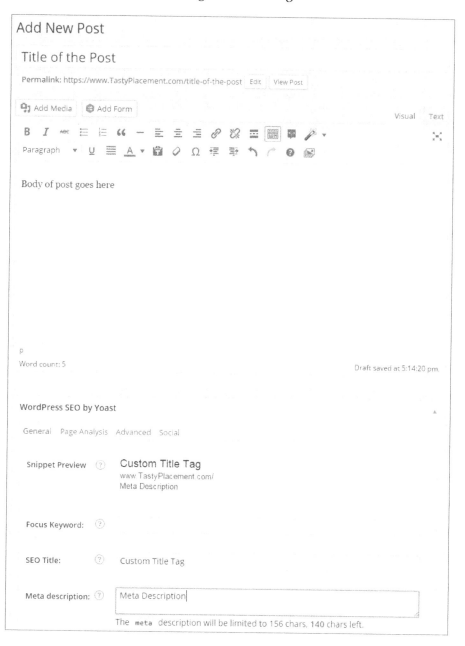

Here's an example. A well-crafted title tag that works wonders in the plastic surgery market around Atlanta is `Plastic Cosmetic Surgery Atlanta Marietta Georgia GA`. This is an actual title tag for a high-ranking page in that market. Yes, it's awkward and repetitive, but it ranks very well in searches that include either Atlanta or the surrounding town of Marietta. However, that title tag would be completely unsuitable as anchor text in a website's internal navigation.

To solve both of these problems with one solution, we'll use the WordPress SEO by Yoast plugin to give our WordPress site the ability to formulate custom title tags (we cover installation of the WordPress SEO by Yoast in *Appendix A, WordPress SEO Plugins*). This plugin is free (though a paid version is available) and is one of the most popular WordPress plugins of all time. Once installed, we'll create separate Page/Post titles and title tags to maximize our SEO power.

Crafting title tags

Title tags are the most powerful of any single on-page ranking factor. Expert care should be applied to crafting title tags—you will be rewarded with high rankings and traffic if you do.

To begin crafting these title tags, keep in mind two concepts with which you should now be familiar: keyword prominence and keyword overlap. Keyword overlap dictates that you should try to collect a small family of keywords with common words, and group them together to create title tags that can capture multiple search key phrases—just as we did a few pages before when discussing how to craft domain names. Keyword prominence rules dictates that the highest value terms go at the beginning of our title tag and the lowest value terms go at the end of our title tag.

We also need to consider that the space in the title tags is limited. Search engines display a page's title tag when that page appears in a search result most of the time. However, search engines only display a limited number of characters. Google displays around 50 to 60 characters, including spaces, of a page's title tag depending on the pixel width of the characters. Bing and Yahoo display roughly the same number of characters. Now, if you exceed the character count, the search engines display an ellipsis (…) to indicate that the entire title tag is not displayed.

From an SEO perspective, this may or may not be ideal. Perhaps (although there is no evidence for this) Google rewards websites that consistently follow the dictates of character length in various elements like title tags and meta tags. On the other hand, an ellipsis tends to suggest *there's more here*, which might cause just a few more users to click through. To distill this down to a hard rule, it's best to keep your title tags to 55 characters or less. If you want to see how your proposed title tag will appear on a search results page, you can try SEO Moz's Title Emulator tool, which you can find here: `https://moz.com/learn/seo/title-tag`.

So, if you exceed the number of characters that the search engines display, viewers won't see those characters in search results. But there's another question: if you do exceed the 55 or so characters, will the search engines read and index the extra characters? In other words, do you earn any ranking power beyond 55 characters? Various tests have revealed different results, and after much disagreement among SEO professionals on this point, a fairly conclusive test by the SEO blogger Hugo Guzman revealed that Google does read and index up to 164 characters of a title tag.

The wise approach, however, may be to keep your title tags within the 55 character boundary. The first words in a title tag yield so much more ranking weight than the last words: a long title tag isn't going to deliver much extra power. Also, who's to say Google won't change its algorithm in the future to exclude or even punish long title tags?

Creating perfectly-sized title tags

To craft perfectly-sized title tags, use any one of dozens of character-counter websites like lettercount.com (`http://www.lettercount.com/`) or wordcountertool.com (`http://wordcountertool.com/`). These tools are also helpful for crafting meta tags, twitter posts, and any text snippet where character length is restricted.

Your brand or company name almost never belongs in the first few words of a title tag if you are trying to rank for keywords. This is a common error that do-it-yourself webmasters and unskilled web designers make. Sure, you want to rank for your own business name, but you can achieve that by placing your business name in a less valuable location than the prime position within the title tag. Just having your business name in the body text of your pages or in the meta description tag will cause you to rank for your business name, not to mention the associative power that a Google Plus business page will generate for your website.

If you absolutely include your business name in the title tag, it belongs at the end, not at the beginning.

Beginning in 2013, Google became sophisticated enough to edit website title tags before displaying title tags in its search results. Specifically, Google can detect a company name at the end of a title tag, and simply reorders the title tag to put the company name at the beginning of the title tag on its search results page. An example will illustrate. Our colleagues at a company called The Search Engine Guys have a title tag that reads, `SEO For Lawyers, Full-Service SEO Firm, Attorney Marketing | The Search Engine Guys`. But note in the following screenshot how the title tag displays in search results:

> ## The Search Engine Guys: SEO For Lawyers, Full-Service ...
> www.thesearchengineguys.com/ ▾
> The Search Engine Guys are an **SEO** company located in **Austin**, TX. We handle web marketing services including **SEO**, web design, PPC, and social media.

So, how do we address Google's inclination to redraft title tags? The best approach is to simply optimize for rankings, and let Google do its work. There is a silver lining to Google reformulating your title tags: it means that you have a strong association for your business name with Google, which is a sign that your website has earned some measure of authority.

With the preceding best practices and guidelines in place, let's look at some real keyword data and undertake the step-by-step crafting of a sure-fire title tag. The following table shows keyword data for key phrases related to air conditioning in Jacksonville, Florida.

Keyword	Monthly Search Volume
Jacksonville air conditioning	82
Air conditioning service Jacksonville	33
Jacksonville air conditioning contractors	33
Jacksonville air conditioning companies	25
Jacksonville air conditioning repair	25

A few important points are immediately obvious. First, Jacksonville is the first word in most of the phrases. Because we typically want to mirror the word order of popular search phrases, we will place Jacksonville as the first word in our title tag. Another lesson that this keyword data yields is that we are fortunate to have a great degree of keyword overlap. That means we can rank for several key phrases by cleverly employing the overlapped portion in our tag. Specifically, the phrases Jacksonville air conditioning, Jacksonville air conditioning contractors, Jacksonville air conditioning companies, and Jacksonville air conditioning repair, all overlap on the phrase Jacksonville air conditioning. This repeated overlap is a bit of luck — typically, key phrases are not so conveniently arranged.

 Break up title tag elements with special characters to aid readers and set apart important elements. The | character (called a **pipe**), is well-suited to separating element of title tags like keywords and your company name. An example would be Utah Ski & Snowboard Vacations | SkiCenter Travel Agency.

However, the phrase Air conditioning service Jacksonville does not share the same word order. How do we deal with it? Well, we have such good overlap and word order with the other four phrases that we don't want to undermine our title tag by trying to rank for all five phrases with one title tag. We can do two things: optimize our title tag for the four overlapped phrases and just hope for the best for the dissimilar fifth phrase, or we could eventually create a separate page with its own title tag for Air conditioning service Jacksonville. However, we always want to create our higher value pages first, and move on to lesser search volumes later.

Now that we have our four search phrases and search data, we can proceed through the exercise. Jacksonville air conditioning has the highest search volume of all the phrases, and is repeated in all the other phrases, so we place that phrase at the beginning of our tag. The remaining phrases have differing search volumes ranging from 33 down to 25 searches per month.

Generally, the high search volumes are the higher value terms, so Jacksonville air conditioning contractors at 33 searches per month is slightly more valuable than Jacksonville air conditioning companies and Jacksonville air conditioning repair, each with 25 searches per month. So, the non-overlapped word contractor is more valuable than companies or repair. As such, a sensible title tag would be the following:

`Jacksonville Air Conditioning Contractor & Repair Company`

In this exercise, we did quite well. We have our high-value terms in the high-value position, and our lower-value terms in the low-value position. We ended up with 57 characters, which will display perfectly and be read by all major search engines. We combined the last two words to `Repair Company` because they were equal in search volume and `Company Repair` doesn't read as well. We capitalized the terms so the title tag looks neat and appealing when displayed on a search results page. One variation we might have employed would be to drop the term `companies` to make room for a brand or company name, but that's optional.

Note that we changed `companies` to `company`. Did we dilute our potential to rank for queries which include the term `companies`? Not really, one of Google's many innovations along the way was to deftly hand synonyms. Google generally treats singular and plural versions of terms equally.

The final step is to enter our finely-crafted title tag into the **Title** edit window in the WordPress SEO by Yoast section of our Page/Post edit page, and WordPress will display our title tag for users and search engines.

Crafting Page/Post titles

Crafting Page/Post titles closely parallels the process of crafting title tags, and should be done in conjunction. We need to think a little differently about Page/Post titles because their function and usage differs from title tags:

- With Page/Post titles, we aren't restricted to 65/69 characters, as we are with title tags.

- Page/Post titles are not hidden tags: WordPress uses Page/Post titles to generate internal navigation anchor text, and the titles appear as titles to content pages. We must, therefore, consider readability.

Internal navigation anchor text is a ranking factor, as is a content page's title. So, we want to be mindful of crafting keyword-rich, or at least keyword-aware Page/Post titles. To return to the `Jacksonville air conditioning` example, we do not want to simply repeat our title tag, `Jacksonville Air Conditioning Contractor & Repair Company`. First, we could risk over-optimization if all of our key elements are perfectly repeated. Second, our title tag, while very effective as a *net* for high-value search phrases, reads somewhat awkwardly. However, we know our title tag is keyword-ready, so we just need to fine-tune a bit. To adjust for these two considerations, we simply need to make our title tag a bit more readable, similar to *Jacksonville A/C Contractor and Repair Company.*

Now our Page/Post title reads nicely. We have adopted a synonym, A/C, rather than Air Conditioning. While we may have lost Air Conditioning as a search term, Google might automatically synonymise these terms — we can certainly just test to see the effect. Importantly though, we have gained readability and we have differentiated our Page/Post title from our title tag. A little variation between elements is a good signal to employ as a general rule.

Optimizing meta tags

Meta tags, like title tags, are *hidden* on-page elements — they appear on the search results pages and in the code of a web page, but otherwise do not display to website visitors within the body of a web page. Many experts now agree that meta tags are no longer capable of any effect on search engine rankings, and there is a vibrant debate on the topic. However, because meta descriptions display on search engine results pages, they have a supplemental function as a click-through conversion tool. Recall that search engines only display a certain number of characters, so your meta description needs to meet certain length requirements. So, the optimum meta description tag falls within a certain character length.

The screenshot of a Google search results entry shows a well-crafted meta description tag. The big money keywords are prominent and proximate to the start of the tag. The tag is readable, persuasive without being trashy, and is perfectly sized for display on search results pages. As a bonus, the tag includes a phone number; a phone number in a meta description can sometimes serve to generate inbound telephone calls without even requiring a visit to your site:

Austin SEO Consulting Company [TastyPlacement]
https://www.tastyplacement.com/ ▾
Tastyplacement is an Austin-based SEO company. We also do mobile sites, WordPress SEO, web development and more. Call 512-535-2492.

This screenshot from SEOmofo shows a fun and interesting approach to title tags. Visit http://www.seomofo.com to see a range of interesting title tag and meta description experiments:

|||||||||||||||||||||||||||||||||||||||||||||||SEOmofo|||||||||||||||||||||||||||||||||||||||||||||||||
www.seomofo.com/experiments/serp/google-snippet-04.html
																																														WORLDS																																																			
																																										GREATEST																																																			
																																											SEO																																																					

Configuring WordPress to generate meta descriptions

In the default setup, WordPress does not generate meta descriptions. In some WordPress templates, however, designers trigger WordPress to generate meta descriptions from either the Page/Post excerpt (but you'll have to remember to create excerpts for all Posts and Pages) or from the body text of the Post or Page. Obviously, having no meta description tags for Pages and Posts is not ideal in a search environment, and generating the tags from body text isn't much better.

So, we again recommend the must-have plugin, WordPress SEO by Yoast. The following screenshot shows the WordPress SEO plugin in use on a Post edit page. This plugin adds two handy features: an automatic character counter is displayed just under the **Meta description** edit field, and a **Snippet Preview** that lets you craft meta descriptions of precise length:

Best practices for meta descriptions

The length of meta descriptions, like the length of title tags, is subject to some rules and best practices based upon how search engines treat them. The first and most important rule is that search engines will only display a limited number of characters when displaying meta descriptions in search engine result pages. Google displays up to roughly 156 characters, including spaces, of a meta description tag. Bing will display up to 185 characters (in rare cases only, it's better to employ Google's standard of 156 characters).

Here's a wrinkle: Google will generally display your meta tag in search result pages, but not always. Sometimes, Google takes it upon itself to generate a custom description for display in search results.

Manipulating these results reliably is difficult, and probably isn't that worthwhile anyway. The most reliable rule; however, for how Google generates these custom descriptions is the following: if the search query is largely composed of terms that appear solely in page content but not in the meta description tag, then Google will generate the description from the text it finds in the body of the web page containing the search query.

The sound approach to meta description tags is to keep them to 156 characters. With WordPress SEO by Yoast's character counter, you can approach that count with perfect precision.

Leveraging your meta descriptions to draw clicks

Consider a bit of salesmanship in your meta descriptions. Meta descriptions should be more than merely repositories for keywords. Because the description tag displays on search engine result pages, it's your opportunity to persuade viewers to click through. Also consider that you might be able to get a customer to call your business without even clicking through your website! In some businesses like locksmithing and taxicab services, users don't care to price shop or compare services, they just want someone to come out and help them as soon as possible. In such markets, consider putting your phone number in the description tag. It's likely that some users will see your website appear in search results and simply call the phone number shown in your description tag.

Because you have a little extra room in your description tag, you have an opportunity to convey some information about your business that will not fit within a title tag. For example, are you the only licensed contractor in your area? Or, are you the only local dealer for a particular product or service? Your meta-description will be displaying along with other organic results, map listings, and paid search ads on a search engine result page, so it is your chance to distinguish yourself from other websites and businesses.

Crafting meta descriptions

With the preceding best practices in mind, we will begin an exercise in crafting an effective meta description tag. We will begin with the keywords and title tag for `Jacksonville Air Conditioning` that we used in the section above on how to craft effective title tags.

By the time you create a title tag for a web page, your meta description is 25 percent complete. Because the keywords that users employ in their queries will tend to draw clicks, we will always want to have our highest value keywords in the first 70 or so characters of the tag, and if your keyword research and analysis are sound, the keyword methodology for creating a meta tag is the same as the methodology for creating a title tag.

In most cases, then, we can simply begin our meta tag with the title tag we've crafted for a page.

However, it is generally wise to make a slight variation between the title tag in the first 65 or 70 characters of the meta description tag: we don't want to risk over-optimization by having the two tags appear exactly the same. One simple solution is to insert a single word at the beginning of the meta description like `best` or `expert` or `24-hour`. If you do follow this idea, make sure the word you add gives some benefit to the tag, such as bringing in a few extra searches or distinguishing you from other businesses. Another option is to change up the word order just slightly.

Our well-crafted title tag for `Jacksonville Air Conditioning` was `Jacksonville Air Conditioning Contractor & Repair Company`. We want to alter the word order slightly and point to the fact that we are licensed. And, assuming we are one of only two outfits in the area that offer emergency service, we might mention that in the title tag to increase customer interest. Finally, we'll include a phone number, and throw in a teaser offer. The resulting title tag is `Licensed Jacksonville air conditioning contractor & repair company. Emergency service, 24-hours. Call 555-1212 for immediate service. Free AC inspection.`

That description measures 153 characters—nearly perfect for displaying in both Google and Bing (it's better to be a few characters short than a few characters too long). We have excellent keyword prominence: our valuable keywords are all near the start of the tag. We've noted that we offer an emergency service, and we've included our phone number. The last three words are a bit of a teaser meant to encourage click through to the website. If you follow these principles when you craft your meta description tags you'll enjoy higher click-through rates from search engine pages.

A dead HTML element – meta keyword tags

Google does not make use of the keyword meta tags in determining web ranking. Google has stated this publicly on several occasions, case closed!

Despite this clarity (which we do not always get from Google), webmasters and even SEO bloggers still cling to the outdated concept of keyword meta tags. And you can still find webmasters mindlessly stuffing hundreds of terms into keyword meta tags in an effort to improve rankings. It has been over ten years since that technique was good for even a mild bump in rankings.

True, some smaller search engines still employ the keywords tag in ordering search results. Notably, Bing publicly acknowledges that it still makes use of keyword meta tags in ordering search results, but warns that because of historic abuse, they'll not give keyword tags much weight. Bing's Product Manager, Duane Forrester, put it this way in a blog post, *Getting it right is a nice perk for us, but it won't rock your world. Abusing meta keywords can hurt you.* Clearly, meta keyword tags also have the potential to trigger penalties and filters if abused. They aren't worth much, so they aren't worth much of your time.

With the preceding post in mind, we'll fashion a few simple and safe rules for creating meta keywords tags (you enter meta keywords when creating a Post or Page in the WordPress SEO by Yoast edit section under the body text edit area):

* Because keyword meta tags don't give much ranking power and should be very limited in number, spend only 15 seconds on them per page
* Utilize only keywords related to the topic of the page—never attempt to extend your ranking to other phrases solely through inclusion in the meta keywords tag
* Include between four and ten keywords or key phrases separated by commas
* Meta keywords aren't mandatory, if you don't have time, skip them

Optimizing your body content

And now we turn to optimization of the body content, the text on the page. One of the ironies of search engine optimization is that the actual words on the page are somewhat overshadowed in ranking power by other elements like title tags and inbound link count. And while you can rank for competitive phrases without the text on the page (with massive link-building campaigns), body text remains a heavily-weighted component of search rankings.

Along with this topic, we will also dig a bit deeper into the concept of keyword density. Keyword density refers to the amount of keywords as a percentage of total words on the page. While keyword density applies to any web page element, it is of particular importance with respect to body content.

First, what is body content? Body content is the visible part of a web page: the text, images, and other elements (video, forms, and so on) that appear to viewers within the four corners of the browser window. This includes text in the form of heading tag elements.

Best practices for optimizing body content

When optimizing body content, you have more freedom than with optimizing title tags and meta elements. The greatest difference is that body content is not restricted in length like the meta and title elements. While you won't be punished for lengthy body content, you'll get more ranking and traffic from 10 individual web pages of reasonable length than you will from one long page.

Body content should meet standards of minimum length. The de facto standard for body content length is around 300 words, perhaps 250 words in a pinch. This is a minimum, and is enough to get a page indexed and ranking, but you'll get slightly more ranking power as your page length gets up to about 1200 words. As a maximum length, pages longer than 1500 words should be split into two or more pages—remember the value of page count to a website's overall authority.

Each page you generate should ideally have a purpose: to rank for a single keyword or a small group of closely related keywords. If you are going to create a page without a ranking goal, then just understand it for what it is: a page that is for your existing readers, but one that isn't going to bring real numbers of new visitors. Keeping each page focused on a single keyword or keyword group helps you keep your content focused. If you try to rank for too broad a group of keywords on a single page, you'll dilute each individual keyword and you won't rank for anything.

For example, in the preceding example for `Jacksonville air conditioning`, it would be appropriate to create a single page to rank for the following group of keywords:

- `Jacksonville air conditioning`
- `Jacksonville air conditioning contractors`
- `Jacksonville air conditioning companies`
- `Jacksonville air conditioning repair`

These key phrases have overlap, so really the total word count of all the terms in this family is five words (because `air conditioning` is for keyword purposes a single word in this instance). Conversely, if this company wanted to rank for HVAC repair — that would ideally require a separate page, because the term HVAC has no overlap with these keywords. Similarly, `heating repair` would require its own page — there is too much dissimilarity in the keywords.

 Body text, like title and meta tags, must follow rules of keyword prominence to some degree. So, you'll want to make sure your keywords appear in the opening paragraph or paragraphs of the body text.

You might consider applying the bold attribute to the keyword the first time it appears — applying bold to text can give a little whiff of ranking power for a phrase or a term.

Another ranking factor that you can employ when creating body text is the use of keywords in the anchor text of outbound links. Search engines know that a link to an external site titled `dance clothes` would tend to indicate that the page is about dance clothes. This can be easily overdone: too many outbound links tend to send away your valuable PageRank and can serve as pathways for your users to exit your site.

Finally, write for search engines — but don't forget to write for people. That's something which SEO professionals always remind themselves. It's easy to get caught up in the technicalities of crafting high-ranking pages and forget that ultimately every page must greet human visitors.

Keyword density in body content

Keyword density, the amount by which a phrase is present as a percentage of all the words on a page, is important for several reasons. First, you need your important keywords to appear enough times to impact the index that search engines keep of your page, so that it can impact rankings. However, repeat your keywords too often and you'll trigger built-in monitoring filters that the search engine employs to sniff out artificially boosted content.

The general consensus currently is that the sweet spot for keyword density is between 2 percent and 5 percent. That means that the keyword phrase for which you are trying to rank should represent between 2 percent and 5 percent of the total words on the page.

You can test the keyword density of your pages (or those of your competition) with several free browser plugins. One such plug-in is the SearchStatus plug-in for the Firefox browser.

Remember that keyword density (like any web page element) can always be tweaked and retested. If you follow the general guidelines set forth here, you'll do quite well while steering well clear of any trouble with the search engines.

We'll dig deeper into content creation in *Chapter 5, Creating Optimized and Engaging Content*.

Optimizing heading tags

Heading tags (h1, h2, h3, and so on) are a great opportunity. It's where the expert optimizers begin to distinguish themselves from the amateurs. Despite the reliability and soundness of heading tags as tools for optimization, they are often not employed by webmasters. With optimization akin to a race where you need do only a *little bit more* than the competition, sometimes heading tags will provide that *little bit more* you need to rise above the fray.

Heading tags were originally intended to operate like newspaper headlines and subheadings. They were, and are, taxonomical clues to both the topic and structure of a web page. As such, they are great food for search engines, and great signposts for you to send to search engines. Curiously, the use of heading tags diminished as the web grew out of its infancy. The rise of CSS as a web technology near the turn of the new millennium let web designers format text with such new flexibility and power that many no longer bothered with the *old* technology of heading tags (of course, heading tags can be flexibly styled with CSS just like any other element). Unsuspecting web clients paid the price in lower rankings.

Crafting heading tags is easy in WordPress: like any word processor, highlight the text to which you wish to apply the tag, and select the heading level from the text formatting pull-down. The following screenshot shows the location of the pull-down menu, indicated by the arrow:

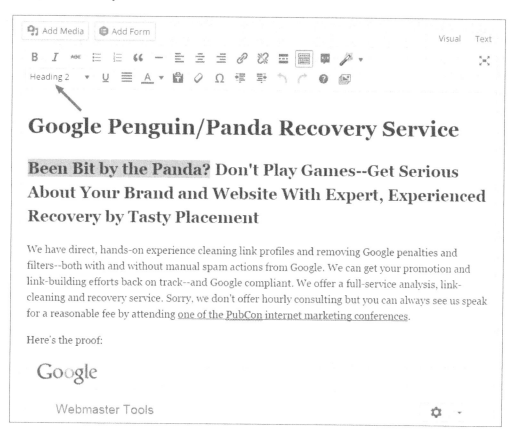

Optimizing WordPress templates

Every Page or Post in WordPress should employ a heading 1 tag as the **headline** of the article. But to achieve this, you'll need to consider if your WordPress template generates page titles automatically, and if it does, does it generate heading 1 or heading 2 tags? WordPress templates nearly always generate Page and Post heading tags automatically based on the Page or Post title. In fact, WordPress' own template design guide dictates that templates work in this way. This is a simple and convenient approach, and better for people just starting out.

But to the skilled optimizer, the more control one can exert over individual web page elements, the greater flexibility and ranking power one can bring to bear. To achieve this power and flexibility, you'll want to generate those heading tags manually. Note that in the previous screenshot, the *headline* of the page has been entered manually, and the author has varied the heading from the page title; the template powering this WordPress site has automatic headings on Posts and Pages disabled.

Here's how to disable automatic page headlines in a WordPress template. The following code snippet demonstrates the typical WordPress approach to Page and Post headlines from a template's `page.php` file:

```
<h1 class="pagetitle"><?php the_title(); ?></h1>
 <div class="entry page clear">
  <?php the_content(); ?>
 </div><!--end entry-->
```

The first line grabs the page title and applies `h1` markup around it. To disable automatic headlines, we simply remove the first line (from the opening `h1` to closing `h1` tag), leaving the remaining code, which will display only the body text of each Page:

```
<div class="entry page clear">
 <?php the_content(); ?>
</div><!--end entry-->
```

Keep in mind that after you make this change, you'll need to manually enter headlines for each Page. And, changing the `page.php` file will only introduce the changes for the Pages. If you want to make the change for Posts, you'll need to make the same edit to a second template file, `single.php`.

Generating page headlines manually

Is your WordPress template wasting a heading tag displaying the blog title on every page rather than being employed specifically to designate the page topic on each individual page? This practice is far from ideal for SEO purposes, yet is all too common.

To remedy this, you can adjust the CSS definition for your blog/site title in your template's `header.php` file. Then follow the tip above to generate your page headlines manually.

Once you have your approach chosen for `h1` tags, what is the best way to approach them?

Starting with heading 1 tags, remember that search engines follow rules of keyword prominence for heading tags. So, your h1 element should include your core keywords in a prominent position (the first few words) of the tag. After all, your h1 element is also the headline of your web page. Again, we'll recommend varying the elements to avoid over-optimization: your h1 element should be just a bit different from your title tag, even if just by a word or two.

Keyword density can also be a factor with heading tags: you might want to avoid 100 percent keyword density with your heading elements when considered as a group (that is, your h1 and h2 tags considered together). Each web page you ever generate should have one, and only one, h1 element.

Now, we will consider h2 elements. As we progress from h1 elements to h2 and h3 elements, and so on, the ranking weight diminishes. Nevertheless, heading 2 elements are highly recommended. h2 elements can also help you organize your page content for readers. You should try to include at least three h2 elements on each web page you create, even if that web page is not lengthy. Use your keywords, but bring in a healthy amount of additional text, it's alright if your keyword density drops in your h2 elements. Also, don't keep your keywords in a perfectly prominent position for all of your heading elements—vary at least one or two of the heading elements to push your keywords farther back in the title tag.

Let's pull all of this together and take a look at the core heading elements and the title tag of a finely-crafted web page, all working together in a successful bid to rank for SEO Austin (and about a dozen variations of that key phrase):

Title	SEO Austin Texas | Search Engine Optimization | TastyPlacement
h1 element	Austin SEO Firm TastyPlacement: Leaders in Design, Performance, and Rankings
h2 element	SEO Clients: the Power of a #1 Search Engine Ranking
h2 element	A Typical SEO Program
h2 element	SEO: Let Our Austin-Area Experts Deliver Superior Search Engine Rankings
h2 element	SEO: Let Our Austin-Area Experts Deliver Superior Search Engine Rankings

This page has it all: the keywords are prominent, but not mindlessly repeated in perfect word order. The page covers both "SEO" and "Search engine optimization". The keyword density is moderate, not aggressive. And, the heading elements still manage to inject some effective salesmanship, yet remain meaningful and human-readable.

Improving rankings with optimized images

Optimizing your images can bring ranking and traffic in two ways. First, in the traditional way, by improving the ranking of the page upon which the image appears. Second, you can bring visitors who use an image-specific search platform like Google Images (`http://images.google.com`) or Bing Images (`http://bing.com/images`). Keep in mind that users who visit your site through image search may not have nearly the same commercial intent as users who visit through a text search query—unless of course your business is selling images.

Image optimization does not carry much ranking power—it's a minor adjustment to a web page that delivers a boost, but does not have enough power to rank for anything competitive on its own. But, to repeat the mantra from *Chapter 1, Getting Started – SEO Basics*, when all on-page optimization techniques, even lower-weight techniques, are all used collectively—the power can be staggering.

Images have several text-based properties that can be harnessed to deliver a slight boost in ranking power: the filename, the alt tag, and the title. First, create image filenames that utilize keywords that underscore the theme of your page. However, it's best to introduce some alternate terms so that you aren't mindlessly repeating your title tags. For example, if you are competing for the key phrase `Fashion Blog`, then you might name an image `fashion-blog-style.jpg`.

The alt tag is intended to provide a text-based description of the image, if for some reason the image is not available. The alt tag serves a secondary purpose as an accessibility feature: special screen-reading web browsers used by sight-impaired folks employ the alt tag to describe the image. Entering alt tags in WordPress is a breeze; the image upload wizard presents a blank alt tag field for you when you upload an image into the media manager. It's impossible to upload an image and miss this feature.

The third text property that you can apply to images is the image title. The image title's purpose is to display a small mouse-over information box with the text of the image. You enter image titles in WordPress just as you do with image alt tags, immediately following upload with the media manager wizard.

Another factor in image optimization is keyword proximity. Keyword proximity refers to the distance in characters or words between two website elements. So, if an image is placed very near a particular keyword phrase on a web page, it tends to indicate that the keyword phrases are the subject of the image. This factor will tend to help the image rank in specialized image search engines, but won't significantly boost your page ranking.

Inserting images and optimizing image properties in WordPress

To insert an image into WordPress, you'll naturally need to be logged in and working on a Page or Post. When you have the Post/Page edit window open, place the cursor where you want your image to appear in the document. Then, click the **Add Media** button that appears at the top of the edit window, indicated by a box in the following screenshot:

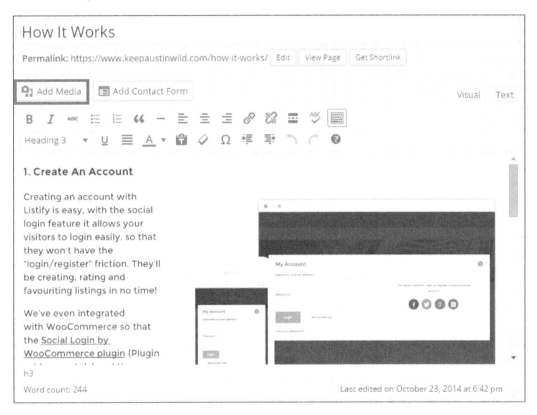

Next, you will see that once you click the graphic icon for image uploads indicated in the preceding picture , the **Insert Media** dialog box pops up. You can upload a picture from your computer (default), or by clicking the **Media Library** tab you can link to a picture already uploaded to your **Media Library**.

If you are uploading a file, you can now drag files into the upload window or click the **Select Files** button. Keep in mind that you can upload multiple files at once—a handy feature introduced recently to WordPress. Simply browse to where the picture is on your computer just like you do when attaching a file to an e-mail. Once you have the file selected, hit the **Open** button. Don't close this window yet—you will enter your title and alt tag parameters in the next step. Once you have hit the **Upload** button, your image will upload (your image is now stored by WordPress on your web server/web hosting), the **Add an Image** dialog window changes dynamically to show you the image properties window. Here, we'll optimize our image for search engines.

The following screenshot shows the last step of the image upload wizard: the **Insert Media** window, formerly the **Image Properties** window before WordPress 4.0. The title field fills automatically based on the filename. The alternate text field (**Alt Text**) is blank by default, and is highlighted:

The WordPress insert media window, shown in the previous screenshot, lets us control several properties for the image in one location, including the title and alt tags for an image.

The **Title** field is the image title. Curiously, WordPress auto-fills this field based on the filename, but strips out the file extension. You can see this effect at work in the previous screenshot; `4904_4_8.png` generates an image title `4904_04_8`. The title property can include spaces, so it's a good practice to clean up the auto-generated title by capitalizing the first letter of the words and replacing the hyphens with spaces.

The next field is the alternate text, the **Alt Text**. This field is blank by default. In our previous example, we've varied the **Alt Text** so that it didn't repeat the filename and/or page title letter by letter. Varying the **Alt Text** is easy, and can actually identify the image with more precision. By including the word `plaid` in the **Alt Text**, we might be very likely to rank for the long tail phrase `android wallpaper plaid`.

The **Caption** field allows you to insert a caption below the image. This can come in handy if you are trying to harness keyword proximity in order to help your image rank in image search engines like Google Images. Generally though, captions will be displayed on the page under the image, depending on your template, so you might not like the appearance.

Setting image alignment and link settings

The next section in the **Insert Media** window is the **Attachment Display Settings** section, where you'll enter image alignment, where the image links to, and the image size.

The **Alignment** parameter lets you align the image to **left**, **right**, **center**, or **none** (text will not wrap for most templates) — you simply select the parameter from the drop-down.

The next field is the **Link To** field. This selection box fills by default to the link location of the image file. If this box contains a URL (by default, WordPress will auto-fill this field with the filename and location of the image), then the image will be a clickable link in your post. Beware of this setting, because for some templates, a user clicking on the image will simply be taken to a page with the image itself, but no text that may not be ideal. If you set this selection to **None** (WordPress will remember this setting thereafter) then your image will not be a clickable link. In most cases, you do not want your images to be clickable links unless you've set up a proper gallery, so if your template is prepared to present images gracefully, you might be wise to set the link parameter to **None**.

The last parameter is **Size** — here you simply select the size, in pixels, for which you want the image to appear. You'll be presented with several sizes: your original size, and a variety of smaller images that WordPress generates on upload.

The last step, once your parameters are set, is simply to hit the **Insert into Post/Insert into Page** button—your image will be inserted into the post in the position where your cursor was when you uploaded your image. If you have made a mistake, simply highlight the image, hit the *Delete* key on your keyboard to remove it, and start over.

Making speedy edits to image properties

You can make changes to image settings on existing posts. To bring up the edit window to make changes to image properties, click on an image in the Page/Post edit window and an edit bar will appear. Click the pencil icon and you'll pull up an edit screen, where you can adjust the image alignment, link settings, alt text attribute, and more.

Let's cover quickly how to make changes to your image properties later. This could be helpful for tweaking alt text and title to squeeze out a few extra ranking positions. WordPress is pretty well set up to make edits to the way your image displays. The preceding screenshot illustrates how to make edits to image properties.

Manipulating image sizes to speed up website load times

Recall that a website's loading time impacts both the user experience and the ranking position—Google has confirmed its interest in fast-loading pages in several public statements. Search engines want sites that they recommend to users to yield a good experience. Websites that are heavy on the use of images can tend to be slower to load; images are bulky in size compared to text.

You want to make sure your images load quickly. So, the smaller you can make your image sizes, the faster they will load. Here are a few simple rules—really, the only rules you need to know that will help you minimize image sizes and thereby minimize loading times:

- BMP files have no place in web design. The files are large and can't be compressed.
- GIF files are most appropriate when large swaths of solid colors are used. GIF files reduce their file size by limiting the number of colors that display within the file. As such, they are ideal for images with fewer individual colors (not ideal for photographs, which can have thousands of colors).

- JPG files are versatile for photographs. JPG files can be made quite lean by adjusting their quality/compression property. Be careful not to compress the files too much, as JPG files employ a *glossy* compression—the quality of the image drops as the files are compressed to a greater degree. JPG files are the best choice for when you must use a very large image because JPG files are capable of tremendous amounts of compression.

- PNG files are ideal for both solid colors and photographs. They display a better image quality than JPG files. Older Microsoft browsers do not display the transparent layer in PNG files. PNG files are a good choice for everyday use, but cannot be compressed to quite the same degree as JPG files.

To manipulate images and make full use of available compression, you'll want to use a good image editor as part of your webmaster toolbox. Adobe's PhotoShop software is the de facto standard, but the open source alternative, Gimp, offers nearly all the same features.

The ultimate WordPress robots.txt file

We learned in *Chapter 2, Customizing WordPress for SEO*, that WordPress generates archive, tag, comment, and category pages that raise duplicate content issues. We can signal to search engines to ignore these duplicate content pages with a `robots.txt` file. In this section, we'll kill a few birds with one ultimate `robots.txt` file. We'll tell search engines to ignore our duplicated pages. We'll go further: we'll instruct search engines not to index our admin area and not to index non-essential folders on our server. As an option, we can also ask bad bots not to index any pages on our site, though they tend to usually do as they wish.

Before we customize our `robots.txt` file, bear in mind that the WordPress SEO by Yoast plugin can help us accomplish the same goal, but not as reliably. Furthermore, `robots.txt` is very handy for all sorts of purposes, so it's a great idea to know how to leverage it.

You can create a `robots.txt` file in any text editor. Place the file in the root directory/folder of your website (not the WordPress template folder) and the search engines will find it automatically because search engine bots are programmed to look for the file.

The following `robots.txt` is quite simple, but can accomplish much in a few lines:

```
User-agent: *

Disallow: /cgi-bin
Disallow: /wp-admin
Disallow: /wp-includes
Disallow: /wp-content/plugins
Disallow: /wp-content/cache
Disallow: /wp-content/themes
Disallow: /trackback
Disallow: /comments
Disallow: /category/*/*
Disallow: /tag/
Disallow: */trackback
Disallow: */comments
```

Line one, `User-agent: *`, means that that this `robots.txt` file is to apply to any and all spiders and bots. The next twelve lines all begin with `Disallow`. The `Disallow` directive simply means *don't index this location*. The first `Disallow` directive tells spiders not to index our `/cgi-bin` folder or its contents. The next five `Disallow` directives tell spiders to stay out of our WordPress admin area. The last six `Disallow` directives cure the duplicate content generated through trackbacks and comments and category pages.

We can also disable indexing of historical archive pages by adding a few more lines, one for each year of archives:

```
Disallow: /2006/
Disallow: /2007/
Disallow: /2008/
Disallow: /2009/
Disallow: /2010/
Disallow: /2011/
```

We can also direct e-mail harvesting programs, link exchanges schemes, worthless search engines, and other undesirable website visitors not to index our site:

```
User-agent: SiteSnagger
Disallow: /
User-agent: WebStripper
Disallow: /
```

The lines request the named bots not to index any pages on your site (although unfriendly bots will often simply ignore your directives). You can create new entries if you know the name of the user agent that you wish to disallow. `SiteSnagger` and `WebStripper` are both services that crawl and copy the entire website so that their users can view them offline. These bots are very unpopular with webmasters because they crawl thoroughly, aggressively, and without pausing, increasing the burden on web servers and diminishing performance for legitimate users.

Fighting bad bots with help from Wikipedia

Check out Wikipedia's `robots.txt` file for an example of a complex, educational, and entertaining use of the tool. Dozens of bad bots are restricted by the file, with some illustrative commentary. You can find it at `https://en.wikipedia.org/robots.txt`.

Optimizing with the XML Sitemaps plugin for WordPress

A sitemap is a page on your website that lists all of the pages on the site, usually in a hierarchical fashion. Having a sitemap on your website makes it easier for the major search engines to find all the pages in your site. An XML sitemap is a sitemap that is generated using the XML coding language. The XML Sitemaps plugin for WordPress allows you to easily add an XML sitemap to your WordPress site.

The XML Sitemaps plugin for WordPress was developed by Semiologic, and can be downloaded for free from their website at `http://www.semiologic.com/software/xml-sitemaps/`.

Once you have downloaded the plugin file, you install it just as you would with any other WordPress plugin. First, sign in to the admin area of your site and then click on **Add New** under **Plugins** on the left navigation in your dashboard. On the next page, click on **Upload**. It is at the top of the page under the header. Next, browse to where you saved the plugin file and click on **Install**. The XML Sitemaps plugin will be installed automatically. Once it is installed, click on **Activate** to start using the plugin.

As soon as you activate the XML Sitemaps plugin for WordPress, it will start generating an XML sitemap. If your site is large, this could take awhile. Once your sitemap is ready, you will be able to view it by visiting your URL, `http://www.example.com/sitemap.xml`, where `www.example.com` is replaced by your own domain name.

It is not absolutely necessary to submit your sitemap to Google. However, using Google's Webmaster Tools to submit your sitemap can help the search engine find it more quickly. If your site is new and has not yet been indexed, submitting an XML sitemap can be especially useful because it may take some time for Google to find the site on its own: you'll almost certainly get your site indexed more quickly. Read the next section for instructions on how to get set up with Google Webmaster Tools.

In addition to Google, other search engines will also read the information in your XML sitemap. All of the major search engines, including Bing, Yahoo!, and Ask. com make use of these files. The sitemap lists every page on your website so that no pages are inadvertently missed when your site is crawled. The search engines do not guarantee that every page listed on your sitemap will be crawled, but having a sitemap does ensure that the search engines can find all of the pages. If you have pages that are not linked from other pages on your site, they may be missed when the search engines crawl your website. Having all of your site's pages listed on your sitemap prevents that from happening.

If you make changes to your website after creating your sitemap with the XML Sitemaps plugin for WordPress, the plugin will automatically update your sitemap and notify Google's update service of the changes—another great benefit! Bing and Yahoo! will also be notified of any changes automatically, so you don't need to worry about pinging the search engines' update services.

When you use the XML Sitemaps plugin for WordPress to add an XML sitemap to your site, you increase your chances of getting all of the pages of your site crawled and indexed in the major search engines, even if they lacked the proper internal linking structure and backlinks to be noticed without the sitemap. These pages probably won't be ranked for anything other than long tail keywords, unless you do something about the linking issues, but it is possible to get quite a bit of traffic from long tail keywords.

Using an XML sitemap is almost certain to increase your website's traffic, which is likely to result in additional revenue, either from advertising or sales. The best part about using the XML Sitemaps plugin to create your sitemap file is that once you have installed the plugin and submitted your sitemap to Google, you are done! You never need to think about it again because everything is done for you automatically.

SEO power tool – Google Webmasters

An indispensable tool in your SEO arsenal is Google Webmasters (formerly Google Webmaster Central, and currently in transition to be renamed Google Search Console). Google Webmasters gives you valuable information that can help you improve your website and your search engine rankings. It is also widely believed, though hard to prove, that simply registering your site with Google Webmasters serves as a trust factor that can bring additional authority to your site and improve rankings. You can use this tool to find out how often your site appears in Google's search results and for which search terms, and to upload a sitemap to ensure that Google can find all of the pages in your website and get information about any errors Google may have experienced while trying to crawl your site.

To sign up for Google Webmasters, point to `http://google.com/webmasters` and log in using the sign-in information for your Google account. If you don't have a Google account, you'll need to create one first. You can do that easily by signing up for Gmail or any other Google service.

When you first log into Google Webmasters, you'll be taken to the home page, where you can click on **Add a site** to add your website to your account. Each time you add a new website, you will be taken to a verification page. You will have to complete the verification process to prove to Google that you are the owner of the site.

There are four ways to verify your website. The first option is to log in to your account with your domain registrar and add a DNS entry to the domain. The DNS information you need to add is provided by Google. The second option is to add a META tag containing your Google site verification code to your home page. The third option is to download an HTML file from Google Webmaster Tools and upload it to the main directory of your site. The fourth option is to link Google Webmaster Tools with your Google Analytics account. Instructions are provided to help you complete whichever option you choose.

Optimizing your site with Google Webmasters

We've discussed XML sitemaps in the prior section, but there are other tools available through Google Webmasters as well. There are a lot of very advanced features in Google Webmasters, we'll cover the simpler tools here.

One of the most valuable is the Search Analytics feature. This feature tells you the search terms for which your website has appeared in Google's search results. It also tells you how many times your site was listed for each search time and how many times a visitor clicked on to your site for each of the search terms. To see Search Analytics for your site, browse to **Search Traffic** and then click on **Search Analytics**.

This information is extremely helpful because if you are already getting traffic for a specific search term, it may not be that difficult to get your website listed higher in the search results, so you get an even bigger share of the traffic. For example, if your site is showing up in the search results for `tiny blue widgets`, you can try searching for that phrase in Google to see what your site's rank is. If you are #12 in the listings, there is room for improvement. By adding more backlinks with the search phrase as anchor text, and modifying your web page if necessary to target it more specifically toward `tiny blue widgets`, you may be able to get your website onto the first page of Google or maybe even into the top few results. This will increase your traffic from that search term significantly.

Google Webmasters will also show you hyperlinks coming to your site from other sites. The list contains the links that are discovered by the Googlebot while it crawls the Internet. This tool may not show every link to your website, but it does show most of them. Some links, such as links to a page that no longer exists, will not appear in the list. You can see the list by navigating to **Search Traffic** on the left navigation bar and then **Links to Your Site**.

The crawl errors section of the dashboard lists any errors that the Googlebot has encountered while attempting to crawl your site. Navigate to **Crawl**, and then **Crawl Errors and Crawl Stats**. By checking these errors, you can find problems such as URLs that cannot be crawled because of restrictions in the `robots.txt` file. This is also where Google will tell you about any page not found errors, timeout errors, or other errors that kept it from crawling the pages on your website.

Another important area is the Content Keywords area of Google Webmasters. Navigate to **Google Index** and then **Content Keywords**. Here, you will find a list of the keywords Google has determined to be most relevant to your website. Reviewing this list will give you an idea of how well you are targeting the content of your web pages to the keywords you're trying to rank for. If you don't see your keywords on the list, you'll need to take a look at your content and reconsider your content strategy. Also be on the lookout for undesirable keywords in this list. If you see terms like `Viagra` showing up on your children's clothing website, there's a good chance that your site has been hacked and you'll need to do something about it.

The **Messages** section is pretty self-explanatory. This is where Google sends alerts related to your account.

You can submit your XML sitemap to Google Webmasters by navigating to **Crawl**, and then **Sitemaps**. After you've submitted your sitemap, Google will display statistics related to your sitemap.

Another important section is the site configuration section, which you'll access by clicking the gear icon in the upper right of the window. Start with **Site Settings**. Here, you can set a preferred domain for your website. By doing this, you let Google know whether you want your site to be displayed in the search engine results as `www.domain.com` or `domain.com`. This helps keep the pages of your website from being duplicated in the search engine results. In order to set this feature, you must have your website added to Google Webmaster Tools twice, once with the `www` and once without. If you have validated both versions, you will be able to specify which one you prefer.

As you can see, Google Webmaster Tools contains several tools that can help you diagnose problems and improve the ranking of your website. Take some time to become familiar with these tools and learn how to use the suggestions provided by Google to get your site ranked higher, and increase your traffic.

Summary

We covered a wide range of technical optimization topics in this chapter. Hopefully, we've illuminated some of the mystery of search optimization and rankings. We have covered a lot of material, and many of these topics are certainly worthy of further study.

We began by learning how to craft a keyword-rich domain name without resorting to the corrupt and expensive secondary market for domain names. We learned how to manipulate WordPress' permalink structure for maximum benefit.

We dug deep into page titles, title tags, navigation anchor text, and meta tags. We learned how to apply sound methodologies of keyword density to our body copy. We also learned some advanced techniques to modify WordPress themes to deliver even greater SEO power. We built a bullet-proof `robots.txt` file to control WordPress' pesky duplicate pages and learned how to employ both the Google Webmaster Tool and XML sitemaps, to increase spider penetration on your site.

In the next chapter, we'll learn how to craft expertly drafted and engaging web content.

5
Creating Optimized and Engaging Content

With this chapter, we begin to fuse our knowledge of search technology, optimization, and keywords together, to create optimized and engaging web content—the *words on the page*. Note the term *engaging*. We have to give greater credence to our human visitors, rather than simply following the rules imposed by search engine algorithms. We don't just want readers, we want engaged readers. We don't want customers, we want engaged customers. We will be writing optimized content, but we will focus on the craft and creative practice of writing itself.

In this chapter, we will focus on the following:

- How to better engage visitors with your content
- How to write effective titles and headlines—how to grab the reader's attention from the start
- How to use WordPress' built-in tag tool to make it easier for users to find our content
- How to create keyword-rich content and how to write with a specific keyword density, as well as when keywords can be taken too far
- How to write for our audience and craft your content to speak to them directly
- We'll discover some techniques to develop a personal writing style
- How to harness WordPress' category taxonomy and hierarchy to organize our content

Some resources and ideas that can help you hire out your writing jobs.

Engaging visitors with your content

Your web content is your front line. Once you have successfully penetrated the search engine and earned placement for your website, then you must engage your visitors with meaningful content. This is true even for a nuts-and-bolts small-business website with a purely commercial message. Customers are engaged with your website when they either have a reason to act (to make a purchase or pursue steps toward a purchase), or have a reason to return to your site. This task will vary greatly depending on the type of website you offer, and hence, can mean many different things.

The following screenshot shows an opportunity missed: a website with zero-visitor engagement. This single-page website is little more than a business card: a half-page logo, a few phone numbers, and a nonsensical theme:

Engaging your visitors can mean many things. It can mean giving them content that they care about or need. Are your visitors tech-savvy entrepreneurs looking for tips and tricks to use with cutting-edge software? If so, then give them valuable and original tutorials, and they'll return in droves. Are your visitors seeking the latest gossip on movie stars? Give them fresh scoops and valuable insights on public figures, that your readers care about.

Now, if you are in the content game already, you probably already know how to give your readers what they are looking for. When you have the content they want, they are likely to return. That is called engaging your readers! What about a purely commercial environment? If you are a plumber, how do you engage your website visitors? First of all, any website can engage visitors. If you are a plumber, you'll return to the same question — what do your visitors care about? Well, if your website visitor has a leaky faucet, they probably care about getting someone out to fix it quickly! It's that simple. This can mean many things. First, don't just display a contact phone number at the bottom of the page. Place your contact number prominently and invite action, *For 24-hour express service, call....*

In a commercial environment, your contact information is an important visual element on your website. It should be present, and in most of the cases, it should be featured prominently.

You can further engage your visitors with trust elements. Trust elements are elements on a website, that send a message of confidence and trust to visitors. Such factors might include a **Better Business Bureau (BBB)** logo, a guarantee seal, or a personal photo but you need to be careful never to clutter a site.

In the following example, a regional pest control company has included a range of certifications and awards, and a BBB logo:

Note also, that the trust logos are not in color—this is by design.

 Trust logos can clutter a site, displaying them in greyscale is an expert way of including them in a design without making them distracting.

See the example website in the next screenshot. Even in the ho-hum world of plumbing, this company has expertly managed to create persuasive, compelling, and engaging content. There are great lessons here for all business owners: a clear and prominent phone number, an invitation to call for emergency repair, and a discount coupon to entice immediate user engagement. They have even personalized the employees and the tone—casual and almost whimsical creates a relaxed and inviting atmosphere.

You can even engage your visitors with temporary coupons that offer savings for a limited time. Savings are always big motivators for consumers. When the savings are temporary, that will tend to cause visitors to act more quickly.

Thinking like a television chef

Another way to engage your visitors is with rich content—how-to's, blog posts, educational content, and free articles. Sure, once in a while a free article might educate a person to undertake personally, what they might have hired you to do, but don't think of it as a lost customer. Think of it as a positive strategy, that increases the size and ranking power of your entire site. Furthermore, you'll establish thought leadership in your business niche—you'll become the expert that customers seek out. This principle is best expressed by television chefs. Mario Batali, the popular television chef, became a household name by sharing his skills with the television viewing public.

Writing effective titles and headlines

When writing for search engine optimization, the title is one of the most important elements of your copy. Titles may not be long, but they have two very important jobs to do. The first thing a good title does is tell the search engines what your article is about. This helps ensure that your page will be listed in the search engine results when someone tries to find the information contained in your article.

For example, let us say you are trying to sell border collie puppies. You have a page on your website informing the reader about the puppies you have for sale, but the title of this page is *Border Collie Puppies*. That might seem like a great title, but it's not specific enough. People who are searching for border collie puppies online could be looking for information about caring for or training those puppies. On the other hand, when someone searches *Border Collie Puppies for Sale*, your content is exactly what they're looking for, but your title does not match. In this case, the search engine may not display your site at the top of the results because it doesn't realize what a good match your page is for the search phrase.

In addition to containing information that will help the search engines correctly place your web pages in its index, the title has another important role. It must entice people to click on the link to read your article. A good title has to grab a reader's attention and make them want to know more. There's a pretty good chance that there is more than one breeder selling border collie puppies. Your title is competing for attention among all of the other titles on the front page of the search results.

Unlike magazine or newspaper articles, which often use catchy or clever titles to pique a reader's interest, Internet titles must be clear and easy to understand. When people look at the search engine results, they tend to scan them, and they are usually looking for words similar to those they typed to get to the results page. For this reason, titles containing the exact match to a search phrase tend to get clicked on more often.

Although the need to include your keyword phrase in the title limits creativity, it does not prevent you from adding something to give your title a sense of urgency. For example, *Border Collie Puppies for Sale – Going Fast!* might entice people to click to make sure they get the best selection. After all, there are only so many puppies in each litter.

It is important to make sure your titles are not misleading. The title must match the content of the page. The search engines don't like misleading titles and neither do potential customers. If they click on your link thinking they have found exactly what they were looking for and are given something else instead, they will be annoyed with you. Most likely, they will hit the back button and click on the next listing, making a mental note to avoid your site in the future.

When writing for search engine optimization, you also need to pay special attention to the headlines you include within the content of each page. The search engines give extra weight to any text that is placed within header tags, so try to include your targeted keyword phrase in your headlines when possible. Most people have a tendency to scan the headlines and read only the sections that they find relevant to their situation. By including headers in your content, you make it easier for your readers to find what they really need.

Transcending bland, keyword-rich titles

Sure, it's great to have keyword-focused titles, but many websites employ page titles that are little more than a bland keyword repository. Such titles can often rank well in search, but do little to engage users. An over-emphasis on keywords can often lead to headings, titles, and text that reads awkwardly, which is not ideal. Let's take a look at one of our finely-crafted pages to see the techniques we are employing to not only earn high search rankings but also to engage visitors and turn them into customers:

THE ULTIMATE WORDPRESS SEO COMPANY/SERVICE: TASTYPLACEMENT

WHEN IT COMES TO WORDPRESS SEO, WE DON'T KID AROUND.

We are the authors of **WordPress 3 Search Engine Optimization** on prestigious publisher Packt Publishing. You can learn more about our book and read reviews by going to the Amazon page for our WordPress SEO book.

We are WordPress evangelists, and we believe strongly in its power as a future-proof, iron-clad platform for both publishing success and SEO/ranking success. If you are currently running a WordPress site or thinking about conversion to WordPress, we can help. And people love us!

There is a wealth of sophistication taking place in the prior page. The page ranks amazingly well in Google within positions 1, 2, or 3 for *WordPress SEO company* and *WordPress SEO service*. The competition for those phrases is fierce.

First, let us look at whether the headlines and the page are keyword-aware, and we can see that they are! The `h1` tag, *The Ultimate WordPress SEO Company/Service: TastyPlacement* has all our target keywords included. Even our `h2` tag, *When it comes to WordPress SEO, we don't kid around* includes the phrase *WordPress SEO*, but doesn't mindlessly repeat our target phrase. This principle is called partial match—we have included important target keywords, but not all of the keywords.

Let's now look a little beyond our keyword coverage. Do our headings engage and speak honestly and without reading awkwardly? Absolutely yes! We have succeeded in persuading users. We have employed some superlatives, `The Ultimate`, and `We don't kid around`. We have also included trust logos from press mentions we have received. The graphic highlights the ultimate accolade: our authorship of this WordPress SEO book. The technique we have applied to this page, can be applied in any industry.

Organizing your content with WordPress tags

WordPress' tag system is a tool that helps make it easier for users to find the content they are looking for on your site. Tags are often confused with categories, but tags work a bit differently. In order to understand how to use WordPress tags, you need to first be aware of how tags differ in categories and how people find your content through tags.

Categories are hierarchical in structure. You can have top-level categories, with subcategories underneath them. Think of categories as a kind of table of contents for your website. For example, if you have a website about crafts, you might have top-level categories that are named for the different types of crafts, such as *Knitting*, *Crochet*, and *Sewing*. Under *Knitting*, you might have subcategories such as *Knitting Patterns* or *Knitting Needles*. You don't want your categories to be too specific because your category list would become unwieldy and you would end up with a bunch of categories with only one entry.

Tags, on the other hand, are meant to be more specific. They help your website visitors find exactly what they are looking for. Perhaps you have a user visiting your crafts site, looking for a pattern to make a pair of baby booties. Baby booties can be knit or crocheted, so rather than looking through both categories, your visitor might find it easier to look through your tags for *Baby booties pattern* or *Pattern for baby booties*.

Unlike categories, tags do not have parents or children, so the tags you choose should be complete enough to give the user a good idea of whether, they will find what they are looking for on that page. You wouldn't use the tag *Pink* for a pattern to knit baby booties, because it doesn't tell your visitor much at all about the post. A post that is relevant to the tag *Pink* could be just about anything.

When you assign tags to a post, think about what terms people would look for if your website was a book, and if they were looking at the index in the back to find out which page to turn to. Those are the terms you should use as tags for the post. In addition, you should add the keyword phrase or phrases that you are targeting in the post.

In addition to helping your site visitors find the information they are looking for, using tags and categories helps increase traffic to your website. These tag and category pages get indexed by the search engines just like any other page on your site. This leads to a warning: tag pages, if overused, can cause large swaths of duplicate content.

Stay focused on a few tags per post. Also, tags should never be used to stuff keywords — to do so will have no effect.

Creating keyword-aware content

It may seem unnatural to focus on a keyword when writing content for your website, but it is absolutely essential for writing your pages in a manner that will get them ranked highly in the search engines. Note that, the title of this chapter includes the phrase *keyword-aware*, rather than *keyword-rich*. Too many inexperienced webmasters, once they discover the magic effect of including keywords in their content, go overboard with keywords. You need not bludgeon the search engines by mindless repeating keywords in singular and plural, and every synonym in between. Google is very sophisticated. A light touch will work best: write content naturally with a few mentions of keywords, and Google will get the message.

That said, no matter how well-written your content is, if it doesn't contain the keywords and phrases that people use to search for your product or service, your pages are unlikely to show up in the search engine results pages.

For this reason, the first step in creating the content for your site is to begin with the right keywords. We learnt in *Chapter 3, Researching and working With Keywords*, how to research keywords, find the big-money keywords and key phrases, and organize and prioritize them. With sound keyword research, writing flows naturally: start with the high-volume, high-value keywords and write high-quality content for your site that focuses on those keywords.

It's best to target one keyword phrase or a group of phrases per content page — this is vital. Recall that keyword overlap can give us a close group of keywords such as *Miami AC* and *Miami AC repair*. In any case, keep each content page very focused on a small group of words.

Whichever phrase or phrases you are targeting, should be used several times, but not dozens of times within the body content. You should make sure to include the keyword phrase in the title and headings, as well as a few times throughout the actual content. It is especially important to include your keyword phrase near the beginning of your content. Most search engines tend to give more weight to words and phrases that appear in the first few paragraphs of a web page. Remember that search engines determine the subject of your page from the words you use on the page. If you don't use the keyword phrase often enough, your page will not rank for that phrase. If your page is selling book covers and you are targeting the keyword phrase; *Buy book covers*, that phrase needs to appear on the page in several places. First of all, it must be included in the title and somewhere in the first paragraph of the copy. In addition, you should try to work it into the rest of the copy at least two to three more times, and into the headings that separate different sections of copy. You can also add the keyword phrase to the alt text for any photos that appear on the page.

Keeping it natural

The main thing to remember about writing keyword-aware content is that, it should appear natural when you read it back. However, some writers are more skillful than others at making a keyword fit with the copy. If you have trouble fitting your keyword phrase into the copy in a way that makes sense, it's possible that you may have better results by outsourcing the writing to someone who specializes in writing for SEO.

If you prefer to write your own copy, you'll find that you will improve as you get more practice. Like anything else, writing SEO website copy is a skill that must be developed. Some people have a knack for it and pick it up quickly, while others require more time and practice to develop the skill.

No matter how skilled you are at writing a copy, you will undoubtedly come across keyword phrases that are awkward and will be hard to work into your website content. This is especially true for search queries that are written in the first person. It's not too hard to come up with a title for *How do I tie a tie*, for example, but once you get past the title and introduction, it becomes difficult to work that keyword phrase into the copy because you have switched gears from asking the question to trying to answer it.

Some people choose to avoid awkward keyword phrases because of the increased difficulty of writing this type of content well enough to avoid losing the reader.

Sometimes, the potential traffic for an awkward keyword phrase makes it worth trying. You'll have to decide for yourself on a case-by-case basis, whether you want to try to rank for these types of keyword phrases.

Another type of keyword phrase that can be difficult to target, is the one with a misspelled word. Although many people have profited from targeting misspelled keywords, it is harder to achieve now because Google has grown adept at correcting misspelled search queries automatically. This practice should be avoided entirely.

Avoiding automated content plugins

Creating fresh, original content for your WordPress site or blog is tedious. For this reason, many people have been enticed into using automated plugins to add content to their sites. Some WordPress plugins that have cropped up to satisfy this misguided demand are AutoBlogged, WP Robot, and MultiPress plugins. However, no automated script can deliver original content for your website. When you employ an automated content plugin on your site, you are getting content that has already been published by another website. This is what is referred to as duplicate content.

Duplicate content does not mean that the content necessarily triggers copyright infringement (although it might); you are not necessarily running afoul of the law by posting duplicate content. In fact, there are hundreds of article directories that encourage you to take their content and republish it on your website. However, duplicate content has little to no value to a search strategy. Most likely, search engines won't even bother to index the content. And, even if the duplicate content is indexed, your pages won't rank well and your site will earn little trust or authority. You are not only competing against the site that originally published the article, but every other site that has used the content.

Another problem with autoblogging plugins is that, some of them pull content that is not freely available for use, in this case, raising legal issues regarding the use of the content. They often pull content from RSS feeds, that include the posts from other people's blogs or websites instead of pulling only from article directories that allow republishing. The companies that sell these autoblogging scripts justify this, by saying that the blogger provided the RSS feed, so they have a right to use it.

However, most bloggers do not intend for their RSS feeds to be used in this way. They are meant to provide a way for their readers to subscribe to their posts, not a means for other site owners to steal their content.

It's good to remember that all original content that appears on other people's sites is covered by copyright laws, and these writers have the right to take you to court if you steal their content to use on your site.

Perhaps the most important reason to avoid using automated content plugins is that, Google warns that sites that use such content may be subject to ranking penalties. In the help section for Google's Webmaster Tools, Google states that it will penalize sites that attempt to rank pages by including content that provides little or no value to the reader. The examples Google gives are affiliate sites that provide no original content but serve only to act as a middleman by sending the visitor to a site where they can buy the product, doorway pages that are only meant for search engines, scraped content, and auto-generated content. The last two of these are exactly what you get, when you use an autoblogging plugin to create content for your website.

When you use autoblogging plugins to post scraped or auto-generated content on your website, you risk having your site removed from the search engine results. In addition, if you use AdSense on this type of site, you could end up having your website, or even your entire account, banned from the AdSense program.

The ranking power of truly original content cannot be denied. In addition, if you write your content to target a specific keyword, it is a good bet that it will be easier to rank your own content for that keyword than anything you scrape from the web. A large portion of the work you need to do to get a web page ranked is getting backlinks; so even though you might be able to get a lot of content on your website quickly by using one of these plugins, you'll still have a lot of hard work to do in building enough links to your pages to get them to rank. If you are going to put that much effort into ranking a page, why not use your own content to begin with and avoid the risk of having your site banned by Google for publishing scraped or automated content?

Writing for your audience

Many people think that all they have to do is learn how to get traffic to their websites, and they will achieve their website goals, but there is more to it than that. Writing web pages that are optimized for the search engines is only half the battle. If you want to make money, you need to write for your audience, not just for the search engines.

Search engines use mathematical algorithms to determine ranking because they have to. No machine can read and think like a human. That's why you need to write content that uses the exact keyword phrase you are targeting, rather than writing like you would talk if you were interacting with your customers one-on-one. However, once a visitor lands on your site, if the content doesn't make sense to them, they will click on the back button and go find what they're looking for elsewhere.

It's the people who visit your site who will determine whether you make any money. They will come to your website looking for something, and if you provide them with whatever they are looking for, they will stick around for awhile and maybe even buy something. It's your job to figure out what they're looking for.

One of the most common things people look for online is information. They may be looking for information that tells them how to do something, information about a product, or information to write a report for school. Regardless of what type of information they need, if they don't find it on your web page, they will not stay long. They will keep looking on other websites, until they find what they need.

Thinking about a searcher's intent

For this reason, you need to think about the keyword phrase you are targeting and determine what type of information the searcher is looking for. If the keyword phrase is a question or starts with the words *How to*, this is a pretty easy task. You can write an article or post that answers the question or provides step-by-step instructions for doing whatever it is the searcher is trying to learn to do, and your visitor will be happy.

Of course, not all search terms are this easy. If someone is searching for *poker*, what do they want? They could be looking for an online poker website, poker rules, or a poker for the fireplace. The best option, in this case, may be to pass up the keyword phrase altogether and target something more specific. However, if you have a keyword phrase you feel could be potentially profitable and fairly easy to get ranked, you might not want to overlook it just because it is vague.

When targeting this type of keyword phrase, you can either try to please everyone or try to guess at the most likely motives of the person doing the search. For example, if you type `poker` into the Google AdWords keyword tool and sort by global monthly search volume, you'll see that the most popular search besides poker that contains that word is `Play poker`. For this reason, you might assume that most people searching for `Poker`, are looking for information on how to play the game. Or, if you want to play it safe, you could create a single page that is targeted to the keyword `Poker` and contains a basic overview of the things, the searcher is most likely to look for, and that links to additional pages that contain more detailed information.

If you have a site that sells products, you will probably have better results if you target buying keywords. These are keywords, that are most likely to be used by searchers who are serious about making a purchase. For example, someone who searches for `New Balance shoes on sale` is ready to buy. They already know what kind of shoes they want. At this point, they are just looking for the best price. Other examples of buying keywords are keyword phrases that include *buy, purchase, under $100,* and other related terms, as well as extremely specific product keywords, such as those containing a model number. People who search for a specific model number have usually already done their research and decided what they want. Now, they just need to find your website to buy it.

Providing quality information

Giving your visitors what they are looking for is a good start, but there are other things you need to consider when writing your content as well, such as providing quality information. Quality information is more than just answering a question; it is answering it well. If you can provide better content for your targeted keyword phrase than anyone else, people will link to your page just because you have great content. This will make it much easier for you to get ranked in the search engines.

Perhaps you are targeting *How to tie a tie,* for example. You've written step-by-step instructions and either drawn illustrations or taken photographs to show each step. That's good, but you can easily make it better by including a video as well. Now, your visitors can decide for themselves whether they'd rather read the instructions, or watch them. That is quality, and after your visitor gets done tying his/her tie, he/she might just share your post on Facebook or Twitter and help you get even more traffic.

Quality content needs to be well-written and free of errors. You don't get quality content for your website by outsourcing the writing to someone to an offshore content factory and slapping it up on your site unchecked. You might save money on the writing by having the work done by someone in a country where labor is cheap, but once you get the articles back, you will either have to edit them or pay to have them edited, which often defeats the purpose of having them written cheaply.

You might get away with lower quality content if you are running a personal blog and monetizing it with AdSense, but if you are building a website for a company that sells products or services online, you will be held to a higher standard. People expect businesses to be professional, and spelling and grammar errors don't send that message. If someone comes to your website to buy something and sees several errors in the copy, they may wonder about the quality of your products or services.

Providing quality information often means providing more than your visitors expect. Most websites that sell products provide the exact same product description, which is usually provided by the manufacturer. You can make your website stand out by offering something more. A video demonstration of someone actually using the product can be a very effective tool for making sales as well as providing unique content for your site that is not available elsewhere.

Writing to get results

Every website has a purpose. If you don't know what the purpose of your website is, you need to figure it out before you write your content. Each page needs to have a goal and the content must be written in such a way that it helps you achieve that goal. There are many different actions users can take when they visit a website, and your copy should steer towards the action you want them to take.

If you have a website that sells products, you want your website visitors to buy something. How do you get them to do that? First of all, you give them the information they need to make a decision. You tell them all about the product, describing all of its features, and perhaps even using a video to demonstrate how it is used. Then you need a call to action. Tell them what they need to do to place an order, and make it easy for them to do so.

It can be tempting to use the description provided by the manufacturer when creating a web page that is designed to sell a product, but remember that this page still needs to get ranked in the search engine results as well. If other websites have already used the product description, you'll be posting duplicate content if you reuse it.

Your website copy will be different, depending on what action you want the user to take. Not all websites sell products. Some make money through advertising and still others exist for the purpose of collecting e-mail addresses for a list, or getting people to request a quote. Whatever your purpose is for the page, the copy should make it clear what you want the visitor to do.

In addition, the layout of your website plays an important role in getting results from your traffic. If you are making money from advertising, you have to rely on the placement of your ads to make sure people notice them because most ad networks won't allow you to ask your readers to click on the ads. This is the one case where you can't use a call to action, to let your readers know what action you want them to take.

The layout of your site can also help if you are trying to get people to sign up for a newsletter or request a quote, but in this case, your copy needs to work together with your website layout. You tell the visitor why they should sign up for your newsletter, and then ask them to do it. A newsletter signup page is usually very simple. There should be a minimum number of ads or other distractions to keep your visitor from filling out the e-mail subscription form. The same is true for a site that is collecting information for other purposes, such as getting requests for quotes. The content of this type of page should be focused on telling the visitor why they should fill out the request, and there should be nothing on the page that will take their attention away from the form.

Once you have decided on a purpose for your website, everything on the site should be designed to serve that purpose. Every element should be carefully planned to get the desired result, and once the site starts getting traffic, it should be tested and tweaked to maximize conversions. Everything from the headline, to the length of the copy, to the size and color of the subscription form can affect the conversion rate. By testing, you will be able to determine which layout and copy gets the best results. We learn about how to test your website in *Chapter 10, Testing Your Site and Monitoring Your Progress.*

Developing your writing style

The tone you use when writing your content will depend on the type of site, as well as your target audience. If you are running a personal blog, the tone can be more casual than if you run a business website. People expect businesspersons to act professionally. This requires a more formal writing style, that has a polished tone.

For a personal website or blog, you can write the same way you would talk to a friend. This will give your site a casual tone, which can help you connect with your readers. They start to feel like they know you because you relate to them in the same way, that you would if you were talking face to face. If you write like you talk, your voice will come through and reflect your personality. This makes it easier for your readers to like you, and they will be more likely to become regular readers, perhaps even adding to the discussion by posting comments of their own.

When writing for a business or professional website, imagine that you are writing a letter to the editor, which will be published in a newspaper or magazine and read by many people. You want to give a good impression, so you choose your words carefully. You make a conscious effort to avoid anything, that will make your writing style seem too familiar.

Some of the things you must avoid when writing in a formal style are slang and contractions. We use these all the time when we're speaking, but these words should generally never be used in formal writing. If you want to convey a professional image, you must be careful to avoid anything that sounds informal. Slang and contractions are among the worst offenders.

In formal writing, empty phrases such as *You may be thinking* or *Do you know that* should be avoided. You should not presume to put thoughts into your readers' heads or try to fill up the page by adding words that don't add any meaning. The length of your sentences is a part of your writing style as well.

Narrative styles

The point of view you use to write your copy also depends on how formal you want your site to be and at what level you want to interact with your audience. If you're writing in a casual style, you'll want to write in the first person or second person style. A more formal writing style requires a formal third person narrative.

When writing in the first person, you write from your own point of view. This style of narrative involves using the word *I* in the copy as related to your readers on a personal level. Many blogs are written in a casual first person style. This style is most appropriate if you are talking about things you have actually done, rather than writing how-to or other informational articles.

The second person style is also considered casual, but when writing in the second person, you avoid using the word *I*, while still referring to the reader as *you*. You are speaking directly to the reader, giving him advice or information that will help him without making it all about you. This style allows you to write as if you are speaking directly to the reader, without drawing attention to yourself.

In the third person narrative, you don't use *I* or *you* in your writing. Instead, you use a more matter-of-fact tone and refer to the people you write about as *he* or *she*. The third person narrative style requires you to write, as if you are a narrator who is detached from the story or article, rather than someone who is involved in it. When you write in the third person, you write as if you are an observer and merely passing on your observations to others.

Once you have decided on a narrative style to use for your website, you should try not to jump around from one point of view to another on various pages of your site. Your writing style should be consistent throughout the entire website to avoid disorienting your readers.

Your writing should also be clear and concise. You can ramble on for hundreds of words without saying anything, but if you do, you will lose your readers. Get right to the point and avoid unnecessary verbiage. Most people don't want to read thousands of words of copy online.

If you have a lot of information to cover, however, you may find that it takes more than the usual 300 to 500 words of a typical web page to say everything that needs to be said. It's fine to write longer copy as long as it isn't filled up with meaningless chatter.

Avoid using clichés in your writing. A cliché is an expression that has been overused to the point that it has become a common expression, such as *older but wiser* and *live and learn*. Readers find these expressions boring, because they have heard them so many times. Try to think of a new and fresh way to say things, and you will keep your reader's attention longer.

You only have one chance to capture your reader's attention and keep it. If your copy doesn't engage the reader, he/she will leave your site and go somewhere else. You need to start with a strong lead paragraph and keep your copy clear, focused, and free of excess words in order to hold the reader's attention long enough to get him/her to take the desired action for that page.

Structuring your content using taxonomy and hierarchy

Setting up the proper structure for your content not only makes it easier for your visitors to find what they're looking for, but it also helps the search engines find and index your content. Although both categories and tags can be used to organize your content, they are not the same thing. Categories break your website into sections that organize your site in a hierarchy, making it easier for users to locate information related to a certain topic through WordPress' built-in navigation. Tags, on the other hand, are free-form identifiers. The tags you use for a given post usually include the primary keyword, as well as any secondary or long tail keywords you hope to be able to rank for with that WordPress Post.

Using WordPress categories

The categories you employ for your site depend on the content. Your main categories should break the site up into manageable chunks without getting too specific. If you own a website that sells pet supplies, for example, you might start by dividing the site into categories by animal. People who have dogs are not going to be interested in bird stuff, so break it down for them. Include main categories such as Dogs, Cats, Birds, and Fish to help people find the pet supplies they need faster.

If your site sells supplies for dogs only, not for other types of animals, you'll need to set your categories up differently. Your top-level categories might include things like Dog Collars and Leashes, whereas the general pet supply store above might use these same labels as subcategories under Dogs. Because categories in WordPress are hierarchical, you can continue breaking categories into subcategories for as many levels as it makes sense to do so.

Because there are many different types of dog collars, it would make sense to break up the collars category even further. Perhaps you might make subcategories for Leather Dog Collars, Dog Training Collars, and Nylon Dog Collars. Do you go deeper and start breaking them up by color or size? That's up to you, and will probably depend on how many items you offer that would fit in each subcategory. If your Nylon Dog Collars subcategory has hundreds of items in it, you might want to break it up a little more. Keep in mind that excessive subcategories can tend to confuse both readers and search engines. It's a good practice to keep category levels no more than three-levels deep unless absolutely necessary.

Keep in mind when creating categories, that people start at the top and browse their way down through your hierarchy.

No one will even see Dog Collars until they click on **Dogs**, so don't try to sneak in a few items for ferrets just to avoid making a new top-level category. If you do, people who visit your site looking for ferret supplies will look at your categories, assume that you don't have anything for ferrets and leave. If you want to avoid having a long list of categories but still cover everything, try making a category for Other and set it to appear at the bottom of the list. That's way, people who are looking for supplies for less popular pets such as ferrets and snakes can still find them.

Managing your categories with plugins

You may find that you don't like the way your categories are displayed by default in WordPress—a common complaint. Perhaps, you want to hide certain categories, change the order in which they appear, or change the way they look when they are displayed on your blog. There are several plugins available that will help you display your categories exactly the way you want them to be shown. Here are a few that you might want to try, if you use the self-hosted version of WordPress.

Advanced Category Excluder

The Advanced Category Excluder plugin allows you to hide selected categories from certain parts of your site while still displaying them on others. If you don't want to display the top-level categories for other animals once your visitor has clicked on **Dogs**, you can use this plugin to do that. This can also help with SEO because excluding these links, which have anchor text listing other animals, can make your dog pages appear more focused on dogs. You can find the plugin at: `http://wordpress.org/extend/plugins/advanced-category-excluder/`.

Multi Column Category List plugin

The Multi Column Category List plugin lets you create a category list that spans two or more WordPress columns. The plugin can be set up to divide your categories at a certain point in the alphabet and it also allows you to set up custom headers for each column. You can find the plugin at `http://www.dagondesign.com/articles/multi-column-category-list-plugin-for-wordpress/`.

My Category Order

The My Category Order plugin lets you change the order in which your categories are listed on your WordPress site, which, by default, is alphabetical. You can find the plugin at `http://geekyweekly.com/mycategoryorder`.

Fold Category List

The Fold Category List plugin helps keep your category list from getting too long. If you have a lot of categories and subcategories, you may find that your category list stretches further than your posts. This plugin allows you to display a list of categories in which only the current category is expanded, while the others are displayed as collapsed, with no children showing. This keeps your category list looking more manageable. You can find it at `http://www.webspaceworks.com/resources/wordpress/31/`.

Hiring a writer

SEO professionals know how to write engaging and keyword-rich content, but most of them have a little secret: they write very little of their own content. These webmasters turn to SEO copyrighters. An SEO copyrighter is simply a writer who has written in a search environment, and therefore knows how to craft titles, headings, and body copy, based on a keyword or keyword group.

Regular writers will certainly do in a pinch; you might need to tweak content provided by regular writers to achieve SEO goals. You can also always employ regular writers when your content is intended for other than purely ranking purposes, such as with ordinary blog posts or company updates.

When you hire an SEO copyrighter, the good copyrighters will ask for a few key parameters before they write, *What are the keywords?* and *What sort of keyword density do you want?* These questions are signs of a copyrighter with SEO experience. Ideally, your writer will let you dictate specific keyword phrases, will write titles and headings in addition to body copy, will let you dictate keyword density, and will even let you suggest the tone, style, and voice of the article.

Where to hire content writers

There are many sources for hiring content writers. The first question is quality; the quality of online content writing varies tremendously. The poorest quality writing (it's also the least expensive) comes from offshore content shops that advertise in webmaster forums. In some cases, such shops scrape original content from existing websites and process the articles through spinning software.

Spinning software takes an existing body of text and *spins* the article to create a variation through the substitution of homonyms. Such software is the source of much of the gibberish found on the Internet. So, *you should seek the counsel of a registered professional* might be spun into something like *one is compelled to aim to the advice of certified expert.*

Once you've seen spinning software in action, such articles are pretty easy to spot. Even if offshore articles are originals, they'll tend to be weak. A 300-word article from an offshore shop can cost between $2 and $5. If you employ such services, don't expect high quality writing, and don't expect quality search rankings.

Responsible webmasters use EFL (English as first language) writers either working as freelancers, through text brokering services, or with an SEO copyrighting service. Here, the prices vary widely. In the local market of Austin, Texas, a 500-word article can cost between $18 and $300. The high end of such pricing is rare, but is offered as a premium service by some specialized SEO copyrighting services.

Some great ways to find solid SEO writers at competitive prices are to either post the position in the **gigs** section of Craigslist.org or simply browse through the services section of Craigslist and find authors advertising their services.

There is another option: text brokering services. There are dozens of websites online that work just like ELance.com—where writing services are offered and sought.

With any writing service, it's touch-and-go. There are good writers and bad writers that populate all such services. You'll have some misses in the beginning, until you find writers that deliver quality products at a good price. Hiring out some or all of your writing can be a great way to build up content quickly.

Summary

Ideally, this chapter illuminated the concepts that can help you implement a sound and effective content development strategy. We considered ways in which you can fully engage your visitors with content and learnt to write effective titles and headlines to gain the reader's attention from the start. We moved on to examine WordPress' built-in tag functionality to expand the reach of your content, and making it easier for users to find.

We learned how to create keyword-rich content that is ready-made for search engines—which users find natural and easy to read. We learned about writing styles: casual versus business, and first-person versus third person. We learned how to adapt WordPress' category structure and hierarchy to organize your content and make it easy to find. Finally, we learned some approaches to hiring out your writing jobs.

With this chapter, we've now got a grasp of the role of content writing in our overall WordPress ranking strategy. Now, we will move on to the all-important arena of link building.

6
Link Building

We now turn to the true source of ranking power: link building. All of our efforts in content writing and on-page optimization will fail if we do not undertake link building. Let's begin with a simple definition: link building is simply the process of encouraging other webmasters to create hypertext links from their website to yours.

Remember the analogy: on-page optimization factors are akin to tuning and building a race car; link building is the fuel that makes the car go. Without on-page optimization, the car will run slowly. Without inbound links, the car will lack the power to move.

One of Google's many ground-breaking innovations was the employment of inbound links as a measurement of the relative value and popularity of a website. The idea was that popular sites were popular for a reason, and if Google returned popular pages in its search results, then it was generally returning the best results to a search query. Google applied the term *PageRank* to the mathematical formula underlying this idea, and the elements of the process and many variants and extensions are now the subject of patents worldwide. Before this innovation, search results were based entirely on on-page factors. Now, inbound linking is a principal component of the algorithms of all major search engines.

And so, link building is a vital element of any search strategy. However, search engines are also keenly aware of attempts to manipulate rankings through link building, so caution is warranted.

In this chapter, we'll begin by covering some general topics in link building, such as do follow/no follow links and authority links. These concepts will color our entire discussion of link building methods. We'll learn about PageRank, Google's trademarked and patented process for counting the inbound votes we receive as links from other websites. We'll learn how to accurately measure the number and quality of inbound links that you garner.

We'll then delve into the craft of link building itself. We'll cover how to evaluate websites as potential link partners. We'll learn several techniques to help build links, including how to request links directly from other webmasters, and how to create the *link bait*.

Understanding the importance of backlinks

A backlink is a hypertext link on another website that points back to your website. Backlinks are also called **inbound links**, whereas a link on your website pointing to another website is called an **outbound link**.

Backlinks are important for two reasons:

1. First, they bring traffic to your website, as web visitors to other sites follow the links to your website.

2. Second, as we have learned, Google and the other search engines examine both the number and quality of inbound links as a measure of a page's quality. Sites with high numbers of quality inbound links are seen as more valuable and are ranked more highly than sites with either lower numbers of inbound links or lower quality inbound links.

Google simply employs the inherent democracy of the Web: sites that other webmasters have linked to are most likely to be the better pages on the Web, and so they represent better quality content. Google stated in the Corporate Information section of its website *Pages that we believe are important pages receive a higher PageRank and are more likely to appear at the top of the search results*. The other search engines employ related approaches.

The mathematics and operation of PageRank

Google's PageRank is part of its search algorithm; the other search engines' ranking algorithms work similarly. Yahoo! and Bing, while they obviously measure inbound link counts as a ranking factor, do not disclose to web users any measure of page value equivalent to PageRank. PageRank works through complex mathematics. Understanding the mathematical intricacies is not vital, but can help illuminate how PageRank impacts your link-building efforts. PageRank works the same on all web platforms, WordPress or otherwise.

PageRank calculations works as follows: Google assigns a numerical value to each indexed page on the Web. When an indexed page hyperlinks to another page on the Web, a portion of that numerical value is passed from the linking page to the destination page, thereby increasing the destination page's PageRank. Inbound links increase the PageRank of your web pages and outbound links decrease PageRank.

PageRank, often abbreviated as *PR*, is expressed as a number from 0 to 10. Google.com and Facebook.com, both of which benefit from millions of inbound links, enjoy a PageRank of 9—very close to the highest available score. In common parlance, a PageRank 10 site is referred to as a *PR10 site*.

Remember that PageRank refers to pages on the web, not just sites themselves. A PR5 site simply means that the site's front page is a PR5.

Let us examine how PageRank is specifically calculated. Every indexed page on the Web enjoys a small amount of PageRank on its own, a PageRank score of 1. This inherent PageRank is the original source of all PageRanks on the Web; it is only through linking between pages and sites that some pages accumulate higher PageRank than others.

The PageRank damping factor

However, a page can never send all of its PageRank to other pages—this is where the damping factor comes into play. The damping factor is simply a number between zero and one (but think of it as 0 to 100 on a percentage scale); it represents the amount of PageRank that can be sent away from a page when that page links out to other pages.

If a search algorithm's damping factor was set to 0, no page would ever send its PageRank away, and the entire PageRank calculation becomes pointless. On the other hand, if the damping factor is set to 1, then 100 percent of a page's PageRank is sent away through outbound linking, and any page with any outbound links retains no PageRank. In this case, the algorithm also fails—the Internet would be populated entirely with the sites of either PR0 or PR10, with no sites in between.

As it happens, the damping factor employed by Google is widely believed to be .85. This means that 85 percent of a page's PageRank is available to be passed to other pages through linking, while 15 percent of a page's PageRank will always be retained. It is believed that Google can alter the damping factor for particular sites.

Consider for a moment that Google manages PageRank calculations for billions of web pages. If that wasn't daunting enough, consider that Google undertakes the even more staggering task of managing the mathematical calculations of immeasurable numbers of links between those billions of sites.

The following graphical illustration, from Wikipedia, of PageRank calculations for a hypothetical group of web pages shows that the PageRank distribution is accumulated in site B because it enjoys a high number of links. C enjoys a high PageRank because of its single inbound link from site B. The sites represented by the small circles at the bottom of the illustration retain only 1.6 percent of the PageRank distribution because they link outward and have no inbound links.

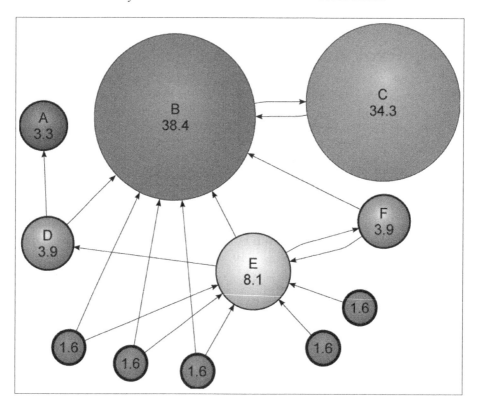

PageRank is shared among outbound links

Also bear in mind that the amount of PageRank available to be passed by a page will be equally divided among all the outbound links on that page. So, if a web page has a total of six links: three internal links (links between pages within the same website), and three outbound links (links to outside websites), then the PageRank passed away by that page will be shared equally among the six links on that page.

What does that mean for the link builder? Well, it means that if you have secured a link on a great PR4 page, but that page has 200 outbound links, then you'll be sharing the available PageRank with the other 199 sites. That's why you want to seek out pages on other websites with low numbers of outbound links. When there are fewer outbound links, your link will enjoy a much greater percentage of the available PageRank.

If the mathematics underlying PageRank isn't complicated enough, there is another facet that you must consider. The PageRank scale of PR1 to PR10 isn't linear, it is logarithmic. Therefore, it takes 10 times as much linking power to rise from a PR2 to a PR3 page. Expressed another way, a PR4 page has 100 times the linking power of a PR2 page. As each level of PageRank is reached, it becomes harder and harder to reach the next level. There are only about 120 to 150 PR10 pages at any given time, and generally this elite class of pages and sites includes Google.com, Microsoft.com, WhiteHouse.gov, and other sites of equivalent popularity and character.

PageRank is historical and only updated every few years or so. Years ago, PageRank was updated much more frequently. When you check the PageRank of a page, you aren't seeing the current PageRank, you are seeing the PageRank reported as of the last PageRank update. You can check the PageRank of any page on the internet by using the free SEO Site Tools extension for the Chrome/Chromium browser.

Learning to discount PageRank

PageRank remains a measure of the value of a link, and the measure of how much link power you've accumulated on your pages. However, as Google's capabilities have grown, Google has layered other ranking factors into their algorithm. PageRank alone is not nearly as important as it once was. Google is quick to point out that it employs over 200 separate signals to rank websites.

Understanding trust as a ranking principle

"A parallel ranking principle that operates alongside PageRank is Trust. Google employee Matt Cutts has made an official statement in a Google Webmaster video (`https://www.youtube.com/watch?v=ALzSUeekQ2Q`) regarding the principle of trust as, "sort of a catch-all term we use...we use several words: reputation, trust, authority...how much are we willing to believe that this is a high-quality page". While PageRank is a component of the trust principle, trust can be indicated in ways other than raw mathematical PageRank."

So, two websites of equal PageRank might send vastly different amounts of trust to a website when they link to it. A website for a local municipality with a PageRank of 4 will send far more trust when it links to another website than a spammy general directory with the same PageRank. A local municipality website is likely to have many trusted links from other trusted sites, like other government and civic websites, perhaps some university websites—trust accumulates in websites much in the way that PageRank does.

Understanding the importance of website category

Another way trust can be earned through link building is to secure links from related websites. A website in the same general topic category sends stronger trust signals and more ranking power when it links to a website in the same topical category.

If you offer online driver training courses on your website, a link from other driver education websites will offer far more ranking power than a link from a fashion blogger. The principle is sound: links are more likely to meaningfully identify important websites and pages if the websites share a common topic. This approach was tested and the results compiled in a technical paper by a Stanford University student, Taher Haveliwala, who later worked for Google as a software engineer. The paper is entitled *Topic-Sensitive PageRank: A Context-Sensitive Ranking Algorithm for Web Search* and can be found on the web at `http://goo.gl/9jH4P5`. The paper is highly technical but concludes that a simple PageRank algorithm can be greatly improved if only inbound links from websites in related categories are used to calculate PageRank. Even if Google did not adopt the exact approach Taher suggested in his study, Google certainly adopted some variant whereby in-category links deliver more ranking power.

Distinguishing between dofollow and nofollow links

But, what if a webmaster wants to link out to another site but not send away its valuable PageRank or trust? That's where nofollow links come into play. A nofollow link is a link that search engines do not record as a link, so no PageRank passes. By contrast, a dofollow link is a link that does pass PageRank. Generally, you want to secure dofollow inbound links to your website when pursuing your link building strategy. That said, nofollow links are an important part of the SEO landscape: they are handy devices in a webmaster's toolbox and can help fine tune your search strategy, as we will learn.

Understanding nofollow links

Here is how nofollow links came into being. Because the effect of PageRank and inbound links is so important to rankings, the Internet became (and still is) fairly polluted with link spam. Link spam is simply a low-value link placed on another website for the purpose of either attracting traffic or PageRank. Common locations for link spam are the comment sections of WordPress or Typepad blogs (called comment spam) and human-edited sites like Wikipedia.

As a way to eliminate the incentive for link spam, Google announced in 2005 that it was adopting a nofollow specification that would operate as an extension of HTML: the nofollow specification was little more than a short bit of code embedded in a hyperlink that let the webmasters signal to the search engines not to pass PageRank for the particular links. The specification calls for the inclusion of a code snippet (`rel="nofollow"`) within the active portion of a link.

How to implement or identify a nofollow link

What follows is a code example of how to implement or identify a nofollow link: it's very simple and takes only a few seconds. The following link shows a standard hypertext link written in HTML:

```
<a href="http://www.tastyplacement.com/">SEO Book</a>
```

To modify the link to make it `nofollow`, we simply add the `rel="nofollow"` code within the opening tag:

```
<a href="http://www.tastyplacement.com/" rel="nofollow">SEO Book</a>
```

When Google encounters a link that includes the nofollow attribute, Google does not pass PageRank or trust via that link. The nofollow attribute says to search engines, *Yes, there is a link here, but I don't want to pass PageRank to this site*. The nofollow standard now applies to all major search engines; quickly after Google's adoption of the nofollow standard, Yahoo! and MSN/Live (now Bing) adopted it as well.

The theory behind the adoption of nofollow links was that if the links on a site were not followed, then spammers wouldn't bother posting links because they would get no PageRank benefits for the links. For the most part, it worked. Big sites like Wikipedia implemented the nofollow standard on all outgoing links, and as a result, the amount of link spam dropped considerably.

Avoiding and identifying nofollow links

Ten years ago, before the adoption of the nofollow specification, all links passed PageRank, so any link you secured for your website increased your ranking power. Nowadays, you need to be aware of which links are dofollow and which are nofollow. When link building, you don't want to waste time securing a lot of nofollow links—such links simply don't carry the same benefit as a dofollow link.

When you are browsing sites looking for potential links, you need to be able to swiftly and reliably identify whether a site offers dofollow or nofollow links. So, say you have found a blog with a relevant post, and you want to add a meaningful comment to the post with a link back to your site. However, you need to know something very important: are the comment links in the particular blog dofollow, or has the webmaster set them to nofollow? There are two ways to tell if a link is dofollow or nofollow:

1. Examine the code. You can manually examine the code to see if the link has the `rel="nofollow"` snippet within the markup for that particular link. Depending on your browser, you can find the menu entry for View source or View source code (all browsers have this functionality somewhere in their menu). The disadvantage to this method is that you may have to dig through a lot of code to find what you are looking for.

2. Get a browser plugin. There are several free browser plugins that will highlight nofollow links on a page automatically. The SEO Site Tools plugin for Google's Chrome browser offers this functionality, as does the Search Status plugin for Firefox.

The screenshot below shows how the SEO Site Tools plugin works in Google's Chrome browser. The plugin, when set to show nofollow links, highlights all nofollow links with a red highlighted background, as shown in the screenshot below:

And so, if the blog's comment section is nofollow, then the link you were thinking of placing probably isn't that worthwhile. You would be wiser to direct your link building efforts to sites that offer dofollow links.

The diminishing universe of followed links

Dofollow links are becoming harder to secure as more and more sites restrict their outbound links to nofollow to combat spam. Major social media sites such as Facebook and MySpace restrict all the user-generated links to nofollow. The link builder's task is harder now than it was several years ago. For this reason, it's important to quickly locate and identify followed links.

Notable dofollow links, while scarce, do exist. You can secure two high-value links on your LinkedIn profile, but you cannot choose custom anchor text: you must select the predefined choices *my website* and *my blog*. The legendary DMOZ directory, a PR7 site, still offers dofollow links for those fortunate enough to gain entry to the directory. We will cover how to apply for a DMOZ directory listing later in this chapter.

Making use of nofollow links

So, how can we employ nofollow links to improve our search strategy? First, we must consider an important principle related to over-optimization. Because nofollow links are so ubiquitous, any website that does not have a healthy mix of dofollow and nofollow inbound links can easily be identified by search engines as having built links artificially. In other words, nofollow links are natural, so you need to have some nofollow links. Because you must have some nofollow links anyway, you might as well secure at least some of your nofollow links from high-value authority sites like Facebook, MySpace, and Wikipedia. Generally, you want to link-build aggressively but naturally. If you pick up a few nofollow links along the way, you need not worry that those links do not pass PageRank, you'll be building link naturally as you should.

PageRank – summary and conclusion

If the complex math of Google's PageRank calculation has your head spinning, do not worry. The math is not what is truly important. What is truly important is that inbound links are the source of ranking power and if you build links naturally and effectively, you will rank naturally and effectively. We can distill the thorny mathematics of PageRank to a few core principles that will help guide our link building efforts:

- Inbound links help accumulate PageRank on your pages and can help you rank better for your chosen keywords.

- Outbound links on your web pages send PageRank away from your site.

- The PageRank calculation operates internally within your site's pages as well. If you want to accumulate PageRank within certain pages or sections of your website, you can direct this flow of PageRank by sending more internal links to particular high-value pages.

- If you secure only dofollow inbound links with no nofollow links, your link profile will not appear natural and your site may be penalized by search engines.

Authority links – what they are and why you want them

There is a measure of power that some links possess that is independent of PageRank, and it is the principle of authority links. The principle is closely related to trust. Authority links are links from websites that have established a substantial degree of trust and authority with search engines as a result of their age, quality, and size. Authority is a somewhat subjective concept. Unlike PageRank, neither Google nor the other search engines offer any public reference or guidelines as to what constitutes an authority site or authority link. Authority sites are going to be the market's leading sites, sites representing established government and educational institutions, large corporations, or leading websites. Authority links can bring tremendous ranking power to a website, if one is lucky enough to obtain one or more.

Authority links are the golden eggs of link building. They tend to be extremely difficult links to get, and, for that reason, most webmasters rarely get them. The best approach to authority links is to be vigilant for opportunities to obtain them, but it is most likely fruitless to waste time in seeking them out.

Our discussion of PageRank and authority links leads naturally to the notion of the relative power of inbound links.

 No two links are the same in terms of power. The degree of authority of a site, the PageRank of the page upon which the link appears, and the number of outbound links on the page where your link appears, will affect the relative value of the links you obtain. That said, almost all links are worthwhile, even lower value links. With what we've learned in the previous few pages, you will have a strong sense of how to evaluate link opportunities and to evaluate the relative strength of links.

Sometimes you'll be forced to settle for low-value links but in higher volumes, as is the case with link directories, though never fall into the trap of thinking that the only links worth getting are high-authority, high-PageRank links. All links are good for your rankings (except links from link farms and content farms, from where you should never seek out links).

Link anchor text

A vital concept in link building is link anchor text. Link anchor text is the word or words that constitute the visible text of the link itself, the *blue underlined text* as it is often called. The anchor text of a link is a powerful ranking factor; anchor text serves as a signpost to Google as to the content and subject of the destination page.

How anchor text appears in HTML code

The anchor text of a link is coded by placing the desired text between the opening and closing markup of the hyperlink, as follows:

```
<a href="http://www.tastyplacement.com/">This Is Anchor Text</a>
```

Controlling the link anchor text of inbound links is vital whenever possible. The problem is that you can't always control the anchor text of inbound links, and unfortunately, the higher quality the link is, the more restricted you'll be in choosing anchor text. A perfect example is the DMOZ directory. A link in the DMOZ directory is a great link to get, but DMOZ dictates that the anchor text you select should be the name of your website or the name of your business. DMOZ does not allow you to stuff keywords into the anchor text. Here lies another good reason to choose a keyword-rich domain name for your website and business. When your business name is carefully crafted to comprise keywords, like *Austin Air Conditioning*, then you can employ those high-volume keywords more easily in your link building efforts.

To continue an example from an earlier chapter, if you have identified the phrases *Jacksonville air conditioning*, *Jacksonville air conditioning contractors*, *Jacksonville air conditioning companies*, and *Jacksonville air conditioning repair* as the keywords around which a specific page is built, then your anchor text selection is nearly complete. You can use the same keywords as your desired anchor text.

When you can control the anchor text, you should craft the anchor text of the links based upon the keywords you have designated for each destination page. With this device used in connection with sound on-page optimization, tremendous ranking power comes into focus. Remember that Google and the other search engines have a primary goal of returning quality search results to their visitors. When anchor text accords with the on-page elements of a web page, that gives search engines confidence as to the subject of that page and, when a search engine is confident about the subject matter, it rewards the page with high rankings.

But be careful with anchor text when gaining links in high numbers. It is unwise to secure hundreds of links, all with picture-perfect anchor text: this manner of link building does not appear natural to search engines. There is a risk of over-optimization when your link anchor text is too perfect. Generally, you never want more than 30 percent of your anchor text for a particular page to be solely based on a small family of perfect keywords. Hence, there is a hidden benefit to garnering links for which you can't control the anchor text, because these links dilute your principal keywords to some extent.

If your anchor text isn't varied naturally, then you should intentionally vary the anchor text. Clever SEO professionals sometimes go as far as to obtain noise links. A noise link is a link with common generic terms used as the anchor text like *Click here* or *Website*.

Not all hyperlinks have anchor text. Images can be hyperlinks, but do not use anchor text. In this case, search engines register the link, but have no anchor text upon which to determine the subject matter of the link. Links in image maps and Flash files suffer from the same limitation. For this reason, such links are less desirable.

Site-wide links and footer links

A site-wide link is a link that you obtain and that appears on every page of a particular website. You often see these links appear as footer links—links that appear in the footer area of a website. Common sources of footer links are the web designers that create websites or website templates.

So you might ask yourself, *If I have a link on every page of a site that has 1,000 pages, do I receive PageRank and ranking power from every one of those pages?* The answer is *No*. The search engines have adjusted their algorithms to the reality of footer links. A site-wide link of any kind, whether in the footer, sidebar, or elsewhere, earns essentially the same power as a single link. The exact operation of the algorithms in this regard is uncertain. Some SEO professionals say that a site-wide link is reduced by the search engines to the equivalent of a single link on the homepage, some say that there is a maximum of three-to-five linked pages that count towards the PageRank count and all other pages are ignored. Regardless of how it is calculated, there is no question that site-wide links carry the rough equivalent of, at best, a handful of links. Nevertheless, site-wide links can bring substantial traffic if placed on the right sites.

Repetitive links from common IP addresses

A supplemental consideration to receiving repetitive links from the same website would be receiving links from the same web server. Shared hosting accounts on web servers all share a common IP address, the numerical Internet identifier that pinpoints all websites. The IP address is like a signature—and it's a signature that search engines can follow. Search engines are wise to monitor IP addresses because link farms and content farms often share the same IP address with each other. Monitoring these IP addresses helps search engines ferret out unsavory link practices.

And so, links from the same IP address are most likely discounted by search engines. You will get credit for one link, but if multiple links originate from the same IP address, the search engines can fairly determine that the same site owner has linked more than once and the subsequent links are discounted.

The IP address of a website looks something like `111.222.333.444`, four sets of numbers separated by periods. The `444` in our example is no different from `445` in the eyes of a search engine—both addresses are seen as sharing the same web server. However, the `333` portion of our example shares a different class C IP address from `334` and is seen by search engines as a separate location. The more varied the class C IP addresses from which your links originate, the better. You can determine the IP address of any website by using the free analysis tool at `http://research.domaintools.com/research/my-ip/`.

How to measure your inbound links

As a webmaster engaged in the process of optimization and link building, you'll want to measure and track your link building efforts. Keep in mind that you won't get a link every time you request one. Not only that, but if the page upon which you secure a link is not indexed by search engines, then you won't get any traffic or ranking power from that link. Some pages will be indexed by one search engine and not others, so your inbound link counts in any particular search engine will differ from all the others. In the past years, Google indexed more pages than other search engines, but that has changed since the mid-tier search engines Yahoo! and Bing began to crawl the web more deeply.

You'll use several methods to measure your inbound links. A great source is the search engines themselves. There is also specialized software for the purpose of measuring and evaluating links.

Measuring inbound links with Bing Webmaster

The quickest and easiest way to get a simple and reliable link count is directly from Bing. This free service, called Bing Webmaster, can be found here `https://bing.com/webmaster/`. You'll need to sign up for an account and add your website and then verify by dropping a verification file into your web hosting account. Once you have verified your website, Bing Webmaster provides a range of information, including inbound links that Bing has identified. Navigate to **Reports & Data** and then **Inbound Links** to see the report. The following screenshot shows a report of inbound links:

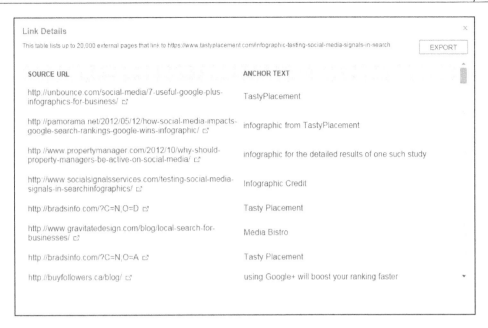

The Bing Webmaster inbound link report is a valuable resource. The report is comprehensive, showing a very complete report of inbound links. A few of the other inbound link measuring tools discussed below give incomplete link reports.

Measuring inbound links with Google

Measuring inbound links with Google is problematic, at least from the standard Google search window: Google does not show accurate link counts from a browser. If you enter the following search string into the Google search box, `link:yoursite.com`, Google will return a greatly deflated link count. A site with tens of thousands of links might only show a few hundred results with this technique. The links shown are not dictated by rhyme or reason, Google appears to return random results. This method is helpful, however, for relative comparisons between sites.

To get accurate link counts, you'll want to check Google Webmaster Tools/Search Console. We learned how to sign up for and install this tool in *Chapter 4, Understanding Technical Optimization*. To get your link counts, log in to your Search Console account at `http://google.com/webmasters`. From the left-hand navigation, expand the menu item **Search Traffic**, and then select **Links** to your site. In the content area, you will see your link counts ordered by the number of links. A bonus feature is the How your data is linked section, in the lower part of the page. This section shows you the anchor text of inbound links that point to your site.

One disadvantage of this tool is that you cannot check Google's link counts for your competitors' sites, because you have to verify site ownership to use the tool.

Measuring inbound links with online tools

There are several online tools that let you measure link counts, both for your site and your competitors' sites. While it's great to have link counts from the search engines themselves (because they are the arbiters of rankings), the online tools generally show you more detailed information about the links.

The king of online link count tools is Majestic SEO, which you can find at `http://majesticseo.com`. While basic functionality is free, you'll need a paid account to see all the available data. To use the tool, simply enter the URL of the site for which you want to check inbound links. The data table that returns contains a dizzying amount of information, all of which is valuable to a webmaster.

Majestic SEO's backlink tools offer a tremendous amount of powerful and valuable information on incoming links. Of particular value is the chart that shows the number of backlinks acquired each month. The key benefit of Majestic SEO is that the tool shows the most links of any link reporting tool. Majestic SEO's spiders crawl the web more deeply, so they show links from the deeper corners of the web.

Among the information returned by the Majestic tool are:

- The link count for any given URL
- The number of indexed pages for a given URL
- The number of .edu and .gov backlinks
- The number of individual domains, including .edu and .gov domains upon which the links appear
- The number of separate IP addresses, including separate Class C subnets upon which the links appear
- A chart that shows the number of cumulative backlinks earned over time

Another paid tool that deserves mention: Moz's Open Site Explorer, reachable by pointing to `https://moz.com/researchtools/ose/`. Open Site Explorer, like Majestic SEO, requires a paid subscription, to be truly useful. A subscription is $100 per month. There are some limitations here: Open Site Explorer does not crawl the web deeply, so it won't show you all of your inbound links. In general, Open Site Explorer will show you only your most valuable links. However, it offers a feature of tremendous value: it scores websites and pages with Moz's proprietary authority scores, domain authority and page authority (PA and DA). Because Google's PageRank has been diluted by changes to the algorithm and is rarely updated, PageRank simply isn't that great a determinant of ranking power any longer. Domain authority and page authority are better indicators of the relative power of a link. The screenshot below shows a sample Open Site Explorer report. Note, the **PA** and **DA** columns, **PA** and **DA** are calculated on a scale of 1 to 100:

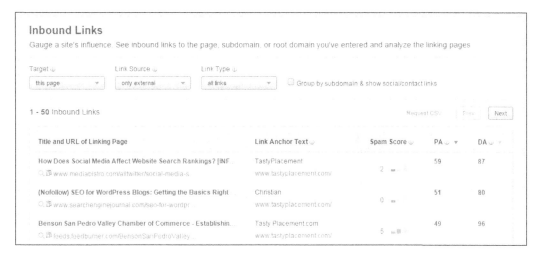

Keep in mind that Open Site Explorer is also a great link prospecting tool. The **PA** and **DA** values are great indicators of the value of a potential link. Now, let's turn to building some links.

Securing links through link directories

Now that we have covered ideas and concepts surrounding link building, and learned about how to measure your link building efforts, we will now turn to the hard work: getting links.

A standard tool in the link builder's arsenal is to secure links through link directories. A link directory is a website that is wholly devoted to categorized lists of links to other websites. The Yahoo! directory (now defunct), the Open Directory Project (DMOZ), and business.com are examples of large established directories, but there are tens of thousands of smaller general, local, and niche directories throughout the world upon which free links are available simply by applying. Before you begin building links with directories, be warned: if you overuse this technique or get links from poor quality directories, you are risking harm to your rankings. We'll outline some best practices.

Link directories were very popular and effective until a few years ago and were once ubiquitous in the world of link building. More recently, however, search engines tend to treat most link directories as link farms. What you want to seek out is only the most premium quality general directories (directories dedicated to all topics), medium to high-quality niche directories, and medium to high-quality local directories.

Similar to any link building effort, making an evaluation of the directory is important before submitting your links. A quick review of any link directory will reveal if the directory has dangerously low standards. Avoid any directories that are polluted with trash links like online gambling, online pharmacies, and so on.

Building links with super directories – BOTW and DMOZ

There are a handful of directories that by their age and reputation represent tremendously valuable link opportunities. The three most important directories are the Open Directory Project, which operates the directory at `http://www.dmoz.org`, Best of the Web, which operates the directory at `http://botw.org`, and `http://business.com`, which we don't recommend.

The king of all general directories is `http://www.dmoz.org`. DMOZ, as it is familiarly known, is often discussed in professional SEO circles if for no other reason, than for the fact that it's nearly impossible to obtain a link within it. A DMOZ directory listing is one of the best free links a webmaster can get.

DMOZ can be frustrating. The directory is human-edited by volunteer editors. One editor might have the responsibility for only one category, or for dozens. For whatever reason, DMOZ often behaves as if it isn't staffed at all. It is common to hear of webmasters submitting their site periodically for years and never gaining admission. There are also rumors of DMOZ being corrupted by self-interested editors who don't allow admission to websites that compete with their own.

The best advice for webmasters seeking to gain a listing in DMOZ is to submit your site using the *suggest URL* link (faithfully adhering to the submission guidelines) every six months and no sooner. Making repetitive submissions will only hurt your cause.

Best of the Web has operated a general directory at `http://botw.org` since 1994. Best of the Web offers strong link power, but is a paid listing. Current pricing is $149 a year, or $299 for a lifetime listing.

> Best of Web offers a 50 percent discount on its listing fees twice a year. On or about April 20 of each year, they offer the discount to celebrate the anniversary of their founding, and in early December. Follow @botw on Twitter to be alerted to the discount.

Best of the Web is a sound, high-quality link, definitely worthwhile if you can get the discount.

Business.com operates a general directory at `http://www.business.com/directory/`. Business.com touts itself as a valuable directory, but the way the site generates URLs, most directory pages on `http://business.com` are not indexed by Google.

> Before you pursue a directory link, make sure the page upon which your link will be placed is indexed by Google. If the page isn't indexed, your link will be useless. Even some pages on DMOZ (usually pages deep within the category structure) are not indexed by Google. To determine if a page is indexed in Google, use the site: operator when making a query at Google.com, as `site:www.dmoz.org/Business/`.
>
> If this query does not return a page or pages in Google search results, then the page is not indexed, and a link on that page is worthless and not worth pursuing.

Building links with mid-tier general directories

There are a few mid-level general directories that can still deliver some ranking power. Typically, they are 10 years old or more and are *human-edited* directories— Google has pointed to this factor being important. There are only handfuls that are worthwhile:

- `http://www.joeant.com/gimpsy.com`
- `http://www.skaffe.com/`
- `webworldindex.com`
- `http://www.avivadirectory.com/`
- `http://incrawler.com/`
- `http://www.dirjournal.com/`
- `http://www.findelio.com/`

Building links with niche directories

Niche directories are link directories that include links solely within a common category. A perfect example is `hg.org/attorney/`, a directory serving solely lawyers and law firms. A niche directory offers some advantages to a webmaster seeking links. First, general directories have no focused category, so a search engine will never treat a link as a link in a particular category. On the other hand, niche directories are by definition focused on a category, so a search engine has no difficulty determining the category. Furthermore, niche directories tend to be less spammy than general directories: general directories are immediately a suspect because they typically grant a link to any website.

Determining if a niche directory offers a high-quality link requires that you apply some analysis. The first test is probably the only one you need: is the directory offering high-quality links generally and not allowing spammy links? If so, it is probably a good prospect for a link. You can look for a PageRank of 4 or above and a Moz domain authority score of 35 or better, maybe a bit lower if links are hard to come by.

Building links with regional directories

Regional directories are simply business directories devoted to a particular city or region. Every city in the United States has dozens of them, you simply need to do a little querying to find a few key prospects. Let us use St. Louis as an example. A query for *St. Louis business directory* yields some promising results, like `stltoday.com/places`. Applying some analysis yields some very good signals: the site is operated by a magazine, the St. Louis Post-Dispatch. It's a good sign when a directory is operated and maintained by a media outlet. A whois.net (`https://whois.net/`) search of the domain reveals that the domain was first registered in 1993 — another great quality signal. The Moz domain authority of the site is a lofty 87, which is spectacular. However, a review of a few random business listings within the directory reveals that the links in business profiles are image links and do not offer anchor text, which is a negative. In this case, the positives greatly outweigh the lack of anchor text and the link is certainly worth pursuing.

Building links with article submission sites and directories

The prior edition of this book recommended link building through article submission websites. This technique, while effective years ago, is no longer a sound links building practice. Google has warned about this technique. In fact, if you have inbound links on article submission sites from years ago, it's a sound practice to remove those links. Even premium article sites like Squidoo and HubPages now deliver no ranking power.

Building links with infographics

An infographic, as the name implies, is a visual image or series of images, such as charts or diagrams used to represent information or data. Infographics are powerful link-building tools. Your goal with an infographic is to entice other webmasters to link to your infographic. Ideally, the sites that link to your infographic will share your niche/category, which lends even more power to the links you'll garner. In a circumstance where your infographic goes viral, you can earn hundreds of links.

But be warned, an infographic is a very serious investment in time and money. The reward, however, is substantial and goes to the heart of a basic principle of link-building: the goal of link building is to secure links in greater numbers and of greater quality than your competitors. Anyone can get directory links, and so everybody does. But an infographic is an example of how extra effort translates into higher quality links, and higher rankings.

Developing your infographic

To develop your infographic, you'll need two things: a set of interesting data, and a talented graphic designer to format the data into a visual representation. The first thing to do is to visit `http://visual.ly`, a website dedicated to the promotion and sharing of infographics, to get a feel for how infographics are put together and what makes a successful one. At visual.ly, you can sort by popularity to see what content is connecting with users. You can also hire an infographic designer through the site.

Generally, infographics feature a data set and some statistical analysis, such as the infographic that displays countries with the most threatened mammals. But other infographics take a more creative approach, such as the infographic featuring the 100 most iconic wedding dresses of all time. You can see both of these examples at `http://visual.ly/100-most-iconic-wedding-dresses-all-time` and `http://visual.ly/map-countries-most-threatened-mammals`.

The real magic trick with infographics is to design them so that the topic area is of interest to webmasters in the same category as your website. That way, any social media buzz or links that you acquire will generate more traffic and ranking power for your site.

Promoting your infographic

Even a moderately successful infographic can go viral and bring a few dozen high-quality backlinks. Creating an infographic—as much work as that is—only gets you halfway there. If you cleverly promote your infographic, you can greatly increase your chances of going viral and generating higher numbers of backlinks. We know because we've done a fair amount of infographic development here at my SEO company, TastyPlacement.

Understanding the quid pro quo of infographics

The name of the game in infographic promotion is that a webmaster gets to display your hard-earned content (the infographic), and in return, you earn a backlink from the website displaying the infographic. A preliminary task in promoting your infographic is to place your infographic where it is easy to find, and in a manner that is easy for webmasters to employ.

Setting up your infographic home

First, pick a home for your infographic—this ideally should be the same site to which you want to send your backlinks. Your home location will house the infographic itself (1,000 pixels wide is fairly standard), and ideally an *on-page display* version for the page itself, for faster loading and easier visibility on a typical webpage (about 540 or 600 pixels wide), a mini-thumbnail for Facebook shares (more on this in a minute) and of course, your recommended embed code (so webmasters can make an easy insertion of the infographic on their website).

Your embed code should be dead easy for any webmaster to simply grab in a block. The embed code should be simple html, and should contain the entire package for the infographic: the on page display version, a link to the full infographic, as well as the author attribution and your desired links.

Here's an example of an embed code that we used to promote one of our infographics:

```
<div style="width: 420px;">
<a href="https://www.tastyplacement.com/wp-content/uploads/Logo-and-Font-Color-Infographic-Full.jpg">
<img src="https://www.tastyplacement.com/wp-content/uploads/Logo-and-Font-Color-Infographic-Reduced.jpg" alt="Fonts & Colors Infographic" /></a>
Infographic authored by TastyPlacement, <a href="https://www.tastyplacement.com/">an Austin SEO and web design agency</a>. To view the original post, <a href="https://www.tastyplacement.com/infographic-fonts-colors-logos">click here</a>.
</div>
```

When we promote infographics, we host the preview image and the full infographic—it's just too complicated to ask webmasters to download the infographic, install it on their site, then update all the links. By hosting the images, you make it easy and idiot proof. Because we are hosting the infographic, and the files are large, we create our infographics in `jpeg` format: this allows us to compress the file down for faster loading and less bandwidth usage.

To see all these elements coming together on a proper infographic home, see the page we've set up for our *Austin Startup Scene* infographic here: `https://www.tastyplacement.com/start-up-infographic`.

Including a Facebook-Ready Thumbnail

You will also notice another element on that page: a square thumbnail of the infographic at the bottom of the page. We added that thumbnail to our infographic page after we learned that when someone posts a share link on Facebook, Facebook will search the page for roughly square-shaped images to offer as a thumbnail choice to represent the share. Because infographics tend to be very tall images, Facebook won't generate a thumbnail from the full infographic. You have to hand-feed an agreeably sized thumbnail.

Promoting your infographic by making it searchable

With our infographic set up and set to share, you want to make sure your infographic can be easily found in the search engines. Make sure you've got the terms *free* and *infographic* in your title tag and body copy. *Free infographic* is searched 2,900 times a month in Google, as reported by the Adwords keyword tool.

Promoting through social media

Promote your infographic through your Twitter account with `#free #infographic` hash tags. Include a shortened URL with a link to your infographic home. You should also post a link to your personal and business Facebook pages. We think it's OK to re-promote an infographic to social media every few weeks.

Promoting through infographic/visual graphic directories

We promote our infographics through infographic and visual graphic directories. These directories exist for the purpose of displaying and housing infographics. You'll get a mix of dofollow and nofollow links from these directories, and you'll get the chance for webmasters to find you there. Below is the list of sites we employ (visual. ly is easily the most popular and authoritative of this group):

- `http://www.infographicsarchive.com/submit-infographics`
- `http://submitinfographics.com`
- `http://infographicsite.com/submit-infographic`
- `http://visual.ly`
- `http://reddit.com/r/infographics`
- `http://www.nerdgraph.com/submit-infographic`
- `http://www.infographiclove.com` (this is a paid submission)

To find more locations for submission, try a Google search for (keep the quotes) `"Submit Your Infographic"`. That query will yield sites with infographic submission forms.

Using Specialized Searches to Find Bloggers and Webmasters

If you really want to take your infographic promotion to the next level, you can do a little curation of specific websites. This technique is going to take a bit more time, but will generate the highest value links.

First, let us search for existing sites that display infographics. It makes sense that a webmaster that already displays infographics would probably post another in the same topic area. For our sleep infographic, we think our content would be valuable to sleep doctors. So we enter a Google query as follows: `sleep doctor` infographic. This query led us to a few sleep doctors and mattress and pillow manufacturers that already display infographics. One mattress manufacturer has an active blog with a PageRank of 4. We'd like to get a link on that site, so the next step is to write an e-mail to that webmaster. So, we wrote the following message:

```
"Hi, we were browsing the site _____.org, and we notice

you display Infographics for your readers. We have a useful

Infographic on sleep science, that you can display for free

on your site. We've already coded the HTML, so all you would

need to do is paste in the code to your website. You can

find the Infographic here: [link to infographic page/embed

code].If you have any questions about how to post the Infographic

on your site, please let me know. "
```

If your infographic is attractive and useful to readers, you should have no trouble in ultimately generating hundreds of links.

Link building by commenting on blogs and forums

Commenting on blogs and posting on forums are two good ways to get backlinks to your website, but you need to be careful to adhere to the proper etiquette and never overuse this technique. If you start spamming blogs and forums with worthless comments, it won't get you anywhere because most of these sites are moderated and your comment will be deleted, along with your link.

Commenting on blogs

Blog commenting is a popular strategy for link building, but there is some debate in the SEO community about whether links from nofollow blogs are counted or not. If you want to be sure that your link carries weight, then you need to find dofollow blogs for blog commenting. The easiest way to do this is to look for telltale footprints that are frequently found on dofollow blogs.

An example of this is the U Comment I Follow logo. Website owners who display this image on their site are making it known that they have modified their sites to use dofollow links in the comments. The easiest way to find these sites is to search for `U Comment I Follow` in Google images. You can also search for the filenames `u-comment-i-follow.jpg` or `u-comment-i-follow.gif`. To narrow the results down a bit, try adding your keyword to the search phrase.

There are also many lists of dofollow blogs online, which you can find by searching for dofollow blogs or dofollow blogs list. Some of these sites are more up-to-date than others, so you may have to look through several of them before you find a good list. Many of the sites that get put on these lists end up getting hammered with comment spam and convert their blogs back to nofollow.

Commenting for good, not for evil

When using blog commenting to get links, you should never spam. Always read the post and make a useful, thoughtful comment that is directly related to the post. Blog comments should always be about the post, never about you. If you try to sell yourself or your site in a blog comment, it is likely to be deleted. Your comment needs to say something more than *Thanks!* or *Great post*. Generic comments like these are frequently left by spammers and experienced bloggers will delete them immediately.

Pay attention to spelling and grammar when writing your comment. People who read the post and find it valuable will often read through the comments too. If they find your comment helpful, they might click through to your website. Your comment is the reader's first impression of you and your site, so make it a good one.

There is some disagreement among website owners about whether it is acceptable etiquette to use your keyword phrase in the name field so that you will get the anchor text you want. Some bloggers delete these comments, while others allow them. You can usually get a good idea of whether it is acceptable on a certain blog by checking to see whether there are other comments published that use keywords in place of a name.

Make sure you use the URL field for your link. Don't paste it directly into the comment text box. This is usually viewed as spam. However, if you are linking to a specific article and explain how it is relevant, it may be considered acceptable. Whatever you do, don't comment on several posts on one site at the same time. This will almost undoubtedly be viewed as comment spam and all of your links will be deleted.

Building links through direct link requests

Getting other websites to link to your site is an essential part of the link building process. You need to find other sites in the same niche as yours to link to you, because this makes it appear that your site has built up some trust among other website owners and it helps build authority with the search engines. However, there are right and wrong ways to go about asking for links. Here are some tips to help you get it right.

Asking for links from the sites in your niche

Don't write to completely unrelated sites asking for links. Would you want links to a beekeeping site on your weight loss site? Most website owners want to link only to content that they feel will be valuable to their readers. For this reason, you should only request links from related sites. You can find other sites in your niche easily enough. Just type one of your main keyword phrases into Google. Yes, these sites are your competition, but they are also potential sources of links.

Telling webmasters why they should link to you

When asking for a link, tell the owner of the site where your site is and why it will provide value to the other site's readers. Suggest a specific URL that you would like the owner to link to, and that will contain the content that provides useful information for his or her readers. Also, make sure your site itself is a quality site. You will have a hard time getting links if your website is all ads and rewritten content. Create something worth linking to.

Requesting links from vendors

A great source for direct link requests that site owners often overlook is from the vendors that supply goods and services to your business. If you are a customer of another business (especially a dealer for a particular product), then a link request is perfectly reasonable. Links from manufacturer sites can also send website traffic from customers looking for local dealers of that particular product.

Reciprocal linking – is it dead?

A controversial topic in the link building is the reciprocal linking. Reciprocal linking refers to the practice of exchanging links directly with another webmaster. It was an early form of building links and while most participants were well intentioned, the practice grew into a source of spam, link farms, and even automated reciprocal link pages. To be sure, reciprocal linking is fairly easy for search engines to detect and so fairly easy to discount within a search algorithm. Google has issued some guidance on this topic. Google warns against *Excessive link exchanges ("Link to me and I'll link to you") or partner pages exclusively for the sake of cross-linking*. What constitutes *excessive*? Google doesn't say, but 10 to 20 links is probably the upper limit of what is safe.

In order to circumvent the obvious problem of detection by search engines, enterprising link builders crafted even more complex reciprocal linking schemes such as three-way links (site A links to site B, site B links to site C, and site C in turn links to site A) and even four-way cross linking. These schemes were too much work to be practical in the everyday world, so they tended to be used within networks of sites owned by one individual or company. These multi-party link schemes are seen as far more reprehensible and worthless in the eyes of search engines than simple reciprocal linking. As such, if detected, these multi-party schemes are almost certain to result in a ranking penalty. Do not be lured into these arrangements.

Simple reciprocal linking is never likely to bring any substantial penalties unless abused, but is never going to bring substantial ranking power. It should also never be used as a principal means of link building. It should only be used as a supplement to a broad-based link building program. The best approach to reciprocal links is to ask *would my customers and visitors really find this link of use?* If the answer is yes, then a reciprocal link might be appropriate.

Building links by creating link bait

Link bait is a term used to describe an article, feature, picture, post, or page that is so good that it attracts links naturally from all over the Web, and certainly infographics fall under the umbrella of link bait. If you've ever read an article that was so useful that you felt the need to not only add it to your browser's bookmarks, but also stumble it, tweet it, and share it on Facebook, then you'll understand the power a great article can have to attract links. That is link bait.

Building link bait is not an easy task, but it will bring in an incredible amount of traffic and links if you can get it right. You can start by brainstorming to come up with ideas for content that would appeal to many readers and make them want to share it with others. Here are some types of pages that seem to attract a lot of links.

Resource lists

If you compile a list of all of the best resources in your industry, you're likely to get some attention from the owners of the websites you include on your list. They may link to your resource page, which will start to get the word out about it so that it attracts even more links. Top 10 lists are probably the most popular of this sort of link bait, that is, *Top Ten WordPress Plugins for Business Bloggers*.

Sharing a humorous story or article

People love to laugh, and if you can make them laugh, they will tell others about you. Try to think of a funny story that you can relate to with respect to the topic of your website. Funny stories and jokes probably get passed on and shared more than any other type of content. Another option is to post a funny picture or cartoon.

Writing about current events

Try to find a way to tie the topic of your website into a popular news story, and you might attract some links from other blogs, especially if you are one of the first bloggers to jump on the story.

Writing something controversial

If you don't mind being in the line of fire, you can get plenty of attention on the Internet by writing a controversial article. If you are the one to start the discussion, you will get links from both the sides—those who agree with you and those who disagree.

Interviewing an expert

Everyone wants to hear what the experts have to say. This tactic will attract links from other bloggers who want to comment on what the expert says in the interview. You'll also get links from the people who learn something from the interview and want to share it with everyone else, and the expert gets the benefit of some free publicity, so they are most likely to accept your request.

Giving something away

Giving something away is a great way to attract links, but the item you are giving away must be worth linking to. It could be a free WordPress theme or plugin or some type of software. It could also be a product that has a substantial value, such as a laptop or other high-priced gadget. If you use a physical product, you can give people entries in the give-away for doing things, like tweeting about the contest and including the URL. Generally, you'll find that the more expensive the product is, the more links you will get.

Testing something

Do you have a theory about something that has yet to be tested? Do the testing yourself and publish your results. Other people who are interested in your niche will link to your page because it contains fresh, new information. Include images or graphs to illustrate your results and make your page more attractive. Review sites— sites that entirely comprise reviews of consumer products—rely on this technique almost exclusively.

Developing How-to Information

Information that tells people how to do something is always in demand. If you can explain things with clear, step-by-step instructions, people who benefit from your instructions will pass them on. For even better results, create a series of articles on the topic or a complete guide that shows every step of the process.

Creating video content

A good video can attract a lot of attention and a lot of links. Try to combine the use of video with one of the other tactics for best results. For example, make the video funny or use it to show someone how to do something, rather than trying to explain it with text and images. Better yet, do it both ways. Then people who have slower Internet connections won't feel left out if they are unable to watch the video. Check out the *Will it Blend* series of viral videos—that company built an entire national viral web campaign with the great idea of putting things like iPods and golf balls into a blender and broadcasting the results in short video clips online.

Creating quizzes

A good quiz can qualify as link bait too. You can either make your quiz interactive or put an answer key at the bottom to help people figure out what kind of wife they are or what Game of Thrones character they like the most. You can come up with a quiz for just about anything.

Using a catchy title

No matter what type of content you use for link bait, you need to have a catchy title to attract readers. Try to make your title stand out somehow so that people will read the article or watch the video. If you have done a good job on the content, they will want to share it, so try to make it easy for them. Include buttons your visitors can click on to post on a link to Facebook, Stumbleupon, Digg, and other social networking platforms.

Examples of effective link bait

The best way to understand what constitutes link bait is to take a look at a few examples. These are pages that have been successful at drawing in links from all over the Internet. You can get ideas for your own site by looking at what other people have done.

Fashionista's 20 Most Influential Personal Style Bloggers

This page lists the website owner's opinion of the top 20 most influential personal style bloggers. As you can probably guess, many of these bloggers linked back to this post from their own blogs. They are not the only ones who linked to it though. This post earned 163 links from 48 root domains, 11,982 likes and 1,500 shares on Facebook, and 1,848 tweets, as reported by Moz's Open Site Explorer tool. Some of the more recognizable sites that linked to it are popsugar.com, and Yahoo!'s own style blog. You can find more about it at `http://fashionista.com/2015/02/most-influential-style-bloggers-2015`

Fast lane—the slide

Pardon the ugly URL, but this YouTube video of a Volkswagen commercial has over 4 million views. It is a great example of link bait. It is something that is fun to watch, and when people are done watching, most of them will share the video on their Facebook page, share it through some other social media site, or e-mail the link to a friend. The backlinks for this video include links from 22 `.edu` domains and 25 `.gov` domains: these are the strongest links you can get. You can find more about it at `http://www.youtube.com/watch?v=W4o0ZVeixYU`

Summary

In this chapter, we learnt about the well-spring of search ranking power: link building. We learnt about the important history and benchmarks for links: how search engines came to regard them as important, how search engines measure link value through PageRank and authority, and how we can harness PageRank for the greatest possible ranking benefit. We covered the important distinction between dofollow and nofollow links. We examined how to evaluate and measure our own link building efforts.

We then undertook the craft of link building itself. We studied how to build links through link directories and article directories, we covered the premiere directories, BOTW and DMOZ. We discovered how to secure links through blog comments. We also covered how to gain links through direct request. Finally, we reviewed some superb examples of link bait.

Link building is the fuel that powers ranking efforts. While it can represent the greatest amount of effort you'll be required to commit to your search efforts, it can be the most rewarding, returning dividend for years. In the next chapter, we'll learn how to employ social media to extend your marketing reach.

7
Using Social Media

In this chapter, we'll learn how to harness social media to promote your company or website and supplement your search strategy. Social media is the cutting edge of search placement: new web properties, new opportunities for placement, and new patterns of Internet user behavior make this a dynamic area. Just like with natural search, social media dominance flows from cleverness and hard work.

Let's begin by taking a close look at the hype-fueled term *social media*. Ostensibly, the term refers to websites and media channels that rely principally upon dissemination, through social interaction between users. Let us use the term *social media* with caution; the definition is shifting quickly and will continue to evolve. For our purposes, we will, to some extent, bow down to the established definition and learn about what are considered typical social media web properties, such as Facebook, MySpace, LinkedIn, Twitter, YouTube, recommendation/sharing/bookmarking sites like Digg, StumbleUpon, and similar properties. However, we'll keep an open mind about what social media really is.

Mastering social media can be elusive. At the core of social media success, is the same principle that underlies web content creation: you must create something of interest to other people. When creating content on social platforms like YouTube or Twitter, if your content flops (and it often will as even experts can attest), you won't make a big splash, but you'll always have another chance to try again.

In this chapter, we'll learn a wide range of techniques for harnessing social media outlets and channels, learn which channels are the best routes for particular kinds of businesses and content, and learn specific tips and tricks for success. We'll begin with an analysis of what social media really is, and how social sites dovetail with traditional search. We'll learn about the power of *viral content* — the true measure of social media content.

We go in depth and learn soup-to-nuts strategies for harnessing the most important of social media tools: Facebook, LinkedIn, and Twitter. We will cover WordPress-specific tools that extend WordPress' functionality into the world of social media and blur the line between your website and your social media presence. We will explore how social bookmarking can extend your site's reach and placement with sites like Technorati, Digg, and StumbleUpon. Finally, we'll look at the awesome power of video sites and video content. By the end of this chapter, you'll be able to implement an effective social media strategy to further build out both your WordPress-based site, as well as, your business generally.

What is a search engine?

This heading, *What is a search engine?* now appears for the second time in this book. We first examined the question in *Chapter 1, Getting Started – SEO Basics*. The reason we have repeated it, is that we now need to extend and re-evaluate our notion of what constitutes a search engine.

Do we even need search engines as much as we did before? In 2010, Facebook.com unseated Google as the most visited site on the Web, as measured by total page views as well as time spent on site. Traditional search engines own a decreasing slice of total Internet visitors and page views compared to just a few years ago, as social sites come to the forefront and consume greater proportions of user interest. Traditional search engines are still massive, without doubt. The social space is growing rapidly and presence on these alternative properties cannot be ignored. So yes, any business owner or blogger needs to continue to rely on traditional search engines for visitors and customers. However, perhaps the better way to think about social sites is that they are just search engines cast in a different light. Digg and YouTube are places where users go *to find interesting stuff*; that's fairly close to the definition of a traditional search engine.

The term *search engine optimization* is the common label for optimizing a site to increase the number of user visits and views. However, as we expand our understanding, the label doesn't fit as neatly. The better way to think of overall optimization is *placement*. We will learn in this chapter, to go beyond placement in search results pages; we'll learn how to enjoy increased placement in a wide variety of web channels, including user's e-mail inboxes.

Going viral with social media

An important concept that permeates all social media is the notion of viral content. Viral content is a site, page, image, or video that, by its own merits, is so humorous, interesting, or otherwise noteworthy, that it extends its reach simply by virtue of being passed on by readers, with no further action by its creator. An example of viral content is *David*, the boy captured on video by his father after leaving the dentist. In the video (if you are one of the few who haven't seen it), a middle school-aged David demonstrates the woozy effects of really powerful painkillers; he asks, *Is this real life?* This video has garnered over 130 million views on YouTube. While this video wasn't created as a promotion for a business, its tremendous popularity has spawned one: the boy's family has launched a website (`http://www.davidafterdentist.com`), that sells a line of t-shirts and stickers based upon the event. That is a demonstration of the power of viral content.

Viral content is the golden egg of Internet marketing. It represents free publicity and can positively affect link building and referral traffic. Viral content and link bait share a common trait: tremendous user interest. It's not easy to do. You have to generate content that is far superior to the Internet's many interesting offerings.

Generating viral content will depend on your chosen niche. For example, `http://www.wreckedexotics.com/` enjoys a naturally sensational niche: photographs of impossibly expensive exotic cars wrecked by hapless owners. That type of content sells itself. For a local plumber, creating outstanding content can be far more challenging, and may be nearly impossible.

Video content is particularly suited to going viral. Videos are easy to share and because they require less effort than reading, are appetizing to viewers. Bookmarking sites like Digg and StumbleUpon can help spread video content like wildfire—which is what you want.

Here are some ideas on how to create outstanding viral content:

- Just as with link bait, create a valuable and useful list of resources for users. People love lists, and they frequently get picked up by social bookmarking sites like Digg and StumbleUpon. They garner plenty of attention, visits, and inbound links. Lists can work for any industry, that is, `Top 10 WordPress Plug-Ins`, or `80 Great Jobs for Recent College Grads`.

- Create an online quiz. You may have seen many viral quizzes come through your e-mail inbox or through your Facebook account.

- Create a viral interactive video. Another popular type of viral content is video and animations. These can be as simple as small flash games or as complex as full videos. A video that teaches users how to do something (upgrade a PC sound card, install anti-virus software, check a dryer vent for dangerous link build-up, wax a car, so on and so forth), is sure to garner some interest.

- Use photography. Any line of work generates matters of particular interest from time-to-time. Add an insightful or humorous caption and share the photographs. The wildly popular Cheezburger Network of sites (`http://icanhascheezburger.com` and a few others) is nothing short of an Internet empire—built entirely from cute and funny photographs. Create a gallery of free desktop wallpaper images from your creations.

- Create an online tool. Online web-based tools are very popular. Tools like mortgage calculators and budgeting tools are very popular online. If you don't know how to program, you can turn to Craigslist and post in the **gigs** section for small programming jobs.

- Issue a press release. Press releases are great ways to get links, spread the word about your company, and go viral. Because press releases are distributed so widely, you get a real head start on distribution that you just can't achieve with just your website. Most press releases will wind up appearing on at least a few dozen websites just through natural distribution. There are dozens of both free and paid press release services, among them, PR.com (`http://www.pr.com/`) and Free-Press-Release.com (`http://www.free-press-release.com/`). Pay a little extra to include a link in your press release and your link will be duplicated by most sites that republish the press release.

Learning to build your personal authority

As you work within social media to build your business, blog, or personal brand, you want to think about the idea of personal authority. Google+, Facebook, and other social media sites like activity: check-ins, friending, following, liking, starring, directions, posting photos, using GPS, and so on. There is no substitute for being a real person doing real things online. Just about anything you do on Google+, Facebook, Google Maps, and on other sites can help your presence online. The power an individual profile enjoys is referred to as **authority**. The more you use your online presence, the more authority you develop. Most of the major recent Google patents speak to the authority of a person interacting with a piece of content (a website, a map listing, and many others), as a measure of value for that content. Be active, and you'll gain authority. What follows are some tips you can employ when you interact in the social media ecosystem:

If your business has a map listing, Google+ activity is vital

Google+ is now fully integrated with Google Maps and has a more powerful impact on your Google Maps listing for your business. Facebook is great for traffic and building customer loyalty, but Google+ activity is important for your Maps listing and for getting your content indexed quickly. If you write a new page or post on your website, post it to Google+ and the Google spider will follow the link in minutes, and you can get your content indexed more quickly.

There's another important element to Google+ and that is the series of patents Google has filed concerning the principal of agent rank. The principal underlying agent rank is that the author or a person sharing content can render particular content more authoritative and trustworthy based upon the inherent authority of the author or sharer. So, content made by a more valued author would tend to appear higher in search results. We saw an early invocation of this principle in 2011 to 2013, when Google was displaying small author photos next to entries in its search results. Google then abruptly discontinued the practice.

Google continues to file patents related to the principle of agent rank, but has not fully integrated agent rank into its algorithm. If you want to read some meaningful and in-depth analysis of Google patents, the leading commentator on this topic is Bill Slawski, who operates the blog SEO by the Sea, which you can find here: `http://www.seobythesea.com`. Certainly, individual personal authority will play an increasing role in search results for years to come.

Make friends

Easy; make friends and connections on all social networks: it expands the reach of your content and raises the authority of your profile. It can also lead to links for your content.

Post photos, then share

If you ever need to share a photo with someone, don't email it—post it to Google+, Facebook, or Pinterest and then share the link with whomever you want. That sends your friends to your Google+, Facebook or Pinterest profile, which these sites see as activity. It's free storage for your photos and you can share entire albums or just individual photos. Again, it increases authority and generates activity and you can post photos to your personal Google+ page or to your Business Google+ page. If it's relevant, post photos to your business page and then share on your personal page.

When you post a photo to your business page, you can track the amount of impressions your photo gets very easily within Google+. Click on **Photo Details** to the right of the photo and views can be found underneath.

Use Google Maps to get directions to your business

This is a power tip for businesses that rely on Google Map listings. This is the subject of a recent Google Patent: customers request directions is a quality signal for a business and also demonstrates that your business is open. When anyone requests directions to your business, that metric is tracked by Google. You (and your customers) can either use the desktop directions or phone-based directions.

Don't go crazy doing one thing

Keep it natural: don't just get directions on Google Maps business dozens of times without getting reviews, likes, and posting photos to your business and personal pages; it doesn't look natural when a business has 90 reviews, yet no one EVER requests directions. You want a natural mix of activities in your personal social space and your business social space.

Review lots of things

You can review any business in Google Maps or Google Plus, and it helps increase the authority of your personal profile—again, the authority of your personal listing means Google sees you as a real person. It also puts your face/name in the review section, permanently, for the business you review, so other customers see your picture and profile—they might click on your profile and follow you.

Activity engenders activity

This is important: the more active you are in social media, the more you appear in other's feeds and on business pages; these social media systems are designed to create little viral swirls of activity around actions people take online. Just one example of hundreds: you post a comment to a clever post on a funny news article that one of your contacts posts—now all of those person's contacts see your activity. They might visit/follow.

There really is no bad activity, just have fun

It's really hard to screw this up because all you need to do, in a sense, is show up at the party. Don't worry about *is this article I am posting to my Google+ page relevant to my business niche?* Sure, some content needs to be relevant, but anything interesting is better than nothing.

Favorite stuff/star stuff

On a Google Maps page, there is a star that you can click—the star turns yellow. This stores the Maps entry to **My Places | Starred**. You can also add a Facebook business page to your list of Favorites. Why not add your business page to your list of personal favorites?

Using LinkedIn to promote your business or website

When it comes to making only business contacts to increase your company's brand, no other social networking site is as valuable as LinkedIn. This is because LinkedIn was created initially as a business networking tool. And today, that is exactly what it continues to be.

The core purpose of LinkedIn is to give its users the opportunity to build and grow business contacts. And with over 80 million members and growing, the contacts your business can make are limitless. One tip for gaining contacts is as simple as joining groups in the same industry in which your company does business. And as you contribute to the group in discussions, you'd be surprised at how many contacts you'll gain. This will expose your company to a bigger and wider audience.

Setting up your company on LinkedIn is a fairly simple process, but in order to get started the right way it is imperative to follow every step precisely. The first thing you need to know about LinkedIn is that a user's account page is known as a **profile**, not a page like the other social networking sites. It's a lot more professional to refer a potential client/customer to your company's profile, instead of your company's page.

To create your company's profile, you will need to provide your company's registered e-mail domain. Your company's registered e-mail domain is the unique name right after the @ sign; for example, @companyname.com. General e-mail domains will not be accepted, and this pertains to e-mail domains for such e-mail providers as Yahoo!, Google, AOL, and so on. The e-mail domain must be unique to your company. And it's worth noting that the only people who can create the company profile are current employees.

When you're all set to create your company profile, follow these simple steps to accomplish the task. To add a company profile for your business, you must do the following:

1. Click on **Interests**, then **Companies** at the top navigation bar of your LinkedIn home page.

2. Click on the **Create** button located in the lower-right section of the page.

3. Type in the full name of your company and your company's e-mail address on the **Add a Company** page.

4. Confirm your company's e-mail address by clicking on the link that LinkedIn sends you via e-mail. After clicking on the link, all that's required to confirm your company's e-mail address is to log in with your current primary e-mail address.

After your company's e-mail address is confirmed, LinkedIn will direct you to the **Create a Company** page. Here, you will be given the opportunity to input details and information about your business. This step is crucial; it is your opportunity to give your company a winning description. Once completed, just click on **Create a Company** to finalize the process. And if you desire to have your company logo on your business profile, click on **browse** to locate your company logo and click on **upload**. LinkedIn requires that your company logo be 300 x 300 pixels in PNG, JPG, or GIF format; 4 Mb is the maximum size allowed.

Expert tip: Keep thumbnails ready!

Many forum sites, social networking sites, press release distribution channels, online profiles, business networking sites, and social bookmarking websites allow you to upload avatar/thumbnail images representing you or your company. Create a set of professional-looking thumbnails representing your brand in typical sizes (80 pixels by 80 pixels, 120 pixels by 120 pixels) and keep them all ready in an easy-to-locate directory on all your computers. You won't be scrambling for a thumbnail, when you add profiles to a website.

Many business owners hesitate to get started with making contacts after setting up their company profile. It is wiser to begin networking as soon as your company profile is completed. And don't worry if you don't connect with hundreds of contacts right away. This is networking, and with any form of networking, making the right connections takes effort and a good amount of time.

The following are a few tips and tricks to build high numbers of valuable contacts on LinkedIn (but the same principles apply to all social networking sites):

- Make sure that your company profile is filled out completely with images, thumbnails, descriptions, projects, and links. A fully completed company profile has a much better chance of attracting reputable contacts than an incomplete company profile.

- Join groups that have similar interests as your business. This will enable you to gain more insight into your industry and will also put you in the position to attract valuable connections. However, remember participation is the key to developing relationships with the other group members. The main thing is to circulate and keep your company's name in front of other member's eyes. If you do this effectively, your contacts will grow exponentially.

- Search for business professionals whom you already know. LinkedIn has an easy, intuitive search feature. Use this method and you'll be surprised by the results. All you'll need to do when you find other people is simply send them a message through LinkedIn introducing yourself. They'll respond, and will be more than happy to add you to their trusted list of contacts.

- Browse your contacts' connections. When someone accepts you as a contact, you gain access to their list of contacts. This is a great feature because maybe your contacts have connections with people you would like to do business with. If so, with a couple of mouse clicks, you can get introduced to a connection. This entails sending a message to the business person you'd like to do business with, as a trusted associate of the business person's contact. Use this networking strategy repeatedly and watch how your trusted list of contacts grows.

- Give testimonials for business contacts that you've worked with. Most likely, the contact will reciprocate, and your profile (which will display on your company profile) will have itself a valuable testimonial on display. Testimonials are a great way to build trust on LinkedIn. They are a clear indicator of your quality of work and professionalism. In a nutshell, testimonials are valuable additions to your profile. When you send a contact a testimonial, LinkedIn will ask the contact to approve it, and if the contact would like to reciprocate.

- Start an event. By taking the initiative of starting your own networking event, it can easily be promoted to your current contacts. You can then ask your current contacts if any of their contacts would be interested in the event. If so, ask your contacts to refer you to the interested parties. This will generate more connections for you and also showcase you as a leader.

Why is LinkedIn so effective for businesses networking? LinkedIn, unlike other social websites, was designed to be a professional business networking tool. While millions of people use it as a personal social experiment, the core of LinkedIn is its business networking platform. Fortune 500 companies are listed, along with top CEOs and numerous movers and shakers from a wide variety of industries. Chances are, you value your company's products and services, and LinkedIn provides the opportunity to share what you have to offer with countless business professionals, clients, and potential customers.

Here are a few specific tips for promoting your business on LinkedIn:

- Create a short newsletter for your LinkedIn contacts to inform them of your company's products and/or services, post it to your LinkedIn feed to share with your contacts.

- Send messages to your LinkedIn contacts that you've targeted as potential customers, with your current sales specials, coupons, and discounts.

- Add value to your company profile by posting your presentations on your company's profile. This can be done by using a presentation application.

- Purchase a LinkedIn direct ad that will only be visible by your target market. The power of LinkedIn's advertising is that you can focus demographically, with great precision, only on those viewers that interest you.

- Offer recommendations to people you know or people you have done business with. This method will give you valuable exposure on their profile. Theoretically, people to whom you give recommendations will return the favor. The more recommendations that you accumulate, the greater the chance you will have that people will want to do business with you.

- Customize your LinkedIn URL. There's a good chance that your company profile may be indexed by the search engines, and LinkedIn profiles actually receive a high rank on Google. LinkedIn provides a default URL on sign-up, but instead of using the default, customize the URL with your company's name. However, if your company is a recent start-up, it may serve you better to use a great keyword that describes your business.

- Use your customized LinkedIn URL to your advantage, by using it as your signature when you leave comments on blogs or business-related websites.

As you can see, LinkedIn is a fully interconnected network that can demand a lot of time in order to achieve success. One person may be able to manage a company profile, but the required time may become a challenge. To avoid this, see if three to four employees can take turns updating and maintaining the profile, under your supervision. Maybe offer an incentive to the employees who are willing to assist with this endeavor.

Another benefit to having a company profile on LinkedIn is being able to post available jobs on your profile. Once you have a sizable list of trusted business contacts, you can ask your connections to refer qualified candidates to you. It can't get easier than that for sourcing great applicants for available positions. It doesn't matter if your company's needs are for customer service reps, sales personnel, engineers, or IT professionals; LinkedIn members are a very diverse group of professionals.

Microblogging with Twitter for business

Twitter is a tremendously popular site that can generate significant numbers of traffic and followers. Twitter is woven into the landscape of the web; hundreds of millions of people use Twitter on desktops, laptops, tablets, mobile phones, and even on smart watches.

Microblogging allows users to communicate updates, opinions, news, reviews, and more in short bursts of information. Internet tools like Twitter help businesses and companies to capture the attention of their customers immediately. Donald Trump recently commented on Twitter calling it `fantastic ... like owning a newspaper without the losses`.

The proliferation of Twitter-enabled smartphones has extended the reach of this important tool. Keep in mind, that Twitter messages are indexed by search engines. Consequently, Twitter messages can yield search traffic independently from your website.

Employing Twitter for your business

Twitter is one of the most widely accessible and reliable blogging tools on the Internet today. In fact, Twitter enjoyed 302 million active users in March of 2015 according to Statistics. In April 2010, around the time of the first edition of this book, it was reported that there were 17 million active users of Twitter. Twitter has helped many small businesses to market their products and services without cost. Twitter differs from traditional blogs, as Twitter only allows 140 characters per message. So your Tweets must be short and sweet. The advantage to a tweet is the immediacy of the contact with your circle of influence and the amount of people you can connect with in the space of a minute or two.

Even if you are a beginner or engaging with Twitter for the first time, what matters is your ability to succinctly offer tidbits of information to the Twitter community and offer your products and services to them in an interesting and alluring way, without being overbearing. Do not make the mistake of aggressively advertising your products or services right off the bat. Make sure you introduce yourself and begin to connect with others before announcing your business services or products.

One benefit that Twitter offers is the opportunity to network with other users who have similar interests. For every person you chat with through Twitter, your exposure through page links and social marketing strategies can expose your business to a circle of `followers`, 10 times the size of your original group of friends or followers. Networking with others who have similar business goals and strategies will help to introduce new and exciting ideas and concepts for your business, as well as opening up the possibility of mutual cooperation on compatible projects. Twitter not only helps to facilitate new relationships, but it also helps to solidify current working relationships. If you take a moment to design an effective marketing plan for using Twitter, the level of exposure your business gains will increase exponentially.

How to get people to follow you on Twitter

The most important rule is to publish information worth reading. As the owner of your business, you have a certain level of expertise to offer your customers. It may be expertise in clothing, traveling, health, or finance. If you offer your followers useful, interesting, and reliable information, they will be much more likely to continue to follow you and may even click on any links you include in your tweet. You'll also want to create a `follow me on Twitter` link on your website or blog, so that your customers can easily choose to follow you on Twitter. You can also gain Twitter followers by following other users—some users will reciprocate by following your Twitter feed.

As with most social media marketing, the key is to gain contacts. In the case of Twitter, a simple way to begin to get followers is to put an invitation on your blog for people to follow you on Twitter. As a follower of yours, they can get a quick notification every time the blog is updated. This will be convenient for your readers, because they won't have to keep checking your blog to see if you have added new content.

You can advertise your Twitter account and blog in a variety of online forums and large social networking sites such as Facebook. Remember to provide useful information to your followers on your blog or website, and update your Twitter followers each time you post an article on your site or profile page.

Twitter has proven to be an effective way to establish a strong brand loyalty. Twitter allows you to recover previous readers of your blog by reconnecting with them as followers on Twitter. You can also post brief tweets to remind your friends or followers of new content on your website. Reminder tweets are much more effective than RSS feeds, because they are so immediate, and are *pushed* to readers, rather than requiring the reader's intervention.

Using Twitterfeed to automatically update your followers of new blog posts

Twitterfeed is a third-party application that will extend the functionality of your WordPress website to push new content automatically to your Twitter followers.

It works by taking your WordPress RSS feed, parsing the title, and creating a Twitter post. In order to use Twitterfeed, you need to sign up for a free account at `http://www.twitterfeed.com`. Then you can configure your Twitterfeed account, to automatically update your Twitter account with posts featuring new content you post to your WordPress site.

Top tips for using Twitter for business

Share links to interesting sites and events in your industry:

- Talk about non-business topics, too.
- Don't answer the question `what you are doing?`; answer the question `what has your attention?"`
- Get your employees to join in and post to Twitter. This will vary the tone and topics of your feed naturally.
- When promoting a blog post, summarize it, don't just dump a link.
- Ask for opinions.
- Follow influential twitterers, and follow people that follow them.
- Use Twitter Search to see who is talking about you.
- Use free URL shortening tools like Bit.ly and TinyURL to keep links short.
- When in doubt, re-tweet what others have posted.
- Don't rely on Twitter alone; it's a supplement, not a principal strategy.

Using Twitter to promote your business

Twitter offers many ways to attract new customers to your business and to gain depth with existing customers. You can influence your target market by building online visibility and maintaining a presence on Twitter. Twitter can lighten your marketing budget, reduce the amount of money you need to invest to win new customers, and engage more deeply with your existing customers.

In order to effectively use Twitter to promote your business, use the social platform to communicate with your target market. Do not just promote your business, but communicate with your followers by providing information they want and need. Increase your level of contact and communication with potential customers and supporters to make it a two-way street. Listen and respond to what your customers are saying.

It is important to provide your supporters with the information they are requesting in a timely fashion. As time goes on, you will develop a reputation in your niche as a reliable and professional expert. By using Twitter to share your knowledge with your followers, you can make very effective use of this burgeoning technology. Consistently offer your readers reliable information and updates. This reliability and professionalism will build a strong relationship with your followers and lead to higher profits for your business venture.

People are quite selective when it comes to who they do business with and they often prefer to do business with someone they know. If done correctly, social networking gives you the opportunity to learn about your customer's perspectives, and will enable you to understand the needs they have and the challenges they face. Through online social networking, you will be able to create a relationship with many people who will then view you as a resource and an expert in your business niche.

Using social bookmarking sites to promote your business

Social bookmarking sites provide one of the most powerful ways to harness the power of the Internet, and drive traffic to your websites and blogs. Social bookmarking sites are sites that empower Internet users to store, organize, and share websites, and other online resources. A typical social bookmarking site lets a user store a profile where their favorite website pages are housed. Ideally, the bookmarking site also allows users to share their favorite properties with other users. As you promote your business online, one of the most effective ways of driving customers to your website is through the use of social bookmarking sites.

Getting started with social bookmarking

As you begin to pursue the arena of social bookmarking websites, a great first step is to visit the main social bookmarking sites such as Reddit, Delicio.us, Digg, Fark, StumbleUpon, and Technorati. Social bookmarking sites each have some degree of focus and you'll want to bear this in mind when selecting a site to pursue. For example, Technorati is focused on technology, while StumbleUpon covers nearly every topic. As an initial investigation, you can join one or more of these sites (focus on just a few at first) and begin to regularly submit content at daily or weekly intervals. On social bookmarking sites, the *content* you submit will be links for the most part to other websites of interest along with your comments and observations. By doing this, you are creating an online presence for yourself in the online bookmarking community. Incidentally, bookmarking sites are great ways to find high-quality web pages and content in topic areas that interest you, which is essentially their purpose.

In order to accurately access the effectiveness of these sites for your particular business, website, or blog, you have to make sure that you submit new links and pages. Ideally, your profile on a social bookmarking site will include dozens of valuable bookmarks to worthwhile websites and pages. You then want to intersperse with your bookmark collection, links to your own website and pages—you never want to have a profile consisting solely of links to your own properties unless your content is truly world class. To do so is not only bad etiquette, but you won't earn any followers with a completely self-serving profile. Maintaining an active membership is one of the main keys to enjoying a healthy level of traffic to your site or blog.

Being an active member confers an obligation to regularly visit the social bookmarking sites you have joined, in order to contribute bookmarks, comments, articles, and advice based on the ideas or business that have a particular relevance to you. By posting regular comments, you are solidifying your online presence in a certain social bookmarking community. If you reply to the comments made by other contributors, they will in turn return the favor and comment on your posts. This means that you will enjoy additional links pointing to your site; some links, but not all, will be dofollow links.

It is crucial that you offer good, reliable, and expert information in your comments and posts. This way, your followers will begin to trust your information and will seek you out via your website or blog, if they have a question about a product or service, in your field of expertise. Also, you do not want to be perceived as posting erroneous comments only to get your own links seen and clicked on by others. This will discredit your reputation as an expert in your niche market.

Choosing a social bookmarking site

The most advantageous social bookmarking sites are the sites that people like and use the most. Your site or blog will move up in the search rankings when more and more people bookmark your page. A higher ranking for a site with healthy traffic translates into a steady flow of fresh, targeted visitors. Additionally, because the social bookmarking sites have become a favorite among bloggers, many people will write about your website and this will in turn generate more and more traffic depending on the quality and usefulness of the backlinks you provide.

Social bookmarking sites allow customers the ability to post their favorite sites with labels, tags, or phrases in order to classify and organize them. The major social bookmarking sites continually offer some of the best array of content you want to share with others. For example, Delicio.us is a social bookmarking site that enjoys a great reputation, due in part to being acquired by Yahoo!. Delicio.us is one of the most popular of the social bookmarking sites. Some other well-known sites include Digg, StumbleUpon, Technorati, Blinklist, and Magnolia. Note that these are just a partial list. Currently, there are over 200 worthwhile social bookmarking sites.

Some bookmarking sites require you to join before you can submit anything, but others allow you to submit and search the site prior to joining. Some of the sites may be better suited to your particular business or field. It is a good first step to visit some of the more popular sites, until you really get the hang of social bookmarking. This will also give you the opportunity to see what each one of the sites has to offer.

One of the most popular and valuable social bookmarking sites is Reddit.com. One notable feature, as copied by other social bookmarking sites, lets users vote on each submitted bookmark. Reddit then ranks bookmarks/stories based on the rating each receives. The votes that an article receives will determine how high or low in the ranking that it appears. The site also lets users comment on each bookmark.

In choosing a social bookmarking site to promote your business, first recognize that you may want to employ a variety of social bookmarking sites instead of just one. Using multiple sites, such as Reddit, Digg, Technorati, StumbleUpon, and others is the best way to diversify your marketing campaign.

Beginning with social bookmarking sites

Before beginning your community participation on any of these sites, you must complete your profile on each site. Nearly all social bookmarking sites offer a profile where you can add a URL; employ this feature to develop a complete profile before you begin to contribute content. Next, select other members with similar interests and become followers of their profiles and bookmarks; most will reciprocate by following you. Next, engage with other users by commenting on their submissions. In turn, those other users will begin to comment on your submissions. Then, you are off and running!

After creating your profile, search the site and bookmark the sites and pages that you like (on Reddit, this is called an **upvote**, on StumbleUpon, this is called a **stumble**). Whenever possible, get a friend or business contact to make any initial submission of your content so that you don't appear fully self-serving. Remember you are creating an identity and reputation for finding great bookmarks from all over the Internet. This will encourage others to eventually follow your newer bookmarks.

Promoting your website through social bookmarking sites

Simply put, social bookmarking is the process of selecting and saving the sites and pages you like in one place, so you don't need to remember the URL. We do this in our browsers, when we *add* a page to our favorites or bookmarks. Social bookmarking sites extend this functionality to include the ability to share and comment on submissions. With that in mind, here are a few tips to harness the power of social bookmarking.

Timing is important

If you submit your bookmark in the middle of the night, when all of your friends are asleep, you will get no immediate points or ranking for your bookmark; it will not drive traffic to your article. The moment you submit, make sure some of your friends are online, so your bookmark gets a chance to be seen on the front page by other users who don't know you. When your friends submit bookmarks, make comments, and reply to the comments made to your bookmarks as soon as possible.

Your ranking matters

Traffic to your site or article from these social bookmarking sites usually occurs only if you make the front page or first few pages of the site, or at least the front page of a popular category within the site. This high ranking usually doesn't last for long. It may not last for more than a day.

Submit a catchy headline or title

When you submit a bookmark, you will be prompted to submit a title. This doesn't necessarily mean you have to submit the exact article title. Ideally, you should submit a title that will attract the attention of your social network; so make it interesting. Also, include a great description of your first paragraph and make it attention-getting. Make a unique title for each bookmark.

Remember to choose an appropriate social bookmarking site for your business

Not all social bookmarking sites are the same. Some lean towards political subjects like Digg, while others lean more towards socializing like Facebook or idiosyncratic interests like StumbleUpon and Clipmarks. LinkedIn, while essentially a business social networking tool, does also operate as a social bookmarking site in the business niche. Choosing the site that matches your business is a fine art and will take you a long way towards online advertising success.

Remember that social bookmarking websites are communities

These websites are communities. The original intention of social networking and bookmarking was to create a community, before it became an SEO trick to drive traffic. When a user joins the community and solely operates to manipulate the community for profit through self-serving promotion, the community doesn't take it kindly. These websites are transparent; your intentions will be difficult to hide if overtly selfish. Join the community first and begin making valuable contributions, before advertising your business or service. Remember that active, regular participation counts.

Leveraging Facebook for a business or blog

Facebook is the largest social networking website online today, and has passed Google as the most viewed site on the Internet. Its popularity is growing dramatically. Almost everyone is familiar with this website, which underscores the increasing importance for online business owners to incorporate Facebook as part of a savvy Internet marketing strategy.

In order to ensure your success, remember that the strength of Facebook is about connecting with people. If you offer a sense of community and connection through your Facebook page, people will become involved very quickly and your business will grow more easily.

Using Facebook to promote a new or existing business or blog

The networking potential of Facebook is enormous in its ability to promote an existing business or launch a new business or blog. Hundreds of millions of users visit the site every day, and each user belongs to several groups and networks of their own. As your online presence on Facebook becomes established, you will be able to connect with people and organizations that will enjoy and benefit from the products and services that you offer.

Facebook does require that a code of conduct be followed when using the site to give exposure to your website. First, you must ensure that your actions do not violate Facebook's terms of service. You should never spam other Facebook users with purely commercial messages.

To successfully use Facebook to promote your business or blog, you need to build your own community around your specific products, services, or profile. For example, if your site is based around real estate in Napa Valley, focus the content on your profile on how much you love Napa Valley, how great the real estate is, events in Napa Valley, or how wonderful the quality of life in Napa Valley is. You can also create a Facebook group using `Napa Valley Real Estate` as the focus.

As people learn to trust you and your voice, they are more likely to respond and choose to use your service or buy your product. If you want to further enhance your presence on Facebook, you can encourage participation by adding or creating a variety of applications, where people can attend virtual meetings or cast their opinions by posting comments to a message board. You can also create a virtual polling place that will allow group members to discuss issues with each other and generate more of a connection to what is happening in your network.

Utilizing the full potential of Facebook

For sheer scale of user activity, no social media website comes close to Facebook. The statistics are staggering: Facebook has well over 1 billion active users. It is also clear that Facebook is not limited to any single age group, indicating the vast potential marketing scope the site has to offer.

One of the most important aspects of using the marketing potential of Facebook, is to use the site to help *brand* yourself. Even if your product is *boring* to the general population, such as running a bookkeeping service, you can add personal touches to your Facebook page, to make your service more understandable and interesting to potential customers. Facebook works optimally when you keep people interested and involved in what you have to offer. You can do this with groups, applications, or attract customers who might be interested in you, based on what you have on your Facebook profile.

A Facebook profile or business page can be used effectively as a means to acquire both new prospects and provide ongoing support to interested parties and existing customers. To use Facebook as an effective marketing tool, business owners should be aware of two distinct features of Facebook: the Facebook business page and Facebook groups.

Using a Facebook business page to promote your business or blog

You should employ a Facebook business page, if you are planning to use Facebook for business promotion. Doing so will allow you to separate your personal profile from your business profile. This is a very effective way of recruiting *fans* (recently changed to *likes*, but it means the same thing) who receive updated information about your company every time you post new information. A business page can succeed by continually publishing new information, such as articles, upcoming events, podcasts, blogs, videos, and links to other relevant information that fans can find important. Your business page should be more of a resource to your fans, instead of a strictly promotional tool, so that *fans* will want to continue receiving updates from you.

Facebook business pages are specifically designed for businesses, professionals, celebrities, and those who want to promote a business, service, or skill rather than a personal profile page. Facebook gives business page users the specific choice to advertise a local business, product or an artist, band, or a public figure. Choose the design that best suits your business. As you follow the steps in creating your Facebook business page, you will be prompted to enter your contact information and other related information.

On each Facebook business page, a visiting user has the option of *liking* your page. This Facebook fan/like option is a great way of generating a system of indirect references, such as friends of the fans of your page. The fan/like option is an easy way to widen your networking circle immensely and generate lots of exposure to your business. A careful, creative, and professional design of your Facebook page goes a long way toward attracting potential customers.

Using a Facebook group to promote your business or blog

When using Facebook in connection with your business, it is important not to posture yourself, your business, and group pages, as purely commercial—it's a delicate balance.

People like new ideas and want to know about them. Facebook users want to find people who share similar interests. If you use the site for commercial purposes, keep this desire for connection in the forefront of your mind, because it will be what makes your business venture successful on a social networking site like Facebook.

Along those lines, making a Facebook group page is a strategy that allows people with a common purpose to build a community. The group can be directly related to your business or community activity that includes your target market. Again, this tactic can be effective if the page is updated regularly with content that the group has an interest in. If you can get your followers more committed, then there is a greater chance that they will remember your company name, and the products and services you offer. If you can find a relevant Facebook group that has fallen into neglect, you can sometimes join the group and jump-start the dialog.

Keep in mind, that a Facebook group is restricted to members of the Facebook website. The Facebook group, unfortunately, does not come with the same option as a Facebook business page, but it does allow people to become members of the group. This greatly reduces the amount of information that can be shared with other potential customers, although it does allow you to enhance the focus of your marketing strategy to a very specific audience. Just like the process of setting up your Facebook business page, Facebook will also lead you through the process of creating your Facebook group.

Sharing content and connecting with others on Facebook – useful features and applications

If you are completing a personal profile as well as a Facebook business page, you want to make sure both profiles are completely filled out. Facebook is a social site and people want to know you, not just your business. Remember, it's called *social* media for a reason; one way to think about how to harness social media is that you want to effectively extend your personal life into a broader community, while acting as an ambassador of your business.

When completing your personal profile, be sure to complete not only your contact information such as e-mail and websites, but also your birthday and where you live. In addition, take the time to complete the sections on your activities, interests, and favorites.

Joining groups

Find groups that interest you, join them, and participate regularly. Many groups will allow you to post information about your business, but do not join a group solely for this purpose. Participate in discussions and provide valuable information. You can also create your own group. The advantage of joining or creating a group is to meet people with similar interests and ideas. Join groups not only with your own personal interests in mind, but also with the interests of your target market as well.

Increasing your circle of friends

The more friends you have on Facebook (up to the maximum of 5,000), the more people you will be able to reach for either personal or business reasons. There is an exponential growth in connections that occur naturally on Facebook, so the more connections you start with, the more you'll end up with.

Start searching for people you know, like people from your school or hometown. Then add them as friends. If you create articles or other online content, invite your readers to connect with you by including a link to your Facebook profile at the end of the article. Include a link to your Facebook profile in your e-mail signature. Do you belong to any other online groups? If so, send them a message inviting the members to network with you on Facebook. You will be amazed at how quickly your group of friends will grow.

Updating your status often

The adage *use it or lose it* applies on Facebook; you have to remain engaged. On your page, you will see a link to update your status. Do this often! Your Facebook friends see this and it will keep you and your business fresh in their minds. Updating your status often, keeps your online exposure high. Your status updates don't always have to be about business, they can be casual. The frequency of your status updates is what is most important to your marketing strategy.

Posting wall comments

You have a wall on your personal Facebook page where either you or your friends can post comments. Enter your own comments or messages on your wall to keep your friends updated on the activities of your business. Often, a musician will post information on an upcoming concert or a retailer will post information about a seasonal sale (don't forget the power of coupons and sale announcements in any social media channel). You can also write comments on your friends' walls. Do not write comments just to promote yourself constantly.

Adding an RSS feed to your page or profile

If you write a blog, add an RSS feed to your page or profile. You can do this easily with the NetworkedBlogs Facebook app. This way, your Facebook friends can see your blog updates. You can also add links to your friends. Do you have a friend with a business that complements yours? Add an RSS feed to your friend's blog. If you are a network marketer, you could help promote another network marketer through your blog. If you promote others as well as yourself, people see you as a valuable contact and leader who has good information to share and your circle of friends and contacts will grow steadily.

Using Facebook Ads

Facebook Ads are pay per click ads that operate similarly to Google AdWords. To get started with Facebook Ads, browse to your business page and follow the link **Create Ads** from the drop-down menu in the upper right of the Facebook menu bar. The advantage of Facebook Ads is that you can get a higher degree of targeting, based on what other people have written in their profiles. Not only can you target the ads geographically, but they will also be targeted based on the information about people's personal interests and so on from their personal profiles.

Linking your external website to Facebook

You should install links on your website, that invite your visitors to sign up on your Facebook business page. You can do this in several different ways:

- By manually inserting a link in a WordPress sidebar text widget

- By manually inserting a link in your WordPress template files

- If you don't want to write any code, you can use the Follow Me plugin which installs a clickable **follow me** tab, that expands when clicked to show a customizable list of social media sites

- Most advanced WordPress templates now have Facebook linking built-in

A more ambitious, aggressive, and effective means of attracting Facebook followers is with pop-up boxes and footer sliders. There's no perfect free plugin for this though, and the coding can be challenging, so if you can't code it yourself, you'll likely want to hire a programmer to implement this strategy.

By integrating your website with Facebook, you will realize many benefits. An interactive website will allow people the option to enter or register on Facebook and share comments on your site and your Facebook page. As your visitors interactively engage with both your website and Facebook, your online visibility will increase dramatically. This increased visibility will ultimately get you more traffic and more customers.

These are just some examples of what you can do to use Facebook to enhance or start your business.

There are many companies that now use Facebook to promote their products or services. A successful online company that is using Facebook as a marketing tool, keeps the idea of building a community at the forefront of its consciousness. If you are using Facebook to promote your business, then start implementing some of these key ideas. It is fairly easy to join groups and start-up pages. The next step is to gradually work on the implementation of the above-mentioned marketing ideas and to increase the number of fans engaging with your pages.

Facebook can be a great addition to any marketing plan. You do not have to use all of the applications that were mentioned. Just find the ones that work best for you. Those who have large social networks or very active community participation, will find Facebook to be a truly effective marketing tool. Even if you do not have a large social network, Facebook can still be used for marketing purposes, as it can give you access to the business pages and groups, where you can slowly win *friends*. Just always remember, that it takes time to build relationships online or offline.

Automating Facebook updates with NextScripts' Social Networks Auto-Poster

NextScripts is a WordPress plugin that automatically publishes your self-hosted WordPress blog posts, to either your personal or business Facebook page (and also can post to a range of other social media and social bookmarking sites). Setup takes only a few minutes, but you will need to follow instructions to create a simple Facebook *App*, and the plugin can be set to run automatically or with one-click manual operation. This plugin saves you the trouble of manually posting all of your blog posts to your Facebook pages. It's a real time saver and keeps your Facebook pages updated and interesting to readers.

To install the plugin, first locate the file by searching the WordPress plugin directory at `http://wordpress.org/extend/plugins/`. Then upload the file by logging in to your WordPress dashboard, following the navigation to **Plugins** and then **Add New**. Once uploaded, click on the **Activate** link just under the NextScripts entry in the plugin list.

To configure the plugin, select **Setting** from the dashboard navigation and click on **Social Networks Auto Poster**. You'll need to add your social media accounts to get started; the plugin offers a simple wizard to get you going. The following screenshot shows the start of the wizard:

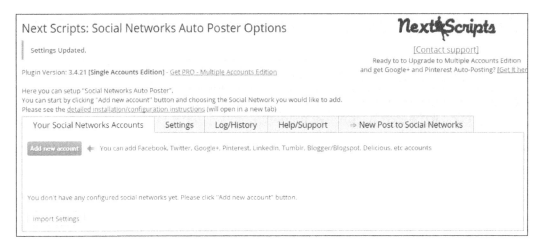

Click on **Add new account** to start the wizard. You'll then need to select **Facebook** from the **Add New Network** dropdown to add a Facebook account. The free plugin is limited to one social media account. The full pro version is of $49, and will let you add several social networks. To continue with Facebook posting capabilities, you'll need to follow the link to Detailed Facebook Installation/Configuration Instructions to create a very basic Facebook app to authorize NextScripts to post to your page.

Once installed, Social Networks Auto-Poster adds Post Options box to your Post edit page. Be certain not to forget you've got the NextScripts plugin installed, posts will be made automatically.

With the NextScripts Social Networks Auto-Poster plugin, you'll harness WordPress' inherent publishing capabilities to extend your content onto the Facebook platform. It's a great and simple way to bring some semi-automation to your content publishing and keep your Facebook business page updated, active, and interesting to viewers. Remember though, that automation isn't always appropriate. Yes, it's a time-saver, but you'll lack the ability to control the specific appearance of the post on social media sites.

Going viral with Facebook sharing plugins

To extend your WordPress' site functionality a bit further, you'll want to consider the wide range of available options for encouraging the sharing of your content on Facebook. Before you install a plugin to achieve this (there are many choices), consider that most modern WordPress templates already have this functionality built-in. Older templates will lack this capability. If you use a modern template from a site like ThemeForest, ElegantThemes, or Mojo-Themes, social sharing buttons are integrated into the template. The following screenshot shows a typical layout of social sharing buttons on a modern WordPress template:

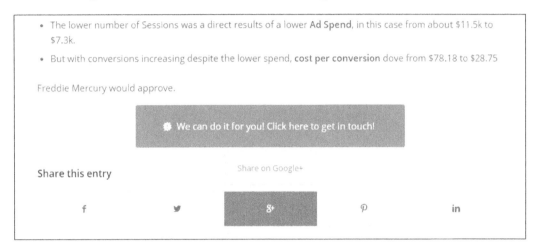

The integration of social sharing buttons is a very powerful benefit of a full-featured WordPress template. Sure, you have the option of adding a plugin to add this functionality, but plugins can cause conflicts with other plugins and don't always look great on all sites; the more reliable way to implement social sharing buttons is to use a modern theme. Of course, this won't be a fit for all websites.

If your blog or business relies on photo sharing, you may consider adding the FooBox photo plugin. This plugin adds gorgeous pop-up functionality to your photos and equally attractive photo sharing buttons. FooBox has a free version, but the paid version offers valuable features. The following screenshot shows FooBox leveraged to encourage the social sharing of an infographic with easy-to-use clickable icons.

Encouraging sharing on Pinterest and photo sharing sites

Pinterest, for those who have never used it, is a social sharing/bookmarking site for the sharing of images. There are other photo sites, but Pinterest is the largest and most important. Here's how Pinterest works: Pinterest users create *boards* based around a common topic and *pin* images from around the web to their boards. It follows the model of a bookmarking site. Each pinned image is also a link back to your site. Here's a board I made for fun: `https:/pinterest.com/tastyplacement/ducati-italian-bikes/`.

Pinterest has grown tremendously in popularity in recent years. For some businesses and bloggers, it can be a goldmine of web visitors. If you sell any type of visual product—clothing, art, interior design, cars—then Pinterest can spread your images like wildfire.

If you want to see how many of your websites' images have been shared on Pinterest, there is a special URL.

Point to `http://pinterest.com/source/yoursite.com` and Pinterest will show you all instances of your websites' images, that have been shared by other users on the site. This valuable tool lets you know how much viral reach your site is achieving.

It's hard to force promotion and virality on Pinterest, but it's very easy for promotion to happen naturally. Images get pinned and re-pinned based on the purely democratic action of user behavior. This behavior can be encouraged. The simple addition of a Pinterest share button, like the one shown in the screenshot above of our infographic, is a vital step. Make it seamless and easy for users to pin your images, and you'll likely do quite well on Pinterest.

Encouraging Twitter posts and the Tweet This plugin

Much in the same way we encourage the sharing of images by including social media sharing buttons, we can also encourage Twitter activity by inviting visitors to tweet our pages and posts.

There are several tools and plugins available that can enable you to either automatically or semi-automatically push your WordPress blog posts to your Twitter feed. Again, most modern WordPress templates and frameworks have Twitter sharing buttons built in. If you want a more customized and powerful solution, one of the most full-featured and popular plugins is the Tweet This plugin. It inserts a very prominent Tweet This link on your Posts, so that readers can quickly and easily share your content via their Twitter feeds, which you can see in the following screenshot:

Blogging for business? These 5 tips can make you Millions

Our support ticketing system is super-simple and super-fast. You simply need to register with the link below, and you'll be able to immediately submit a support ticket. Our ours are 8 to 5:30 weekdays in the central time zone. We'll be notified immediately of your support request.

Blogging for business? These 5 tips can make you Millions.

Powered By the *Tweet This* Plugin

 Tweet This

The power of Tweet This lies in the prominence of the sharing button. You are more likely to earn tweets with a prominent call to action, although; see the warning just below about overdoing it with sharing buttons.

Taking social media too far

Social media can, and often is, taken too far. Examine the screenshot below, which was taken from the ecommerce listing of a major US company:

Two social media buttons are present. The vendor expects its users to share a link of a 24 cent screw on Facebook, seriously? Even the social media link to share on Pinterest is hopelessly unrealistic. This is a clear example of a company misunderstanding how social media can impact sales. Social media buttons should only be used when they are relevant to the content on the page. Now, if the vendor in the above example used the same buttons on a piece of content they created instructing how to install an outdoor deck, the social media buttons would be appropriate and effective.

Keep your calls to action focused on the core actions you want your users to take. Yes, it's great to have many Facebook likes for your business page, but a Facebook like is an indirect conversion. When you sell a product, that is the principal conversion that you should be seeking.

Promoting your business or blog with YouTube

As you probably know, YouTube is a video-sharing site where anyone — including you and your business — can post videos for others to view. YouTube, just behind Facebook and Google.com, is the third most popular website worldwide in 2015, as reported by the Alexa ranking service, `http://www.alexa.com/topsites`. Youtube also serves as a search engine in its own right. It also happens to be owned by Google, so Google has an interest in driving search traffic to YouTube and Google does in fact include YouTube content in search results — but you have to know how to optimize your video submissions.

The leverage you'll enjoy from promoting your business with video will depend on your niche and the quality of the videos you produce. Video content, like any content, must be quality content. The biggest mistake business owners make when publishing videos online is that the videos are amateurish productions of poor quality. A low-quality video can do more harm than good; if you are a new or small business competing against larger, more established competitors, an inexpensive video can simply highlight your shortcomings. The proliferation of inexpensive video cameras is only compounding this problem.

A high-quality video requires several elements: quality shooting and editing equipment and software, quality lighting, sound equipment, and copy writing. If you use a human subject, you'll want a successful performance. Finally, the video must be compiled for display on YouTube or through an embedded video player. Quality video production, like quality website design, is a specialized skill set. The result you achieve will depend greatly on the team you assemble to get your video or videos produced.

Always aim for quality. You'd have probably noticed when you use YouTube that when you finish watching a video, YouTube shows you several thumbnails of related videos, and video thumbnails are displayed constantly in the sidebar; understandably, YouTube want to keep you on the site. If you generate a high-quality product, your video will be seen by more people because higher ratings, and comment activity will cause YouTube to offer the video to viewers, when they are watching related videos.

Using YouTube as a hosting and delivery platform

There are two ways to display a video on your WordPress site: you can upload your videos to YouTube and embed a few lines of code where you want the video to display, or you can host the video yourself within your WordPress installation with a video player plugin. Embedded YouTube videos are easier to implement, but have some disadvantages.

One big advantage to YouTube is that you can upload nearly any video file format and YouTube automatically processes it into their widely-accepted Flash format. Thereafter, YouTube hosts the file on their server and allows you to embed a display code in your Pages and Posts to display to your viewers. If you've ever tried to host your own video, there are serious challenges: you need to install video player software on your website, and delivering video consumes large amounts of bandwidth. Hosting your videos on YouTube solves most of these technical challenges.

However, there is a trade off. When you host your videos at YouTube and embed a YouTube player on your website, you'll be forced to accept whatever in-play or post-play advertising YouTube serves up with the video. A user watching an embedded video on your website will be served up popular alternative videos, when your video has finished playing. Those videos could conceivably be videos created and posted by your competitors; you could quite possibly be serving up your competitor's content on your own site! Also, YouTube is one of the most widely popular sites on the Internet. Your viewers might simply be distracted away to something they remember seeing or hearing about on YouTube—and you've lost your visitor.

Embedded YouTube videos come with a cost: you get free bandwidth and ease of use, but when the video is done playing, your website's visitors are presented with alternate videos to view. This is not ideal because you want to keep your visitors tuned in to your message.

Using video delivery alternatives to embedded YouTube videos

Serious Internet marketers generally don't embed YouTube videos on their sites— these professionals don't want alternative choices presented to their hard-earned website visitors. All website owners should aim for conversions; when users exit to other websites, the conversion is lost. Luckily, there are options that can help you serve up video content without YouTube's mandatory advertising.

One option is hosting your videos with Vimeo, a competitor to YouTube. Vimeo offers a paid service ($195 per year) that lets you submit a nearly unlimited number of videos. Vimeo provides an interface for managing your videos, and some special features, like the ability to display a call to action when the video reaches its end. Vimeo delivers video quickly, in high quality, and displays on all devices. Vimeo also gives you an easy to install link for insertion of videos into your content.

You can also use one of many plugins to self-host your video, you simply install the plugin and upload your videos to your website. This arrangement is inexpensive, but not ideal. These plugins often do not display videos correctly in all templates, and may not show videos properly on all devices. If you are using a modern template, you might have the feature already built in, which may solve all of your formatting issues.

Employing YouTube as a search engine

Despite the method that you choose for the delivery of your video content, you have to throw into the mix that YouTube video pages sometimes can rank on their own, and are available through YouTube's search field. So, a YouTube video can be a destination page in itself, almost like having a separate website. If you have a video produced and self-hosted, you'll certainly want to post it on YouTube, in addition to displaying the video on your own site.

To make your video accessible to Internet users through a search engine query, through a search on YouTube, or to display correctly in YouTube categories, you need to submit a proper title, description, and tags for the post. To make your YouTube submissions search-friendly, you'll want to include keywords within the title, description, and tags sections of the edit window when you make your submission. Try a few sample searches in YouTube and you'll see that writing a title and description for a YouTube video is much like writing a title and description for a piece of content on your website. After you submit a video to YouTube, you are presented with the video settings page.

Video success story – Will it Blend?

One of the truly shining examples of clever leveraging of YouTube as a marketing platform is the series of *Will it Blend?* videos by Blendtec. Blendtec makes what they tout as commercial quality blenders for home use. In their *Will it Blend?* series of tongue-in-cheek YouTube videos, they blend everything from mp3 players to golf balls and glow sticks.

This campaign has been phenomenally successful, and the creators have gone on to speak at conferences about techniques related to viral success online. Simply through the natural viral effect of users sharing the videos, dozens of the videos have more than one million plays and several videos have play counts in the six to nine million range. Blendtec's YouTube channel alone has over 825,560 subscribers.

What Blentec has achieved with this masterful campaign is the equivalent of a consistent national advertising campaign — but with a budget of thousands of dollars instead of millions of dollars.

Promoting products and services on YouTube

Always make full use of any videos produced naturally in the course of your business. Perhaps, you already have seminars or lectures you have produced. Perhaps, you sell a DVD — an excerpt of the DVD would be a suitable subject for a YouTube video. Despite our warnings about video quality above, when displaying video within your own site, for a YouTube-only video, you can lower the quality bar slightly; it's probably better to have something on YouTube even if it isn't top-quality.

In the entertainment business, you can post content from one of your performances. If you work in the trades, many companies have had great success by posting instructional videos; teach readers how to use a tool, or perform a repair. Product reviews are a great way to develop inexpensive content. The online tool retailer ToolBarn.com has had great success on YouTube by creating short, inexpensively-produced video reviews of tools that they sell. We learned about ToolBarn's YouTube videos when searching for reviews of a popular hand tool.

The key is to create a video that users actually want to watch. This means producing something educational, useful, or entertaining. Generally, straight-ahead commercials will not perform well on YouTube. In the world of social media, it's about creating user interest naturally; there are no couch potatoes on the Internet. If your content doesn't interest them, they'll watch someone else's video.

Summary

In this chapter, we looked at how to harness the growing power of social media to extend and supplement your website presence. We learned how social media is changing the nature of search as more users turn to social networks and specific web properties to find information. We examined the concept of getting your content to go viral, as well as, how to create and publish content so that it catches fire within the social community.

We learned how to employ the *big three* social media sites for business owners, LinkedIn, YouTube, and Facebook, and how to set up accounts and maximize their potential. We learned about some powerful WordPress plugins that can help you connect your WordPress site to these social networking websites, and extend the reach of your website farther than before.

We discovered how to harness social bookmarking sites such as Digg and StumbleUpon to stretch your website and brand's reach even further. Finally, we examined how to make the most of video content and the YouTube platform.

Social media and social networking are a rapidly-evolving area of search marketing, but can, with a fair degree of effort, produce a great return on investment. In the next chapter, we'll learn about the unsavory world of forbidden search techniques and how to avoid them.

8

Avoiding Black Hat Techniques

The term black hat SEO, generally refers to any manner, by which visibility, rankings, or traffic is improved through illicit or forbidden techniques, tools, or methods. There are a wide variety of techniques that fall under black hat: Spamming forums, spamming blog comment areas, automated link exchange schemes, browser hijacking, cloaking, link farms, keyword stuffing, article spinning, paid links, and many more. The goal of this chapter is to help you sort the good from the bad, and avoid the worst techniques and the websites that employ them.

The search engines push back against the black hat methods; they've gotten better and better at detecting and punishing illicit techniques. Generally, when black hat methods are discovered, Google and other search engines will impose either a penalty or a filter (we'll learn about the distinction between those two concepts) by making an automatic or a manual adjustment to the search results.

There's a continuum at play in the world of black hat. Some techniques, such as browser hijacking (where viruses that infect thousands of user's PCs manually change the search results), and cloaking (where the true content of a web page is not shown to the search spiders) are among the most heinous of methods. On the other end of the scale, link exchanges are less sinister, but still frowned upon by the search engines. The lighter techniques are often called gray hat techniques.

In this chapter, we'll take a tour through the seedy side of SEO. We'll examine a wide range of black and gray hat techniques—and why it is imperative that you avoid them. The greatest risk to you and your business from engaging in such forbidden techniques is that your site will be penalized or filtered in Google's search results.

Typical black hat techniques

There are a wide range of black hat techniques fully available to all webmasters. Some techniques can improve rankings in the short term, but generally not to the extent that legitimate web development would, if pursued with the same effort. The risk of black hat techniques is that, they are routinely detected and punished. Black hat is never the way to go for a legitimate business, and pursuing black hat techniques can get your site (or sites) permanently banned and will also require you to build an entirely new website with an entirely new domain name. We will examine a few black hat techniques to help you avoid them.

Hidden text on web pages

Hidden text is the text that through either coding or coloring does not appear to users but appears to search engines. Hidden text is a commonly used technique, and would be better described as a gray hat. It tends not to be severely punished, when detected. One technique relies on the coloring of elements. When the color of a text element is set to the same color as the background (either through CSS or HTML coding), the text disappears to human readers, while still visible to search spiders. Unfortunately, for webmasters employing this technique, it's entirely detectible by Google.

More easily detectible is the use of the CSS property `display: none`. In the language of CSS, this directs browsers to not display the text that is defined by that element. This technique is easily detectible by search engines. There is an obvious alternative to employing hidden text: simply use your desired keywords in the text of your content and display the text to both users and search spiders.

Spider detection, cloaking, redirection, and doorway pages

Cloaking and spider detection are related techniques. Cloaking is a black hat SEO technique whereby the content presented to search engine spiders (via search spider detection built in to any web server) differs from the content presented to the users. Who would employ such a technique? Cloaking is employed principally by sellers of products typically promoted by spam, such as pharmaceutics, adult sites, and gambling sites. Since legitimate search traffic is difficult to obtain in these niches, the purveyors of these products employ cloaking to gain visitors.

Traditional cloaking relies on spider detection. When a search spider visits a website, the headers accompanying a page view request identify the spider by name, such as Goolgebot (Google's spider), or Slurp (Inktomi's spider). Conversely, an ordinary web browser (presumably with a human operator) will identify itself as Mozilla, Internet Explorer, or Safari, as the case may be. With simple JavaScript or with server configuration, it is quite easy to identify the requesting browser and deliver one version of a page to the search spiders and another version of the page to the human browsers. All you really need is to know the names of the spiders, which are publicly known.

A variation of cloaking is a doorway page. A doorway page is a page through which human visitors are quickly redirected (through a meta refresh or JavaScript) to a destination page. Search spiders, however, index the doorway page, and not the destination page. Although the technique differs in execution, the effect is the same: human visitors see one page, and the search engines see another.

The potential harm from cloaking goes beyond search engine manipulation. More often than not, the true destination pages in a cloaking scheme are used for the transmission of malware, viruses, and Trojans. Because the search engines aren't necessarily reading the true destination pages, the malicious code isn't detected. Any type of cloaking, when reported or detected, is almost certain to result in a severe Google penalty, such as removal of a site from the search engine indexes.

Linking to bad neighborhoods and link farms

A bad neighborhood is a website or a network of websites that either earns inbound links through illegitimate means or employs other *black hat on-page* techniques such as cloaking, and redirects them. A link farm is a website that offers almost no content but serves solely for the purpose of listing links. Link farms, in turn, offer links to other websites to increase the rankings of these sites.

A wide range of black hat techniques can get a website labeled as a bad neighborhood. A quick test you can employ to determine if a site is a bad neighborhood, is by entering the domain name as a part of the specialized Google search query, `site:the-website-domain.com`, to see if Google displays any pages of that website in its index. If Google returns no results, the website is either brand new or has been removed from Google's index — a possible indicator that it has been labeled a bad neighborhood. Another quick test is to check the site's PageRank and compare the figure to the number of inbound links pointing to the site. If a site has a large number of backlinks but has a PageRank of zero, which would tend to indicate that its PageRank has been manually adjusted downwards due to a violation of Google's Webmaster Guidelines.

If both of the previous tests are either positive or inconclusive, you would still be wise to give the site a **smell test**. Here are some questions to ask when determining if a site might be deemed as a bad neighborhood:

- Does the site offer meaningful content?

- Did you detect any redirection while visiting the site?

- Did you get any virus warnings while visiting the site?

- Is the site a little more than lists of links or text polluted with high numbers of links?

- Check the website's backlink profile. Are the links solely low-value inbound links?

If it isn't a site you would engage with when visiting, don't link to it.

Google Webmaster Guidelines

Google Webmaster Guidelines are a set of written rules and prohibitions that outline recommended and forbidden website practices. You can find these webmaster guidelines at `http://www.google.com/support/webmasters/bin/answer.py?hl=en&answer=35769`, though you'll find it easier to search for `Google Webmaster Guidelines` and click on the top search result. You should read through the Google Webmaster Guidelines and refer to them occasionally. The guidelines are divided into design and content guidelines, technical guidelines, and quality guidelines.

Google Webmaster Guidelines in a nutshell

At their core, Google Webmaster Guidelines aim for quality in the technology underlying the websites in their index, high-quality content, and also discourage manipulation of search results through deceptive techniques. All search engines have webmaster guidelines, but if you follow Google's dictates, you will not run afoul of any of the other search engines. Here, we'll discuss only the Google's rules.

Google's design and content guidelines instruct that your site should have a clear navigational hierarchy, with text links rather than image links. The guidelines specifically note that each page *should be reachable from at least one static text link*. Because WordPress builds text-based, hierarchical navigation naturally, your site will also meet that rule naturally. The guidelines continue by instructing that your site should load quickly and display consistently among different browsers.

The warnings come in Google's quality guidelines. In this section, you'll see how Google warns against a wide range of black hat techniques, such as the following:

- Using hidden text or hidden links, elements that through coloring, font size, or CSS, display properties to show to the search engines, but do not show them to the users.

- The use of cloaking or *sneaky redirects*. Cloaking means a script that detects search engine spiders and displays one version of a website to the users, while displaying an alternate version to the search engines.

- The use of repetitive, automated queries to Google. Some unscrupulous software vendors sell software and services that repeatedly query Google to influence Google autocomplete.

- The creation of multiple sites or pages that consist solely of duplicate content that appears on other web properties.

- The posting or installation of scripts that behave maliciously towards users, such as with viruses, Trojans, browser interceptors, or other badware.

- Participation in link schemes. Google is quite public that it values inbound links as a measure of site quality, so it is ever vigilant to detect and punish illegitimate link programs.

- Linking to bad neighborhoods. A bad neighborhood means a website that uses illegitimate, forbidden techniques to earn inbound links or traffic.

- Stuffing keywords onto pages in order to fool search spiders. Keyword stuffing is *the oldest trick in the book*. It's not only forbidden, but also highly ineffective at influencing search results and highly annoying to visitors.

When Google detects violations of its guidelines

Google, which is nearly an entirely automated system, is surprisingly capable of detecting violations of its guidelines. Google encourages user-reporting of spam websites, cloaked pages, and hidden text (through their page here: `https://www.google.com/webmasters/tools/spamreport`). They maintain an active anti-spam department that is fully engaged in an ongoing improvement in both manual punishments for offending sites and algorithmic improvements for detecting violations.

When paid link abuses are detected, Google historically always punished the linking site, not necessarily the site receiving the link—even though the receiving site was the one earning a ranking benefit. This position changed over the period of 2011 to 2013, and Google now issues penalties to sites receiving links when it detects that some of the links are *unnatural*. We'll discuss how to handle this circumstance below.

When an on-page black hat or gray hat element is detected, the penalty may be imposed upon the offending site. The penalties range from a ranking adjustment to an outright ban from search engine results. Generally, the penalty matches the crime; the more egregious penalties flow from more egregious violations.

We need to draw a distinction, however, between a Google ban, penalty, and algorithmic filtering. Algorithmic filtering is simply an adjustment to the rankings or indexing of a site. If you publish content that is a word-for-word duplicate of the other content on the Web, and Google doesn't rank or index that page, that's not a penalty, it's simply the search engine algorithm operating properly. If all of your pages are removed from Google's search index, that is most likely a ban. If the highest ranking you can achieve is position 40 for any search phrase, that could potentially be a penalty called a *-40 penalty*. All search engines can impose discipline on websites, but Google is the most strict and imposes far more penalties than the other search engines, so we will largely discuss Google here.

Filtering is not a penalty, it is an adjustment that can be remedied by undoing the condition that led to it. Filtering can occur for a variety of reasons but is often imposed following over optimization. For example, if your backlink profile comprises links of which 80 percent use the same anchor text, you might trigger a filter. The effect of a penalty or a filter is the same: decreased rankings and traffic. In the following section, we'll look at a wide variety of known Google filters and penalties, and learn how to address them.

Diagnosing a Google ranking ban, penalty, or filter

If you undertake black or gray hat techniques, you run a fair chance of having your site penalized in the search results. But even if you are not engaged in these techniques yourself, your site may be punished for associating with black hat purveyors. Hosting on a shared server or sharing the domain registration information with bad neighborhoods can lead to ranking problems, if not punishment. Certainly, linking to a bad neighborhood can lead to discipline. If you purchase a domain, you'll nearly always inherit any penalties or bans imposed on the prior version of the website.

There is a wide range of penalties and ranking filters that search engines impose, and a still-wider range of effects that those penalties produce. In diagnosing and correcting ranking problems, more than half the battle is about figuring out which penalty, if any, is imposed and for what violations. Ranking problems are easy to fix, but are arduous to diagnose with precision. Sudden drops in rankings might lead you to suspect that you've received a penalty, but it might not be a penalty at all.

In the following section, we'll look at some specific penalties, filters, conditions and false conditions, and how to diagnose ranking problems.

Understanding a Google ban

The worst punishment that Google serves upon webmasters is a total ban. This means the removal of all pages on a given domain from Google's index. A ban is not always a punishment: *Google may temporarily or permanently remove sites from its index and search results if it believes it is obligated to do so by law.* Google warns that punishment bans can be meted out for *certain actions, such as cloaking, writing text in such a way that it can be seen by search engines but not by users, or setting up pages/links with the sole purpose of fooling search engines, may result in removal from our index.* Note the seriousness of those offenses.

One of the most newsworthy instances of a total ban was when Google, in 2006, issued a total ban to the German website of carmaker BMW (`http://www.bmw.de`). Their offense was cloaked doorway pages stuffed with keywords that were shown only to search engines, and not to human visitors. The incident became international news, ignited at least partially by the SEO blogging community. BMW immediately removed the offending pages and within a few weeks, Google rescinded the ban.

Diagnosing a total or partial ban

To diagnose a total or partial ban penalty, run the following tests and exercises:

- Check Google's index. In the Google search field, enter the following specialized search query: `site:yourdomain.com`. Google then returns a list of all of your site's pages that appear in Google's index. If your site was formerly indexed and now the pages are removed, there is at least a possibility that your site has been banned from Google.

- Check if Google has blacklisted your site as hacked or unsafe for browsing (type `http://www.google.com/safebrowsing/diagnostic?site=mysite.com` with your domain at the end). You may also be alerted to hacking by messages in your Webmaster Tools account, as shown in this screenshot:

ⓘ **Hacking suspected: http:/'**

Unfortunately, it appears that your site has been hacked.

A hacker may have modified existing pages or added spam content to your site. You may not be able to easily see these problems if the hacker has configured your server to only show the spam content to certain visitors. To protect visitors to your site, Google's search results may label your site's pages as hacked. We may also show an older, clean version of your site.

Sample URLs

http://1   com/wafhds/v93205.html

Recommended actions:

- Sign in to Webmaster Tools and check Security Issues to see details of sample URLs that may be hacked.

- Read our resources for hacked sites for detailed information on how to fix your site.

- Remove the hacked content from your site. Use the Fetch as Google tool to confirm the hacked content has been removed.

- Fix the security issue that allowed your site to be hacked. Otherwise, your site is likely to be hacked again.

- Request a review in Security Issues when your entire site is clean and secure. Once we determine your site is fixed, we will remove the hacked label.

Need more help? Ask questions and get more support in the Webmaster Help Forum.

- Check for nofollow/noindex settings on your pages. It might seem obvious, but check to make sure you haven't accidentally set your WordPress site to noindex. To check, go to your WordPress Dashboard and click on **Settings**, then **Reading**. If the setting **Discourage search engines from indexing this site** is set, then your site will promptly fall out of Google's index. A stray entry in a `robots.txt` file or in your WordPress template file can instruct search engines not to index your entire site.

- Check Google Webmaster Tools. Sometimes, but not always, Google will notify you through your Webmaster Tools account that your site has been penalized. But you won't always receive this message, so you can still be penalized even if you don't receive it. See the following screenshot for an example message:

PageRank adjustment/PageRank penalty

An alternative penalty short of an outright ban is a PageRank adjustment. The adjustment can be partial (a drop from a PR4 to a PR2) or it can be full (a drop to PR0). With a PageRank adjustment, Google simply adjusts or removes the PageRank value for a site. Google often imposes this punishment upon low-value general directories that sell links. Part of the difficulty with diagnosing and repairing a PageRank penalty is that the PageRank that Google shows to its users is historical; sometimes six months pass between PageRank updates.

Diagnosing a PageRank penalty

To diagnose a Google PageRank penalty, run the following tests and exercises:

- Check your inbound links. Whenever your PageRank drops, the most likely reason is that you've lost valuable links. Check your link profile on Open Site Explorer. Have you lost any premium, high-PR links you had formerly? Use the reliability of the PageRank algorithm to help diagnose: if you have a PR4 link pointing into one of your pages, and that PR4 link has only one outbound link, that one link alone will be strong enough to make the destination page a PR1 or a PR2. If despite such a link, your page remains a PR0, that raises the likelihood of a PageRank penalty.

- Check all pages. Be sure to check every page on your site, you might just have your PageRank shifting around within your site. It is true, however, that generally your home page will have the highest PageRank value of any page of your site. So, if you've got a PR0 on all pages including the homepage, a PageRank penalty is suspected.

- Check canonicalization. Recall the www and non-www distinction, and that search engines see these as separate domains in some cases. WordPress handles this automatically, but some online tools don't check this for you so you have to be sure you're checking both, the www and non-www versions of your domain.

- Compare PageRank. Compare Google's reported PageRank score for your pages with SEOmoz's Page Authority. Typically, these two scores will correlate loosely (within about 10 percent). If the Google score is much lower than the SEOmoz Page Authority score (remember that PageRank is from 0 to 10 and Page Authority is 0 to 100), it's likely that Google is trimming some PageRank. You can see the SEOmoz Page Authority score by visiting http://opensiteexplorer.org/.

- Check the internal links. In Google Webmaster Tools, Google reveals its profile of internal links on your site. If your site has 100 indexed pages, but the Google Webmaster Tools references only a handful of links, it means that Google is not properly processing your internal links. We need to be careful here, because a range of conditions can cause this. It can potentially arise from a PageRank penalty, but also from poor internal navigation structure.

The -950 ranking penalty

Google occasionally employs a -950 ranking penalty to individual pages (but not to the entire site) for particular search queries. The -950 penalty means that for a particular search, your page would have 950 positions added above it. So, a term for which you ranked on page one of Google's search results at position three, you'd now rank on page ninety-five of the search results at position 953. Sound harsh? It is, and Google has made faint references to it as a penalty for over-optimization. Some SEO professionals contend that they have seen the penalty imposed for shady link building practices.

How to diagnose a -950 ranking penalty

Diagnosing a -950 ranking penalty is easy: try search terms for which you formerly ranked (hopefully you noted their exact former position) and follow the search results out to page 95 or 96. Remember that you can always set Google to display 100 results instead of 10 by using the advanced search option at Google.com, which is convenient for checking a ranking position in the 100s and above.

The -30/-40 ranking penalty

Google often serves up another variety of penalty: it's the -30 or -40 position penalty. This is an often-imposed penalty, and is applied by Google to the entire site, not just particular pages and not just for particular search queries. This penalty is common enough to trip up legitimate webmasters for very minor oversights or offenses. Most signs point to the -30 penalty being applied algorithmically and is *forgivable*, so changing the condition that led to the penalty automatically reverses the penalty. This penalty has historically been imposed upon sites for serving up poor quality content. For example, the penalty has been imposed upon sites that display thin content. Thin content is the content that is partially generic, as with an affiliate site repeating common descriptions of products it sells. Low-value directories have also been served this penalty.

Diagnosing a -30/-40 penalty

If you suspect that your site has been hit with a -30/-40 penalty, there is one surefire test to determine if you tripped the penalty. Perform a Google search for your domain name without the www, and without the .com, or .net, as a part of the domain. This search, in normal circumstances, should return your site at or near the first position (depending a bit on the competition of that term). If this test yields your site showing up in a position dropped to the 40s or 50s, it almost certainly is a -30/-40 penalty.

False positives that aren't penalties

Don't assume you've been penalized by Google just because your rankings drop or because your rankings remain poor for a new site. Ranking positions can jump around naturally, especially just before algorithm updates, when Google updates its search engine rules. You may also have lost one or more valuable inbound links, which can lead to a drop in rankings. You may also be alternating between Google's personalized search modes. Personalized search is a Google feature that returns results based on your personal browsing habits. So, if you've visited your own website in the past few days, Google will return your website near the top of the results, figuring that it's one of your personal favorites. Personal search is a convenience tool, but it doesn't return true rankings. To see actual ranking results you need to make sure that personalized search is off. To do this, clear your browser history and open an incognito (private browsing) window and then test results.

Google penalties are almost never imposed for no reason at all. Yes, Google imposes penalties on light offenders while more egregious violations go unpunished. While that might not seem fair, it doesn't change the fact that if you have perfectly complied with Google Webmaster Guidelines, you are extremely unlikely to be penalized. If you've been penalized, there's a reason.

Clearing a Google penalty

Google penalties can literally mean the death of your business. In a business climate where such high percentages of consumers use Google for search (Google's share of total searches hovers around 65 percent), a Google penalty can reduce your website traffic to a trickle. There are three paths to clearing a Google penalty. First, automated penalties and filters correct themselves when the error is corrected. Diagnose the problem, fix it, and you are back in business. Sometimes webmasters miss this point. They assume they have been penalized and request reconsideration from Google and wait for a response, only to realize later that the answer to their penalty was simply to correct the error that led to it.

Whenever you suspect a penalty, you must review Google's guidelines thoroughly. To correct an automated or manual penalty, you must make your site 100 percent compliant with Google Webmaster Guidelines.

The second path to correction is for more serious penalties: serious penalties will require you to fix the violation and request reconsideration of your site from Google; such a request can take more than a year to be heard. We'll explain how to submit a reconsideration request in the following section. The final path to clearing a penalty is to abandon the tainted domain, and begin with a new site.

Until your Google penalty is lifted, you have a few alternatives. Bing's share of the search market is growing, especially following their partnership with Yahoo!, so Bing can deliver meaningful traffic, although much less than what Google would deliver. There are always paid click programs such as Google's AdWords and Bing's AdCenter. Also, you may take advantage of pay per click campaigns in specific web properties, such as LinkedIn and Facebook. But without doubt, a Google penalty is a harsh sanction that will cost you the traffic and business.

Abandoning your existing domain and starting over

While it sounds drastic, you may be better off, in some cases, to abandon your domain when struck with a Google penalty. Requesting reconsideration from Google is where the trouble lies: it can take over a year to clear a penalty attached to a domain and delays of up to three years are not uncommon. Then there is the possibility that the penalty will languish indefinitely. Note that Google penalties that attach to a site solely because it is infected with malware or other viruses do not fall into this category. Such penalties are lifted within hours.

Here's how to evaluate the choice between abandoning a domain and sticking with the domain, and requesting reconsideration. First, bear in mind that Google penalties follow the domain, they do not follow the specific content. So, if you secure a new domain and rebuild your site, page by page, your new site will not inherit the Google penalty. WordPress has a convenient export/import feature (available under **Tools** in your WordPress dashboard), so rebuilding a site on a new domain takes little time.

What you need to consider is how valuable is the old domain? Does it have a difficult-to-obtain DMOZ listing? Is the domain a valuable domain with powerful branding awareness with the public? Does it have thousands of links, which would take months or years to rebuild? Or, can the link references be easily changed to point to your new site? Is your penalized domain a newer domain? A newer domain is less valuable than a domain with years of history and authority with the search engines. You should also consider that you will need to update any local listings that appear in Google Maps and Yelp, to point them to the new domain.

In some cases then, the work to create a new domain is less than the delay and trouble you'll endure by going through the reconsideration process.

Cleaning your site and requesting reconsideration following a Google penalty

If your website has, with certainty, been penalized, and abandoning your old domain isn't feasible, you'll need to begin the work to make your site, and all its inbound links compliant with Google's webmaster guidelines. You can also request reconsideration directly from Google, but only if you've received a manual penalty notice in your Google Webmaster Tools dashboard. If you did not receive a manual penalty, all you can do is clean your site and wait. Here are the steps to move toward the reconsideration of a Google penalty.

Step 1 – Sign up and verify with Google Webmaster Tools

If you haven't already, you must create a Google Webmaster Tools account to request reconsideration or diagnose a Google penalty effectively. If you haven't done so already, visit http://www.google.com/webmasters to sign up for a free account. Then, verify your site by either uploading an HTML file, adding a tag to the header of your site, linking to a Google Analytics account, or by adding a DNS entry to your domain configuration. The reconsideration request process is handled entirely within the Google Webmaster Tools area. Naturally, you'll want to look in the **Messages** area with Google Webmaster Tools to see if you've received a penalty notice.

Step 2 – Clean your site

Before requesting a reconsideration, you must correct whatever violation or condition led to the penalty. The key to this step is thoroughness, and you'll need to meet a higher standard than simply meeting the bare minimum rules set forth in Google's guidelines. Your site will be reviewed manually by a Google representative, so you need to make sure your house is in order. That means all your content needs to be original, no thin content affiliate pages or duplicate content.

Your site should be validated to the current HTML standards (use W3C's free HTML validator tool at http://validator.w3.org/). Any scripts that run on your site will be scrutinized extremely thoroughly. Even if such scripts are harmless, if Google can't determine that, they'll let your penalty stand. You should thoroughly check your site for malware and malicious code. Google provides a free tool for this, the Safe Browsing Diagnostic Tool. To use this tool, enter your website URL manually into the following string http://www.google.com/safebrowsing/diagnostic?site=http://yoursite.com.

The Safe Browsing Diagnostic Tool will return a report on any malware or malicious code hidden in your site. If you want a second opinion, you can also run your site through AVG's free web page scanner `http://www.avg.com.au/resources/web-page-scanner/`.

Your chance for a review might take four weeks or way longer, so make sure your site is clean when Google comes to visit.

Step 3 – Requesting reconsideration

Once you have verified your site in Google Webmaster Tools and cleaned your site of any problems, you are ready to request a reconsideration from Google. Log in to your Google Webmaster Tools account and navigate to **Manual Actions**. Here is a sample of a manual action message from Google:

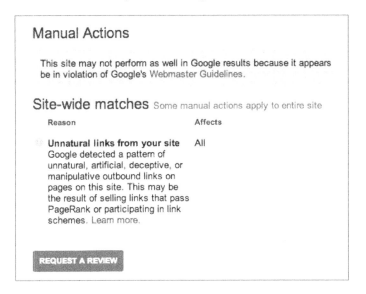

The **REQUEST A REVIEW** button initiates the review process. You'll be asked to *acknowledge that my site does not violate Google's Webmaster Guidelines*, and present a narrative of the actions you took to address the violations set forth in Google's manual action. There may be minor variations in the text of the acknowledgement, but it will be in a very similar format. An example follows:

Request a review

Tell us how you have addressed the specific issues we have listed, including all relevant information.

> I acknowledge that my site does not violate Google's Webmaster Guidelines.

Request a review   Cancel

Step 4 – Drafting the reconsideration message

The narrative you submit will be determinative. If you don't submit a complete description of the actions you've taken, you will receive a message in a few weeks saying that the penalty will remain in place with an invitation to request a review again.

Here's a sample of a reconsideration message that successfully removed a Google manual penalty based on a spammy link profile; we began with a summary, just to guide the reviewer:

Summary of Compliance Efforts

-We have removed 37 links, which we feel were not compliant with Google's webmaster -guidelines.

We have contacted 14 webmasters without success.

We then thought it would be a good idea to reaffirm our commitment to Google's quality guidelines.

Current Compliance and Future Commitment to Quality Guidelines

We have read, and fully understand the Google Webmaster Guidelines. We see now that some of our links clearly violated Google's Webmaster Guidelines. We have committed substantial time and effort to cleaning out bad links. We accept full responsibility, and we are fully committed and promise to observe Google's guidelines in the future.

Next, we presented our link removal efforts in detail, entering each link line-by-line. We've truncated our long list of removed links in this example:

Compliance Efforts in Detail

Successful Link Removal

We have successfully removed or nofollowed the following links:

-http://21stguru.com

-http://www.alastdirectory.com/detail/link-1954.html

-http://www.aoldir.com/link-krasner-hughes-and-long-188586.html

Of course, we didn't successfully remove all the bad links, so we pointed out that although we weren't successful, we did put effort into at least trying. So, we continued.

Unsuccessful Link Removal, and Our Efforts

We were unsuccessful in removing the following links, and made repeated contacts. We have included here the dates upon which we contacted these webmasters.

-http://www.add-top-links.com/listing/Society/Law/10067

--9/22/13

--10/8/13

--10/22/13

Step 5 – Wait

After submitting the reconsideration request, you simply need to visit Webmaster Tools every few days to see if your reconsideration request was granted. In the example just above, we received a message in Webmaster Tools about two weeks later that our reconsideration request was granted and that the manual spam action had been revoked. The time for processing consideration requests varies greatly, longer times tend to be bad news:

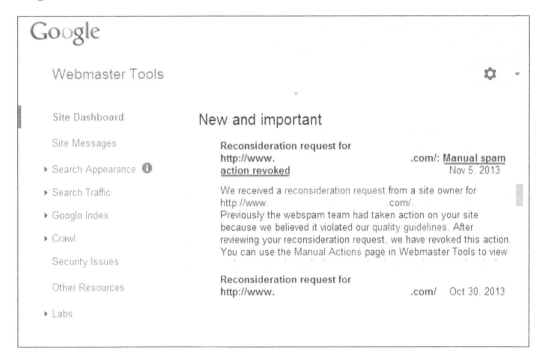

If your request gets rejected the first few times, just keep trying. You'll need to review your site again for violations and resubmit your reconsideration request. Trying to e-mail Google or posting in the Google Webmaster forums isn't likely to yield any results, and certainly won't yield any specific information in your case. You might also consider hiring a professional with experience in handling reconsideration requests.

Avoiding black hat techniques and purveyors who promote them

Books like this one are of little use to black hat webmasters, who rely on shortcuts to web rankings and traffic, so we suspect our audience is predisposed to our warning about black hat techniques. You are more likely to be lured into a black hat scheme than concoct one yourself. If you honor the Google Webmaster Guidelines and produce valuable original content, you are extremely unlikely to be penalized.

But black hat providers prowl the Internet for business constantly. You may already have received e-mails about link exchanges and automated content services. Nearly 100 percent of all mass marketed traffic, link, and content services are black hat services, and should be avoided. As you promote your site and become more visible online, the number of inbound inquiries you receive will increase.

The standard black hat scam – Link exchange

This is a standard pitch you might receive through an e-mail. An innocent-sounding webmaster proposes a link between your site and theirs. Naturally, they'll open with a generalized compliment about your site. Here's an actual e-mail, completely representative of this type of come-on:

```
Hi,

My name is Lauren Robinson, Web Marketing Consultant. I've greatly
enjoyed looking through your site and I was wondering if you'd be
interested in exchanging links with my website, which has a related
subject. I can offer you a home page link back from my related
websites all in Google cache and backlinks which are:

transcendtechnology.biz    PR4
```

You should never pursue such a link exchange. No matter how innocent-sounding and personal, these e-mails are sent to hundreds of thousands of webmasters, if not millions. The sites promoted by such e-mails are nearly always bad neighborhoods or link farms. The risk of penalization for linking to such sites is high.

The standard black hat scam – Website submission service

Website submission services often promote their services through e-mails or on online forums. As the pitch goes, they will submit your site to *the major search engines* for a fee. They offer specialized software as well as automated services. These services haven't been necessary for at least 10 years, as now the major search engines find the sites by crawling the Web, not through manual submissions. These purveyors still exist despite the fact that the service is completely unnecessary. At worst, these services will spam the search engine submission forms with your domain name. You should never subscribe to a search engine submission service. There is no value to the service, and it will be worse than doing nothing at all.

The standard black hat scam – Offshore link building

This is a common e-mail-based pitch. Most of these e-mails originate in massive link-building shops based in India, or that part of the world. Link building is a major industry in India and the prime source of revenue are the American-based, and European-based businesses. Nearly all of the offshore purveyors of link building services offer very low-quality, assembly-line link building services that are more likely to trigger the ire of search engines than build up your website's rankings or popularity.

The standard pitch usually sounds very similar to the following, from an e-mail received at our consultancy, with minor variations, nearly 500 times in the past two years:

```
Dear Sir \ Madam,

We are a Smart and fast growing Web Development Services company from
Delhi(India).

We provide complete natural quality Link Building services in a fully
professional manner and at a very competitive cost.

We get one way high pr relative links from commenting on dofollow
blogs and forums. However, all these benefits leads to one goal:
"Increase in Sales".
```

The standard black hat scam – Autoblogging

While less common, sellers of autoblogging software and services do market services online through e-mails, websites, and pay per click ads. Here's an actual e-mail that is fairly typical of the pitch for autoblogging services:

```
Generate Automatic Income While You Sleep—Auto Blog  S a m u r a i
Software 'automatically' creates content and updates your blog every
day - once your blog is set up, you're done!
```

Start Earning Monthly Residual Income On Autopilot—The software seamlessly integrates with and generates profits from most popular affiliate networks such as Google AdSense, Amazon Associates, eBay Partner Network, and ClickBank.

Autoblogged content is, by definition, duplicate content, and we've learned that it is strongly discouraged by Google Webmaster Guidelines.

Beyond the specific services outlined here, there are others. If you follow Google Webmaster Guidelines and follow your instincts, you should have no trouble steering clear of Google penalties.

Summary

In this chapter, we learned about a range of black hat techniques and why the obvious course is to avoid them religiously. You must always remain vigilant in honoring Google Webmaster Guidelines. Stay right with Google, and you'll be rewarded with high rankings and steer clear of damaging ranking penalties.

In this chapter, we examined the full spectrum of forbidden black hat and gray hat techniques, such as hidden text, cloaking, sneaky redirects, doorway pages, and more. We dug into Google Webmaster Guidelines and learned how and when Google will act on a violation. We discovered the difference between penalties, filters, and bans, and how to distinguish them. We learned how to diagnose and repair specific Google penalties.

Finally, we learned how to avoid the black hat techniques by steering clear of purveyors of these forbidden techniques. By following the guidelines set forth in this chapter, you will keep your rankings and traffic shielded from penalty. In the next chapter, we'll learn about common SEO mistakes and how to avoid them.

9
Avoiding SEO Mistakes

We have come to learn that search optimization is a complex task, riddled with both opportunities and pitfalls. In this chapter, we'll examine some of the most common search ranking mistakes webmasters make while building their sites, and how you can avoid these errors.

Every technique that we admonish in this chapter is undertaken commonly, but always with innocent intent. Unlike the active, forbidden techniques we warned of in the last chapter on black hat techniques, here we cover methods that are applied without malice. Nevertheless, however, there are certain techniques and methods that can undercut your ranking power that you will want to avoid. For example, Adobe Flash animation graphics on websites seem innocent and effective: Flash graphics are popular, widely used, and attractive. Unfortunately, search engines don't read Flash effectively and reliably. And so, Flash-based websites don't perform well in search engines. Ideally, webmasters should incorporate Flash elements in a way that does not include any navigation links or any targeted, high-value content.

Sadly, it is typically professional web designers that serve as proponents of placement-robbing design methods like Flash graphics and image-based navigation menus. With web technology, just because it can be done, doesn't mean it should be done.

Thankfully, WordPress won't let you make the most serious SEO errors, assuming, of course, that your WordPress template is well drafted. WordPress builds sound, hierarchical, text-based navigation that keeps most webmasters from making the gravest of errors. There are, however, mistakes that WordPress will not prevent you from making, and we'll discuss those here.

We will examine errors in keyword research that can lead to ranking troubles well into the future. We will learn to avoid common mistakes with poor internal anchor text. Next, we'll turn to Flash, JavaScript, image links, and other non-readable content. We will look at the complex challenges surrounding site architecture and look into some common mistakes that webmasters make. Then, we will turn our attention to over-optimization in both link building and on-page factors. We'll learn about sandboxing and jumping the gun—special challenges that webmasters face with brand new sites.

We will continue with a warning about using free hosted domains. Next, we'll look at some often-ignored tools: local directory listings and free verification tools. We'll explore the risky (but sometimes necessary) practices of paying for clicks, when you already enjoy organic rankings. We'll then look into the common errors of leaving stray pages in search engine indexes. We'll end with a warning to remain vigilant in the production of new content.

Pursuing the wrong keywords

Keyword research lies at the foundation of all search marketing efforts. As webmasters, we must always be mindful of what users are searching for, in what relative volumes, and whether those keywords are relevant. WordPress will not research keywords for you. You need to perform thorough and sound keyword research to make sure you can grab the relevant traffic that ties web searchers with your content. The error of pursuing the wrong keywords can infect the earliest stages of your web marketing plan, if you choose a poor domain name, based upon a misconception about what customers are searching for.

Perhaps the most common keyword-related mistakes come with webmasters and business owners that make instinctual guesses at keyword volumes. SEO professionals know that the truth is in the keyword data, not in the instinctual guess made by a business owner. The high-volume and high-relevance terms are where you'll find hidden profits, so that's where your efforts need to be focused. Search volume data is never what you'd expect; the data always returns surprises, both pleasant and unpleasant. Also, consider that some search traffic is seasonal, so you need to constantly monitor keyword volumes for trends and adjust your strategy as necessary.

Bear in mind that, the total volume of search traffic is not the only determinant of a keyword's value. The search query must be relevant. A search term like *AC service* is relevant both to home air conditioning service companies as well as automobile repair service companies. On the other hand, *HVAC service* is a nearly 100 percent relevant keyword to a business that does home AC service. You have to begin with search volume data and analyze it yourself for relevancy.

Google has, for several years now, been correcting spelling errors in searches, yet desperate webmasters continue to include common misspellings on pages in the hopes of capturing errant searches. Your keyword research must be done thoroughly and at the inception of your marketing plan, not in the middle. You can make use of the tools mentioned in the previous chapters, like Google Keyword Planner, Google Trends, and so on, for keyword research.

Poor internal anchor text

As we have learned, the anchor text that forms a part of a link is an important ranking element for the destination page. The anchor text serves as a signpost to the search engines as to the content and subject of the destination. This principle applies with respect to both external links and internal links.

Links with anchor text such as `Click here`, `Go home`, and `Read More` are missed opportunities. The search engines index this anchor text and attempt to divine the content of the destination page.

You can see this principle at work, by performing a Google search for the phrase `Click here`. The number three result is the download page for Adobe's Acrobat Reader. The reason? Over 935 million web pages have linked to the Acrobat Reader download page and some have used the non-descriptive anchor text `Click here`. Google's algorithm works properly here, but can only return the result based on what it reads.

In your web marketing efforts, avoid this result by simply creating anchor text that signals the subject of the destination page. This task might simply be a matter of selecting different words as anchor text that is already present in your text. See the following screenshot that illustrates two different approaches to the anchor text using the same sentence. The anchor text employed in the first example sends no keyword signal. In the second example, the anchor text leverages keywords:

> You can click here for information on pool cleaning service in Sarasota.
>
> You can click here for information on pool cleaning service in Sarasota.

The principle also extends to your navigation menus. Perhaps, the most commonly used example of poor anchor text is the use of the anchor text Home in site-wide navigation, to point users back to your home page. This error is compounded by the fact that your home page is (or should be) your most important page reserved for your principal keywords. Even worse, the Home link is often the first link on all pages of a site, which implicates the controversial first link priority rule. The first link priority rule refers to some testing results announced (but the underlying data was not released) by the Stompernet team of SEO trainers, that discovered that the first link read by search engines on a page is given more weight than subsequent links on a page. The marketers at SEO.com later tested the theory and released a small but definitive study here: https://www.seo.com/blog/testing-link-priority-rule/. In theory, the principle demands that extra attention be paid to that first link, which is often a top bar, site-wide navigational link back to a website's home page. Keep in mind that, the principle of first link priority is widely disputed.

However, whether the first link priority applies or not, you should never employ Home as the anchor text anywhere on your site. True, users are accustomed to seeing a Home link or button in order to navigate within a site. The effect on ranking, however, is too substantial to ignore. If you must use the word Home for navigation, remember that you can add Home in parenthesis along with your keyword-aware anchor text. So, your Home link might read WordPress SEO Company [Home], instead of Home by itself.

This is an error that WordPress will thoughtlessly make for you, if you choose Home as the title of your home page. The best use of site-wide links to your homepage is with anchor text that includes your primary keyword or keywords.

Flash, JavaScript, image links, and other non-readable content

Search engines do not read the text in images and do not reliably read JavaScript navigation and Flash files. Also, the iPad doesn't support flash. Presenting non-readable content to search spiders is a fundamental error that must always be avoided, even at the expense of a website's appearance. Google Webmaster Guidelines dictate:

Make a site with a clear hierarchy and text links. Every page should be reachable from at least one static text link. Try to use text instead of images, to display important names, content, or links. The Google crawler doesn't recognize text contained in images. If you must use images for textual content, consider using the ALT attribute to include a few words of descriptive text.

Despite the clear logic and strong dictates of this rule, this is an area where uninformed web designers can often undermine their clients' rankings. Flash-based websites are sometimes the worst offenders, because they often incorporate almost no text that can be read by search engines. Designers that specialize in Flash-based websites dazzle clients with animation while eventually destroying their rankings.

Webmasters of WordPress-based sites may typically worry less about Flash navigation. The default WordPress template and all free templates on WordPress.org do not employ Flash navigation. That said, there are commercial WordPress templates available, that incorporate Flash navigation, and there are certainly web developers willing to incorporate Flash elements into a WordPress installation, for those who request it.

Next, we turn to the use of images to display content within site navigation. As we have learned, Google does not read the text in images. We should note, however, that Google has made some hints that it ultimately will apply **optical character recognition** (**OCR**) technology, in order to read the text in images, but that innovation is far off. For the foreseeable future, you may fully expect that any text that appears in images will be totally ignored by search engines. While Google Webmaster Guidelines instruct that, *if you must use images for textual content, consider using the ALT attribute to include a few words of descriptive text*; this solution isn't ideal. Google might read the ALT attribute, but it won't give great weight to your ALT tags, and you should never use ALT tags to include long passages of text.

The warning against the use of images to display text is further compounded when images are used to display text, that is also the subject of site navigation. Not only will the search engines have no text to read, but they will have no link anchor text to read either. Recall that the anchor text of a link serves as a signpost to Google as to the subject of the destination page. If the hyperlink anchor is an image, Google will index a blank entry for the anchor text, and that's a missed opportunity to employ a powerful ranking factor.

Poor site architecture

Another example of a common SEO mistake that you should endeavor to avoid is poor site architecture. Site architecture is the skeleton of your website: it is the design and navigational framework that dictates the flow of both the user behavior and search engine spider behavior on your site. Site architecture needs to be considered at the planning stages of your website. Effective site architecture should display a visible and comprehensible navigational structure to both the users and search spiders, that echoes your content hierarchy. Sound site architecture will yield thorough search engine spidering, engaged visitors, and higher PageRank flow to your primary pages. Poor site architecture can mean that search engines can't crawl your site effectively, and users can't find what they need to convert into customers.

Many SEO professionals will concede that website architecture is one of the most difficult SEO skills to master. Site architecture demands that a webmaster deftly blend and balance the skills of conversion science, usability, coding, and PageRank sculpting. WordPress does about half the work of site architecture for you; for the other half, you'll need to think thoroughly about your site hierarchy.

WordPress performs some important architecture tasks automatically:

- Your content hierarchy is echoed semi-automatically into your navigation menus (as long as you employ WordPress' custom menu features). All published pages appear in your navigation without requiring further action. Thus, no Pages or Posts can be accidentally forgotten or left out of your navigation.

- Your WordPress navigation menus are text-based by default, ensuring thorough spidering.

- Nearly all WordPress themes display your navigational hierarchy in a visually intuitive way. For example, Pages that are children of parent pages are visually indicated in navigation through indentation or a reduced font size. This helps your readers understand the relationship between site elements. Furthermore, child pages are coded by the WordPress engine in a way that indicates to search spiders their position in your site's hierarchy.

However, WordPress will rely on you for the following:

- You must make sure both Pages and Posts display throughout the site. A WordPress template that lacks a header navigation area (rare, but they do exist) might require you to manually add sidebar widgets to display Posts and Pages. If you can reach all of your Pages and Posts from anywhere on your site, you have done this correctly.

- WordPress themes with custom templates and multiple sidebar widget areas can be problematic: such themes require you to be vigilant to make sure you have adequate navigational links in all areas of your site. Beware of *shifting navigation* — navigation that changes as users pass through different areas of your site. Shifting navigation confuses both the users and search spiders.

- Your site hierarchy, the relationship, and the structure of Pages, Posts, tags, and categories to each other and to the whole, all fall solely upon you. All WordPress can do, is faithfully present the content and categorization that you submit to it.

Don't forget what we've learned about WordPress' propensity for duplicate content on archive and tag pages — that content should almost always be no-indexed through the use of a `robots.txt` file.

WordPress' default navigation is fairly bland — it presents a single navigational entry for each Page or Post. To highlight particular areas of your site, or to push extra link power to the important sections of your site, you'll want to add some links manually. We cover this advanced technique in the following section.

Expert site architecture with manual links and PageRank sculpting

If you want to drive extra traffic and ranking power to a few of your most important, primary keyword-based pages, you can achieve it with a few extra manual links. In your sidebar or footer, use a WordPress text widget to craft three or four extra navigational links to your highest-value pages. You can title the widget `Popular Pages`, to draw additional user interest and traffic to the pages. In addition, you'll send extra PageRank (and hence the extra ranking power) to these high-value pages. The use of navigation to either send or restrict ranking power to sections or pages of your site is called **PageRank sculpting**.

The following screenshot shows some PageRank sculpting (and heightened usability) in action. Note, the key links are placed prominently in the footer of a WordPress site with the use of a text widget. These links highlight the website's most popular pages. In addition, these links send extra PageRank to those key pages:

ADDITIONAL SERVICE AREAS	POPULAR SERVICES
› Fort Worth, TX	› Dallas Fence Company
› Arlington, TX	› Dallas Fence Materials & Supplies
› Plano, TX	› Temporary Fence Rental in Dallas
› Frisco, TX	› Dallas Commercial Fence Contractors

Over-optimization

Over-optimization refers to the excessive use of optimization techniques, that ultimately yields either penalization or poor rankings. We've touched on over-optimization throughout this book, and it always remains a danger if one is actively optimizing and promoting a site. A good way to think about over-optimization is *Unnatural optimization*. Put another way, the search engines want to present search results that represent naturally-written content. They don't want to display content that specifically manipulates rankings. For example, would it be natural that an article on Houston apartments would have the phrase *Houston apartments* repeated 20 or 30 times in the article? Of course not. This is where the over-optimization component of the search engines' algorithms come into play.

Over-optimizing of on-page factors – Guidelines

You must ensure that your on-page factors (text, headings, bold, ALT tags, and so on) are not over optimized. If you write your pages naturally, you'll most likely never trigger over-optimization. However, aggressive optimization in competitive markets will typically require that the content be written with a keyword focus in mind. It's easy to get somewhat carried away with optimization, and you'll want to follow some established guidelines, to make sure you don't go too far. Mathematical rules for optimization are not published (for obvious reasons), but some sound best practices have emerged.

Some sound guidelines to follow to ensure that you aren't over-optimizing, are the following:

- The keyword usage on a particular page of body text should comprise about 5 percent of the total words on the page; more than 8 percent to 10 percent of total words on the page is risky and isn't going to present a very nice user experience anyway.

- The keyword usage in heading tags should not comprise more than 35 percent to 40 percent of the total words within the heading tags.

- Vary your keyword prominence. Your keywords should not be used as the first words in 100 percent of your website elements. To do so appears completely unnatural, and is easy for search engines to detect. A general rule: never use the same phrase of two or more words as the first words in more than one-third of your website elements.

- All of the major elements of a website, taken as a whole (title tag, meta description, meta keywords, body copy, image ALT tags, heading tags, body copy, and outbound links), should never contain the exact keyword phrase, even if diluted with other terms. Some of your website's lower-weight elements like ALT tags and lower-lever heading tags should have no keywords present within them.

- Don't employ perfectly matching elements. You should never have individual website elements be exact matches of other elements. For example, you do not want to have an exact match among your `title` tag, `h1` tag, and `h2` tag. Vary the text, so that the page does not appear machine-generated.

- Don't mindlessly repeat keywords in your site navigation. If your site has 20 pages and they appear in your navigation as *Used Cars Dallas*, *Used Cars Houston*, *Used Cars Plano*, and so on, that pattern is easy to detect and you should avoid it.

- The more important the element, the more likely you'll trigger over-optimization. It's almost impossible to trigger over-optimization by tinkering with italics, bold text, and ALT tags, while the more powerful elements like title tags and headings can more easily trigger problems.

- Over-optimization becomes more likely as the scale of your site grows. For example, five pages with repetitive text in the site navigation anchor text is not nearly as risky as fifty pages with repetitive text.

Over-optimizing inbound links – Guidelines

The over-optimization inquiry does not end with your on-page factors. You must also consider the effect of over-optimization of inbound links. This is the most common area where webmasters misstep and trigger over-optimization troubles with Google. The notion of *natural* optimization again applies here; you want your inbound links to appear as if they were built naturally by other webmasters, that selected your site as link-worthy, because of the quality of your content. Again, mathematical rules on the over-optimization of inbound links are neither published, nor helpful, but sound guidelines have emerged.

Over-optimization in link building can be distilled to a single principle: don't secure all your links with the same anchor text. Now, because you'll garner some links naturally without any input from you, you'll gain links that have whatever anchor text the other webmasters select. Inbound links for which you are able to choose your anchor text (such as directory submissions), must be varied.

A sound general rule to follow is that you never want more than 20 percent of your inbound links (measured by either number of links or by link power) to share the same anchor text. The 20 percent figure is a personal guideline; were you to ask 100 SEO professionals, you would get 100 different opinions. An exception to this rule is the obvious: your company or blog name. If you have a company called Midwest Pediatric Associates with a domain MidwestPediatrics.com, then it is safe to have a high proportion of links with your business name as the anchor text.

Note that, the 20 percent suggestion applies to both numbers of links and power of links. If you have 1,000 inbound links, you want no more than 200 of those inbound links to share the same exact anchor text. However, the guideline also applies to the power of your inbound links. So, if you have 800 poor quality links but 200 very high-powered, high PageRank links and if all of these 200 links share the same exact anchor text, then you are running the risk of over-optimization.

Jumping the gun and the sandbox

Brand new websites can sometimes be subject to the sandbox effect. The sandbox effect is a highly debated observation, about the way Google serves relatively poor rankings for new websites in the first months of launch. No observer can seem to agree on whether the sandbox effect even exists, let alone how it operates. Google has been tight-lipped (Google almost never reveals specifics about its algorithm).

What is reasonably certain is that the sandbox effect often doesn't apply to all niches. Brand new sites can rank quite well, but typically in less competitive markets. So, if the sandbox effect is being algorithmically imposed by Google, it is being imposed only upon certain categories and niches. It is also possible that the sandbox effect is triggered by some external trigger, such as garnering too many powerful links too quickly.

Don't fight the sandbox effect. In the first months of your website's life, you need to build the links slowly. Don't simply rush out and secure dozens of high-powered links right away. However, a large number of high-value links can look unnatural. The general consensus among SEO professionals is that securing high-powered links immediately upon a website's launch, can trigger very poor rankings for a period of up to one and a half years.

The better approach to link building in the first few months of your site's life is to roll out links gradually, building up slowly through the first six months. Some SEO professionals will build 15 links in the first month, 30 links in the second month, and 50 links in the third month. Now, if you achieve prominent rankings quite quickly, you are very likely to have avoided the sandbox effect, and you can safely begin full-scale link building. Tread gently at first, and watch your rankings. Once the rankings come through, you are on the safer ground.

Using free hosted domains

Free hosted platforms like Blogger.com and WordPress.com provide a valuable service, but they aren't appropriate as the primary destination for a business that works in a competitive SEO market. WordPress' free blogging service (available through WordPress.com instead of WordPress.org) offers users a free, full-featured blog on the WordPress platform. The free service offers hosting on a subdomain (`http://yoursite.wordpress.com`), but a custom domain is available for about $99 a year. Be warned: the custom domain feature requires some sound knowledge of domain mapping.

No free hosted domain will ever match the design flexibility and ranking power of custom domain. You'll be limited as to the themes and plugins you'll be able to install. Without the freedom to install plugins, you'll limit the SEO power available to you. And, if your site resides on a subdomain of WordPress.com, you'll be poorly regarded by search engines and customers alike. Search engines don't rank free hosted domains very highly, and customers know they are free, so they might not take your business seriously.

Forgetting verification tools

`Yoursite.wordpress.com` offers much more than insight into how the search spiders interact with your site. It also provides a verification function. Verifying your site through Google Webmaster Tools, lets Google know that your site has an active and engaged webmaster. The same goes for Google Analytics. Having Google Analytics installed on your site sends a signal to Google, that an active webmaster is at the helm. The same dictate applies to having an XML sitemap that resides in your site's root directory. Your sitemap, even if not needed for indexing purposes, lends additional credence to your website.

Ignoring local directory listings

Organic search results are not the only game in town. Local directory listings are now served up by all three major search engines as well as by dozens of independent sites such as Yelp, HotFrog, MerchantCircle, and InsiderPages. In some local business niches, local directory listings can deliver up to 35 percent of total web traffic.

You can broaden your overall reach by securing complete listings on any or all directory sites. Google, Yahoo!, and Yelp are the most important, although Yahoo! is in the process of selling off its local features. With a few dozen business directory listings, you'll stand a better chance of blanketing the first page of Google's results when users search for your business' name. If you are highly effective at creating complete, keyword-rich local directory listings, your listings themselves might rank for primary and secondary keywords. What follows are some guidelines for supplementing your natural search results with strong, high-ranking individual business listings.

Always assigning as many categories as possible

This is paramount. Google Places allows you up to five categories into which you can place your business listing. With most local business directories, each business category under which you register, will create an individual entry on an individual category page. So, your entry might appear in five different places in a directory. Each page is a backlink for the traffic, and for the PageRank value (assuming the link is followed, in Google Places it is not), and your listing will quite simply be seen more often.

Getting reviews

Reviews from happy customers can help boost your rankings within the local directory. Google Places is the greatest example. While their ranking system for local entries is a secret, Google obviously favors entries that have received reviews. I'll bet you've done a favor for a client at one time, right? Ask them for a review. Send them a clear and concise e-mail with instructions and a link to write the review. Besides the ranking power within the directories, reviews will increase the conversion power of the local entry; readers are more likely to follow up on your ad, if they see a positive review from a member of the community.

Also, positive reviews can offset a present or future negative review. If a negative review does get written, a positive review can soften the blow.

Uploading pictures to your local listings

The larger local business directories are quite advanced, and most of them include the ability to upload pictures. Always upload the maximum number of pictures. A full and complete listing is always more likely to rank higher within the directory. And again, viewers are far more likely to act on a complete listing, rather than a sparse one.

Completing all optional fields

When creating a local business entry, you may have noticed many optional fields such as business hours, payment types accepted, and languages spoken. These fields are optional and most folks just skip them.

You should always fill out every optional field possible. In some directories, the extra fields have the effect of enlarging the directory entry, while omitting it would just display nothing. So, your listing might be 5 or 6 inches tall on a results page, while your competitors — those who skipped the optional fields — will have a simple two or three line entry.

Also, some directories allow (or will allow in the future) users to use the optional fields as search criteria (that is, the ability to search for companies that accept Google Checkout, and so on). Naturally, you'll want to come up in any such search result.

Making multiple entries for multiple locations

If you have multiple business locations, make separate entries for each location. However, don't create multiple entries unless each entry has a separate phone number. Google Places often merges listings, if it encounters a common phone number. With multiple entries, each location will show up in searches separately (many folks search by ZIP code). Each entry will represent a backlink.

Writing a compelling business description with keywords

This goes without saying, but 75 percent of the folks don't bother. A compelling business description will convert viewers and draw them to your site. And, if your description is focused on your primary keywords, then your local business entry will likely to be ranked for those keywords.

Paying for clicks when you rank organically

Don't cannibalize your natural rankings with expensive paid search ads. There is an interaction between natural search entries and paid ads. Say you rank organically in Google for the term `Stop smoking ad`, and you also have paid ads competing on the same search results page. The paid clicks you purchase might be clicks you could have had already. It's a judgment call. Are the clicks 20 cents or 10 dollars? And, even if you do pay for some of your traffic, are you earning a positive return on investment in the paid click channel?

Perhaps, the most egregious example of the cannibalization of organic traffic is the purchased paid clicks for one's own business name. This practice almost certainly directs users into paid clicks, when the organic entry is clearly visible. National brands often employ this technique. Brands such as Dr. Pepper and Federal Express purchase paid clicks in the Google Adwords program. This practice is almost never necessary for smaller businesses and will nearly always result in higher search costs, than are necessary. There are only two instances where such a practice is advisable: when the bid prices for clicks are in pennies, or when competitors are bidding on clicks for your business name.

Leaving stray pages in Google's index

If you have Flash files and PDF files on your site, Google will eventually find those pages and index them—even if you don't intend for them to be searchable pages. Eventually, you'll have a slew of ugly, unappealing indexed entries in Google's search results. These pages will often compete in search results for your primary terms. You can check Google's index of your site by entering the `site:yourdomain.com` query in the Google search box.

You should monitor the index that Google maintains for your site, to make sure that no low-value pages have made their way into the index. To remove the files from Google's index, simply create an entry in your `robots.txt` file instructing the search engines to ignore particular pages.

Failing to produce fresh new content

Fresh content can be almost anything. It can be regular blog posts related to the topic of your site. It can be photographs of the work you've done, or events in which you've participated. It can be announcements of new products or services you've added to your offerings. It can even be coupons and specials, that you offer on your services. New content can have purely commercial intent, although you'll get more mileage if most of your new content is meaningful to users.

When a website remains static, the search engines recognize that nothing has changed, and the spiders will visit at less frequent intervals. The value of the site as a whole will diminish in the eyes of the search engines. New content sends a completely different signal. New content serves as a signpost, that your site is an active and engaging community. The search engines will send spiders more often to crawl your site and your rankings will rise.

Remember that, you can schedule content to publish in the future with WordPress. When you create a new Page or Post, you simply need to click the **Edit** link next to **Publish** immediately in the **Publish** box when creating new content. If you have three articles of new content, don't post them all immediately; you can schedule them so that they publish at one week intervals in the future. Regular posting of new content is preferable to posting chunks of new Pages and Posts every few months.

It's tough to stick with a regular blogging routing. Writing content takes time, and writing quality content takes even more time. The rewards are so obvious and reliable, however, that creating new content is a mandate for success online.

Summary

In this chapter, we covered the most obvious, common, and avoidable SEO mistakes. With the information in this chapter, you'll easily steer clear of the most typical errors.

We examined the practice of pursing the wrong keywords and continued with the common practices of selecting poor anchor text. We learned about a wide range of content that search engines can't reliably read: Flash animations, JavaScript, and image files. We looked at poor site architecture and examined what WordPress accomplishes for you, and where you'll need to step in to assure your site architecture is easily spidered by search engines and sensible to users. We furthered this inquiry to explore the advanced topic of PageRank sculpting.

We explored over-optimization of both the on-page factors, as well as the inbound links. We warned about the common practice of *jumping the gun*—securing inbound links that are overwhelmingly powerful when your site is brand new. We discussed the proper way to ease yourself into favor with the search engines.

We warned against the use of free hosted domains like Blogspot.com and WordPress.com. We reminded you of the importance of the supplemental verification functions provided by Google Webmaster Tools and Google Analytics. We also learned not to ignore parallel search channels like the local directory listings. We continued with an examination of the danger of paying for clicks, when your site already enjoys robust organic rankings.

Finally, we learned how to identify and clear stray pages from Google's index, and discussed the importance of producing regular fresh content. Armed with the warnings and instructions in this chapter, you will easily avoid the most common SEO mistakes and you won't hamper your rankings as you pursue your Internet marketing plan. In the next chapter, we'll learn how to test your site and monitor your progress.

10

Testing Your Site and Monitoring Your Progress

Once you have built your website and started promoting it, you'll want to monitor your progress to ensure that your hard work is yielding both high rankings, search engine visibility, and web traffic. In this chapter, we'll cover a range of tools with which you will monitor the quality of your website, learn how search spiders interact with your site, measure your rankings in search engines for various keywords, and analyze how your visitors behave when they are on your site. With this information, you can gauge your progress and make adjustments to your strategy.

Obviously, you'll want to know where your web traffic is coming from, what search terms are being used to find your website, and where you are ranking in the search engines for each of these terms. This information will allow you to see what you still need to work on in terms of building links to the pages on your website.

There are five main tools you will use to analyze your site and evaluate your traffic and rankings, and in this chapter, we will cover each in turn. They are Google Analytics, Google Search Console (formerly Webmaster Tools), HTML Validator, Bing Webmaster, and Link Assistant's Rank Tracker. As an alternative to Bing Webmaster, you may also want to employ Majestic SEO to check your backlinks. We'll cover each of these tools in turn.

Google Analytics

Google Analytics monitors and analyzes your website's traffic. With this tool, you can see how many website visitors you have had, whether they found your site through the search engines or clicked through from another website, how these visitors behaved once they were on your site, and much more. You can even connect your Google AdSense account to one or more of the domains you are monitoring in Google Analytics to get information about which pages and keywords generate the most income. While there are other analytics services available, none match the scope and scale of what Google Analytics offers.

Setting up Google Analytics for your website

To set up Google Analytics for your website, perform the following steps:

1. To sign up for Google Analytics, visit `http://www.google.com/analytics/`.

2. On the top-right corner of the page, you'll see a button that says, **Sign In to Google Analytics**. You'll need to have a Google account before signing in.

3. You will have to click **Sign up** on the next page if you haven't already, and on the next page you'll enter your website's URL and time zone.

 If you have more than one website, just start with one. You can add the other sites later. The account name you use is not important, but you can add all of your sites to one account, so you might want to use something generic like your name or your business name.

4. Select the time zone country and time zone, and then click on **Continue**.

5. Enter your name and country, and click on **Continue** again. Then you will need to accept the Google Analytics terms of service.

After you have accepted the terms, you will be given a snippet of HTML code that you'll need to insert into the pages of your website. The snippet will look like the following:

```
<script>
   (function(i,s,o,g,r,a,m){i['GoogleAnalyticsObject']=r;i[r]=i[r]||fu
nction(){
   (i[r].q=i[r].q||[]).push(arguments)},i[r].l=1*new Date();a=s.
createElement(o),
   m=s.getElementsByTagName(o)[0];a.async=1;a.src=g;m.parentNode.
insertBefore(a,m)
   })(window,document,'script','//www.google-analytics.com/analytics.
js','ga');  ga('create', 'UA-xxxxxx-x', 'auto');
   ga('send', 'pageview');</script>
```

The code must be placed just before the closing `head` tag in each page on your website. There are several ways to install the code. Check first to see if your WordPress template offers a field to insert the code in the template admin area — most modern templates offer this feature. If not, you can insert the code manually just before the closing the `</head>` tag, which you will find in the file called `header.php` within your WordPress template files. There is yet a third way to do this, if you don't want to tinker with your WordPress code. You can download and install one of the many WordPress analytics plugins. Two sound choices for an analytics plugin would be Google Analyticator or Google Analytics by Yoast; both the plugins are available at Wordpress.org.

If you have more than one website, you can add more websites within your analytics account. Personally, I like to keep one website per analytics account just to keep things neat, but some like to have all their websites under one analytics account.

To add a second or third website to an analytics account, navigate to **Admin** on the top menu bar, and then pull down the menu under **Account** in the left column, and then click **Create a New Account**.

When you are done adding websites, click **Home** on the top menu bar to navigate to the main analytics page.

From here, you can select a web property. This is the screen that greets you when you log in to Google Analytics, the **Audience Overview** report. It offers an effective quick look at how your website is performing:

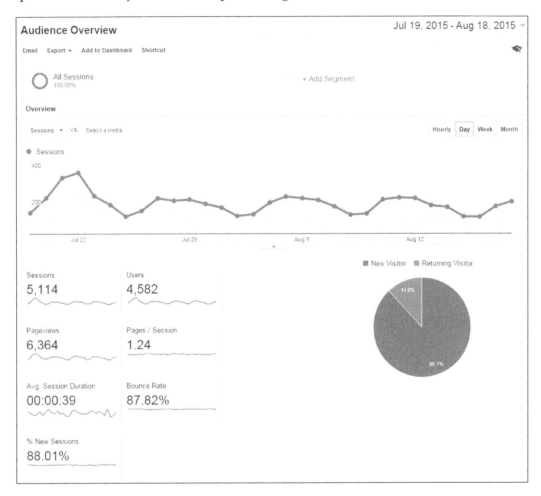

Using Google Analytics

Once you have installed Google Analytics on your websites, you'll need to wait a few weeks, or perhaps longer, for Analytics to collect enough data from your websites to be useful. Remember that with website analytics, like any type of statistical analysis, larger sets of data reveal more accurate and useful information. It may not take that long if you have a high-traffic site, but if you have a fairly new site that doesn't get a lot of traffic, it will take some time, so come back in a few weeks to a month to check to see how your sites are doing.

The **Audience Overview** report is your default report that is displayed to you when you first log into analytics and gives you a quick overview of each site's traffic.

You can see at a glance, whether the tracking code is receiving data, how many visits (sessions) your website has gotten in the past 30 days, the average time visitors stay on your site (session duration), your bounce rate (the percentage of users that come to visit your site and leave without visiting another page), and the percentage of new sessions (users that haven't visited before) in the past 30 days.

The data displayed on the dashboard is just a small taste of what you can learn from Google Analytics. To drill down to more detailed information, you'll navigate to other sections of analytics using the left menu. Your main report areas in analytics are Audience (who your visitors are), Acquisition (how your visitors found your site), Behavior (what your visitors did on your site), and Conversions (did they make a purchase or complete a contact form).

Within any of the main report areas are a dozens of available reports. Google Analytics can offer you tremendous detail on almost any imaginable metric related to your website. Most of your time, however, is best spent with a few key reports.

Understanding key analytics reports

Your key analytics reports will be the **Audience Overview**, **Acquisition Overview**, and the **Behavior Overview**. You access each of these reports by navigating to the left menu area and each corresponding overview report is the first link in each list.

The **Audience Overview** report is your default report, discussed earlier.

The **Acquisition Overview** report drills down into how your visitors are finding your site, whether it is through organic search, pay per click programs, social media, or referrals from other websites. These different pathways by which customers find your site are referred to as channels or mediums on other reports, but mean essentially the same thing. The **Acquisition Overview** report also shows some very basic conversion data, although the reports in the **Conversions** section offer much more meaningful conversion data. The following screenshot is an **Acquisition Overview** report:

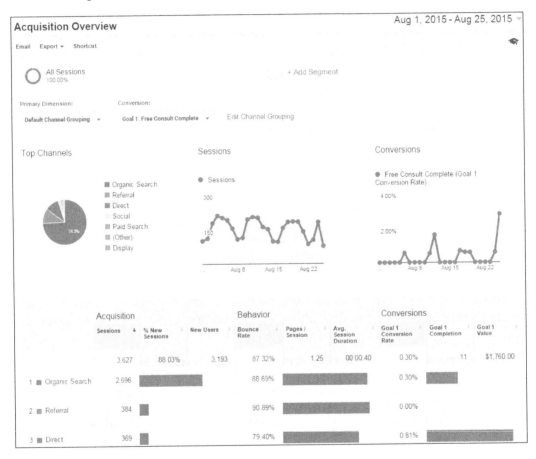

Why is the **Acquisition Overview** report important? It shows us the relative strength of our inbound channels. In the case above, organic search is delivering the highest number of users. This tells us that we are getting most of our users from the organic search results—our organic campaign is running strong. Referrals generated 384 visits, which means we've got good links delivering traffic. Our 369 direct visitors don't come from other websites, it's a fresh browser page where users type our URL directly or follow a bookmark they've saved. That is a welcome figure because it means we've got strong brand and name recognition, and in the conversions column on the right side of the table we can see that our direct traffic generated a measurable conversion rate. That's a positive sign that our brand recognition and reputation is strong.

The **Behavior Overview** report tells us how users behave once they visit our site. Are they bouncing immediately or viewing several pages? What content are they viewing the most? Here's a sample **Behavior Overview** report:

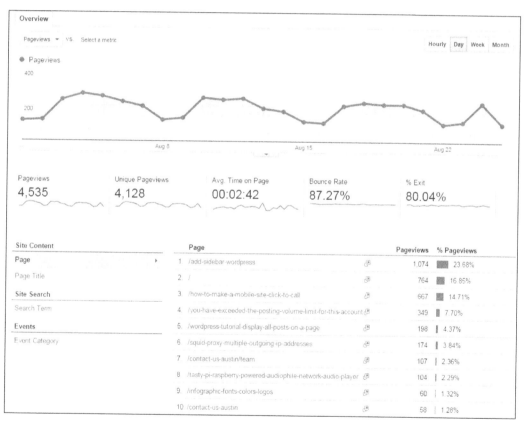

Some information is repeated on the **Behavior Overview** report, such as **Pageviews** and **Bounce Rate**. What is important here is the table under the graph. This table shows you the relative popularity of your pages. This data is important because it shows you what content is generating the most user interest. As you can see from the table, the page titled **/add-sidebar-wordpress** generated over 1,000 pageviews, more than the home page, which is indicated in analytics by a single slash (/).

This table shows you your most popular content—these pages are your greatest success. And remember, you can click on any individual page and then see individual metrics for that page.

One way to maximize your site earnings is to focus on improving the performance of the pages that are already earning money. Chances are, you earn at least 80 percent of your income from the top 20 percent of the pages on your site. Focus on improving the rankings for those pages in order to get the best return for your efforts.

With any analytics report, by default the statistics shown will all be for the past month, but you can adjust the time period by clicking on the down arrow next to the dates in the upper right hand corner.

Setting up automated analytics reports

You can also use Google Analytics to e-mail you daily, weekly, or monthly reports.

To enable this feature, simply navigate to the report that you'd like to be sent to you. Then click the **Email** link just under the report title. The following pop-up will appear:

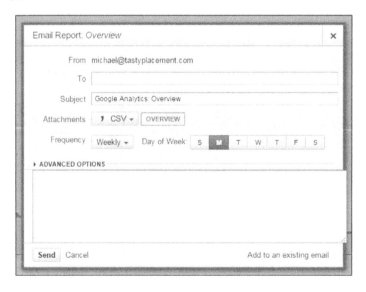

The **Frequency** field lets you determine how often the report is sent, or you can simply send the report one time.

Google Webmasters/Search Console

The process of setting up an account with Google's Search Console (formerly Google Webmasters, and formerly Google Webmaster Tools) has already been covered earlier in this book, along with a basic overview of the different tools available. Now, we are going to go into a bit more detail, and show you how to use Google Webmaster Tools to obtain information that you can use to improve your website.

Understanding your website's search queries

The Search Console now shows you data on what search queries users entered in Google search to find their way to your website. This is valuable: it teaches you what query terms are effectively delivering customers. To see the report, expand **Search Traffic** on the left navigation menu and select **Search Analytics**. The following report will display:

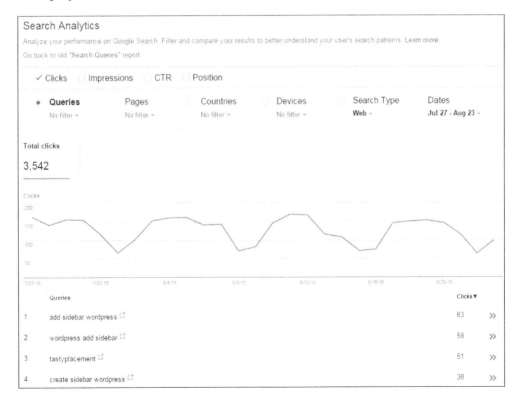

Examine the top queries that Search Console shows you are getting traffic for, and add them to your list of keywords to work on, if they are not already there. You will probably find that it is most beneficial to focus on those keywords that are currently ranked between #4 and #10 in Google, to try to get them moved up to one of the top three spots.

You'll also want to check for crawl errors on each of your sites while you work in the Search Console. A crawl error is an error that Google's spider encounters when trying to find pages on your site. A dead link, a link to a page on your site that no longer exists, is a common and perfect example of a crawl error.

Crawl errors are detrimental to rankings. First, crawl errors send a poor quality signal to search engines. Remember that Google wants to deliver a great experience to users of its search engine and properties. Dead links and lost pages do not deliver a great experience to users.

To see the crawl error data, expand the **Crawl** link on the left navigation bar and then click **Crawl Errors**. The crawl error report will show you any pages that Google attempted to read but could not reach. Not all entries on this report are bad news. If you remove a piece of content that Google crawled in the past, Google will attempt for months to try to find that piece of content again. So, a removed page will generate a crawl error. Another way crawl errors get generated is if you have a sitemap file with page entries that no longer exist. Even inbound links from third party websites to pages that don't exist will generate crawl errors.

Other errors you find might be the result of a typo or the other error that involves going into a specific page on your website to fix. For example, perhaps you made a mistake typing in the URL when linking from one page to another, resulting in a 404 error. To fix that, you need to edit the page that the URL with the error was linked from and correct the URL.

Other errors might require editing the files for your template to fix multiple errors simultaneously. For example, if you see that the Googlebot is getting a 404 (page not found) error every time it attempts to crawl the comments feed for a post, then the template file probably doesn't have the right format for creating those URLs. Once you correct the template file, all of the crawl errors related to that problem will be fixed.

There are other things you can do in Google Webmaster Tools, for example, you can check to see how many links to your site Google is detecting.

Checking your website's code with a HTML Validator

HyperText Markup Language (HTML) is a coding standard with a reasonable degree of complexity. HTML standards develop over time, and a valid HTML code displays more websites more accurately in a wider range of browsers. Sites that have substantial amounts of HTML coding errors can potentially be punished by search engines. For this reason, you should periodically check your website for HTML coding errors.

There are two principal tools that web professionals use to check the quality of their websites' code: the W3C HTML Validator and the CSE HTML Validator.

The W3C HTML Validator (`http://validator.w3.org`) is the less robust of the two validators, but it is free. Both validators work in the same way: they examine the code on your website and issue a report advising you of any errors.

The CSE HTML Validator (`http://htmlvalidator.com`) is not a free tool, but you can get a free trial of the software that is good for 30 days or 200 validations, whichever comes first. This software catches errors in HTML, XHTML, CSS, PHP, and JavaScript. It also checks your links to ensure that they are all valid. It includes an accessibility checker, spell checker, and a SEO checker. With all of these functions, there is a good chance that if your website has any problems, the CSE HTML Validator will be able to find them.

After downloading and installing the demo version of CSE HTML Validator, you will be given the option to go to a page that contains two video demos. It is a good idea to watch these videos, or at least the HTML validation video, before trying to use the program. They are not very long, and watching them will reduce the amount of time it takes you to learn to use the program.

To validate a file that is on your hard drive, first open the file in the editor, then click the down arrow next to the **Validate** button on the task bar. You will see several options. **Selecting Full** will give you not only errors, but messages containing suggestions as well. **Errors only** will only show you actual errors, and **Errors and warnings only** will tell you if there are things that could be errors, but might not be. You can experiment with the different options to see which one you like best.

After you select a validation option, a box will appear at the bottom of the screen listing all of the errors, as well as warnings and messages depending on the option you chose. You might be surprised at how many errors there are, especially if you are using WordPress to create the code for your site. The code is often not as clean as you might expect it to be. However, not all of the errors you see will be things that you need to worry about or correct.

Yes, it is better to have a website with perfect coding, but one of the advantages of using WordPress is that you don't have to know how to code to build a website. If you do not know anything about HTML coding, you may do more harm than good by trying to fix minor errors, such as omission of a slash at the end of a tag. Most of these errors will not cause problems anyhow. You should look through the errors and fix the ones you know how to fix. If you are completely mystified by what you see here, don't worry about it too much unless you are having a problem with the way your website loads or displays. If the errors are causing problems, you'll either have to learn a bit about coding or hire someone who knows what they're doing to fix your website.

If you want to be able to check the code of an entire website at once, you'll need to buy the Pro version of CSE HTML Validator. You can then use the batch wizard to check your website. This feature is not available in the Standard or Lite versions of the software. To use the batch wizard, click on **Tools**, then **Batch Wizard**. A new window will pop up, allowing you to choose the files you want to check. Click on the button with the large green plus sign, and select the appropriate option to add files or URLs to your list. You can add files individually, add an entire folder, or even add a URL.

1. To check an entire site, you can add the root file for your domain from your hard drive, or you can add the URL for the root domain.
2. Once you have added your target, click on it.
3. Now, click on **Target** in the main menu bar, then on **Properties**.
4. Click on the **Follow Links** tab in the box that pops up, then check the box in front of **Follow and validate links**.
5. Click on the **OK** button and then click on the **Process** button to start validating.

Checking your inbound link count with Bing Webmaster

Bing Webmaster allows you to get information about backlinks, crawl errors, and search traffic to your websites. In order to get the maximum value from this tool, you'll need to authenticate each of your websites to prove that you own them. To get started, go to `https://www.bing.com/webmaster/` and sign up with your Microsoft account. As a part of the sign up process, you'll get a HTML file that you'll install in the root directory of your WordPress installation. This file validates that you are the owner of the website and entitled to see the data that Bing collects.

One core use for Bing Webmaster is that it presents a highly accurate picture of one's inbound link counts. If you recall, Google does not present accurate inbound link counts to users. Thus, Bing Webmaster is the most authoritative picture from a search engine that you'll have of how many backlinks your site enjoys.

To see your inbound links, simply log in and navigate to the **Dashboard**. At the lower right you'll see the Inbound Links table shown here:

INBOUND LINKS 36552 ⓘ	
Links pointed at your website	
TARGET PAGE	**COUNT OF LINKS**
http://www.tastyplacement.com/	19,944
https://www.tastyplacement.com/infographic-testing-social-media-signals-in-search	139
https://www.tastyplacement.com/	89
	See all 59

The table shows you the inbound links to your website for each page of content. This helpful feature lets you determine which articles of content are garnering the most interest from the other webmasters. High link counts are always good, but you also want to make sure you are getting high quality links from websites in the same general category as your site.

Bing offers an additional feature: link keyword research. Expand the **Diagnostics & Tools** entry on the navigation bar on the left, and click **Keyword Research**.

The search traffic section will give you valuable information about the search terms you should be targeting for your site, as well as allowing you to see which of the terms you are already targeting are getting traffic. Just as you did with the keywords shown in Google Analytics and Google Webmaster Tools, you want to find keywords that are getting traffic, but are not currently ranked in the top one to three positions in the search engine results pages. Send more links to these pages with the keyword phrase you want to target as anchor text in order to move these pages up in the rankings.

Monitoring ranking positions and movement with Rank Tracker

We've tried in this book to present as many free tools as possible to help you with your optimization. Rank Tracker is a paid tool and we've included it because it is tremendously valuable and noteworthy. Rank Tracker is a software tool that can monitor your website's rankings for thousands of terms in hundreds of different search engines. Even more, it maintains a historical ranking data that helps you gauge your progress as you work. It is a valuable tool that is used by many SEO professionals. There is a free version, although the free version does not allow you to save your work (and thus does not let you save historical information). To really harness the power of this software, you'll need the paid version. You can download either version from `http://www.link-assistant.com/rank-tracker/`. After you install the program, you will be prompted to enter the URL of your website. On the next screen, the program will ask you to input the keywords you wish to track. If you have them all listed in a spreadsheet somewhere you can just copy the column that has your keywords in it and paste them all into the tool. Then Rank Tracker will ask you which search engines you are targeting and will check the rank of each keyword in all of the search engines you select. It only takes a few minutes for Rank Tracker to update hundreds of keywords, so you can find out where you are ranking in very little time.

This screenshot shows the main interface of the Rank Tracker software. For monitoring progress on large numbers of keywords on several different search engines, Rank Tracker can be a real time-saver:

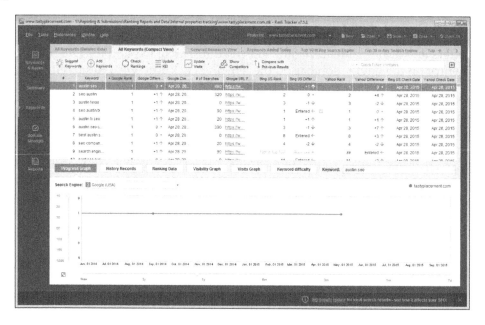

Once your rankings have been updated, you can sort them by rank to see which ones will benefit the most from additional link building. Remember that more than half of the people who search for something in Google click on the first result. If you are not in the top three to five results, you will get very little traffic from people searching for your targeted keyword. For this reason, you will usually get the best results by working on the keywords that are ranking between #4 and #10 in the search engine results pages.

If you want more data to play with, you can click on **Update KEI** to find out the keyword effectiveness index for each keyword. This tool gathers the data from Google to tell you how many searches per month and how much competition there is for each keyword, and then calculates the KEI score based on that data. As a general rule, the higher the KEI number is, the easier it will be to rank for a given keyword. Keep in mind, however, that if you are already ranking for the keyword, it will usually not be that difficult to move up in the rankings, even if the KEI is low. To make it easier to see which keywords will be easy to rank, they are color-coded in the Rank Tracker tool. The easiest ones are green, and the hardest are red. Yellow and orange fall in between.

In addition to checking your rankings on keywords you are targeting, you can use the Rank Tracker tool to find more keywords to target. If you navigate to **Tools** and then **Get Keyword Suggestions**, a window will pop up that will let you choose from a range of different methods of finding keywords. It is recommended that you start with the Google AdWords Keyword Tool. After you choose the method, you'll be asked to enter keywords that are relevant to the content of your website. You will only get about 100 results no matter how many keywords you enter, so it's best to work on just one at a time. On the next page, you will be presented with a list of keywords. Select the ones you want to add and click on **Next**. When the tool is done updating the data for the selected keywords, click on the **Finish** button to add them to your project.

You can repeat this process as many times as you want to find new keywords for your website, and you can experiment with the other fifteen tools as well, which should give you more variety. When you find keywords that look promising, put them on a list and plan on writing posts to target those keywords in the future. Look for keywords that have at least 100 searches per month, with a relatively low amount of competition.

Rank Tracker not only allows you to check your current rankings, but it also keeps track of your historical data as well. Every time you update, a new point will be added to the progress graph so you can see your progress over time. This allows you to see whether what you are doing is working or not. If you see that your rank is dropping for a certain keyword, you can use that information to figure out whether something you changed had the opposite effect that you intended.

If you are doing SEO for clients, you'll find the reports in Rank Tracker to be extremely useful (if not mandatory). You can create a monthly report for each client that shows how many keywords are ranked #1, as well as how many are in the top 10, 20, or 100. The report also shows the number of keywords that moved up and the number that moved down. You can use these reports to show your clients how much progress you are making and demonstrate your value to the client.

If you want to take advantage of the historical data, you'll have to purchase the paid version of Rank Tracker. The free version does not support saving your projects, so you won't have data from your past rankings to compare and see whether you are moving up or down in the search engine results. You also won't be able to generate reports that tell you what has changed from the last time you updated your rankings.

Monitoring backlinks with Majestic SEO

If you want to see how many backlinks you have pointing to your site, along with a range of additional data, the king of free backlink tools is the powerful Majestic SEO backlink checker tool. To use this tool, go to `https://majestic.com/` and enter your domain in the box at the top of the page. The tool will generate a report that shows how many URLs are indexed for your domain, how many total backlinks you have, and how many unique domains link to your website. For heavy-duty link reconnaissance, you'll want the paid upgrade. Underneath the site info, you can see the stats for each page on your site. The tool shows the number of backlinks for each page, as well as the number of domains linking to each page. You can only see 10 results per page, so you'll have to click through numerous pages to see all of the results if you have a large site.

Majestic SEO offers a few details that you won't get from Google or Bing Webmaster. Majestic SEO calculates and reports the number of separate C class subnets upon which your backlinks appear. As we have learned, links from sites on separate C class subnets are more valuable because they are perceived by search engines as being truly non-duplicate links. Majestic SEO also reports the number of `.edu` and `.gov` upon which your links appear. This extra information gives you a clear picture of how effective your link building efforts are progressing. Majestic offers another feature of note: Majestic crawls the web more deeply, so you'll see higher link counts. Majestic is particularly useful when doing link cleanup because it scrapes low-value sites that Google and Bing don't bother indexing.

This screenshot highlights some of Majestic SEO's more robust features: it shows you the number of backlinks from .edu and .gov domains as well as the number of separate Class C subnets upon which your inbound links appear:

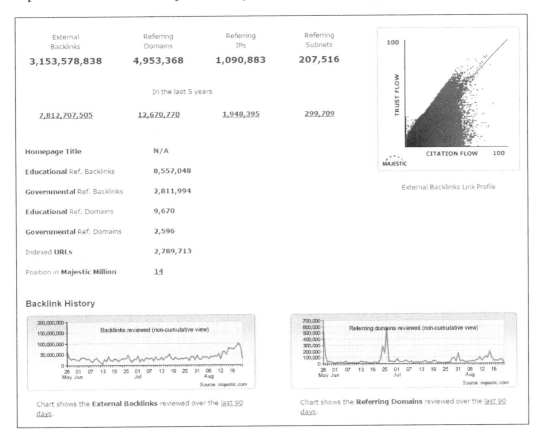

Majestic SEO offers one more special feature, it records and graphs your backlink acquisition over time. The graph in the preceding screenshot shows this feature in action.

Majestic SEO is not a search engine, so it will show you a count of inbound links without any regards to the quality of the pages on which your links appear. Put another way, Bing Webmaster will only show you links that appear on indexed pages. Lower value pages, such as pages with duplicate content or pages in low-value link directories, tend not to appear in search engine indexes. As such, Majestic SEO reports higher link counts than Bing Webmaster or Google.

Summary

In this chapter, we learned how to monitor your progress through the use of free and paid tools. We learned how to set up and employ Google Analytics to measure and monitor where your website visitors are coming from and how they behave on your site. We learned how to set up and use Google Webmaster Tools to detect crawling errors on your site and learned how Googlebot interacts with your site. We discovered two HTML validation tools that you can use to ensure that your website's code meets current HTML standards.

Finally, we learned how to measure and monitor your backlink efforts with Bing Webmaster and Majestic SEO. With the tools and techniques in this chapter, you can ensure that your optimization efforts are effective and remain on track.

WordPress SEO Plugins

WordPress takes a lot of the work out of website design, coding, monitoring, and SEO, by allowing you to install plugins to accomplish a variety of tasks for you. There are WordPress plugins for almost every conceivable task. There are plugins that can automatically add meta tags, generate internal links, check for broken links, and more. In this Appendix, we'll cover some of the most helpful and powerful plugins that can help you take your WordPress site to the next level. Keep in mind, however, that plugins are only available for self-hosted WordPress sites; plugins are not available for WordPress.com websites.

So what's changed in the plugin environment for WordPress over the past few years? First, plugins have become generally more sophisticated and stable, which is good news for the webmasters. Second, there has been a growth in the scope of many plugins. For example, in previous years you might need a general SEO plugin for controlling titles and meta tags, another plugin to clean up the WordPress head (like the HeadSpace plugin), and yet another for controlling the noindexing of category and tag pages. Today, the Yoast SEO plugin performs all these functions.

All in One SEO Pack

All in One SEO Pack is a WordPress plugin that helps you optimize your WordPress blog for SEO. There are several SEO plugins for WordPress, but the All in One SEO Pack has emerged as one of the most popular and effective plugins, although it does take second place to the immensely popular and successful Yoast SEO plugin. If you are hung up between installing All in One SEO Pack and Yoast SEO, Yoast is probably the better choice. Never install two full-featured SEO plugins, you'll encounter problems.

If you're not sure what you want it to do, you can just install and activate it, but for the best results, you really should learn about the options that are available, and how they affect the SEO of your website. The All in One SEO Pack supports canonical URLs, optimizes your titles, automatically generates meta tags on each page, and helps you avoid duplicate content. You can download the All in One SEO Pack at `http://wordpress.org/extend/plugins/all-in-one-seo-pack/`.

Yoast SEO

Yoast SEO is the granddaddy of all SEO plugins. With nearly 21 million downloads, it's easily the most widely used SEO plugin. We've discussed it throughout this book. Yoast SEO optimizes title tags, meta tags, and even adds open graph code to your pages and posts. There is a bit of a learning curve with Yoast SEO, so it'll take longer to set up.

You can download Yoast SEO at `https://wordpress.org/plugins/wordpress-seo/`.

Gravity Forms Contact Form Mailer

The Gravity Forms plugin allows you to create a form on your WordPress site, and have the information submitted by the users sent to any e-mail address you choose automatically, whenever a user submits the form. You can use this plugin for anything, from a simple contact form to a long survey containing hundreds of questions. For marketers concerned with reliable delivery of customer contact forms, a great mailer plugin is a must. Gravity Forms is certainly reliable, easy to use, full-featured, and is a common choice among serious professionals. It is, however, a paid plugin, available for $39. Curiously, the plugin is not available at WordPress.org. The Gravity Forms Contact Form Mailer can be downloaded from `http://www.gravityforms.com/`.

Contact Form 7

This plugin provides an easy way for you to insert a contact form on your WordPress site. This plugin functions much like the Gravity Forms Contact Form Mailer plugin described above, but offers less functionality than the fully paid version of Gravity Forms. Contact Form 7 can handle multiple contact forms on the same site and supports Akismet spam filtering and CAPTCHA. The plugin is available for download at `http://wordpress.org/extend/plugins/contact-form-7/`.

Duplicate Post

The Duplicate Post plugin allows you to create quick duplicates of both Pages and Posts. This plugin is handy for creating quick alternative Pages for, say, if you want to create six service pages for six different cities in your region. The plugin duplicates not only the text, but all the tags, custom fields, title, and meta entries (if you are using a SEO plugin).

The plugin gives you two different ways to create a duplicate version of any Post or Page on your website. From the **Edit** posts or **Edit** pages navigation pages within the dashboard, you can click on the **Duplicate** link for the post or page you want to copy. You can also make a copy while you are in edit mode, by clicking on **Copy to a new draft**, which appears above the **Move to Trash** link.

Of course, once you have created a duplicate of your post using the plugin, you'll need to edit it so that it is not exactly the same as the original. The duplicate post gives you a good place to start if you are publishing a similar article, but you should rewrite some portion of the content, so that the search engines will index both copies. If you have two identical articles on your site, the search engines will pick one to display and may ignore the other completely. The Duplicate Post plugin is a useful tool to have if you frequently publish content that is similar to other content on your website, such as the localized versions of the same sort of information for different cities. You can download the Duplicate Post plugin from `http://wordpress.org/extend/plugins/duplicate-post/`.

Broken Link Checker

One of the best kept secrets among power bloggers and serious SEO professionals that work in the WordPress environment is the Broken Link Checker plugin. The Broken Link Checker plugin constantly monitors your site for broken links, and offers you speedy and simple choices for addressing the invalid links. The Broken Link Checker plugin will monitor both your internal and outgoing links, even links in the user comments and images.

See the following screenshot showing the Broken Link Checker's admin area:

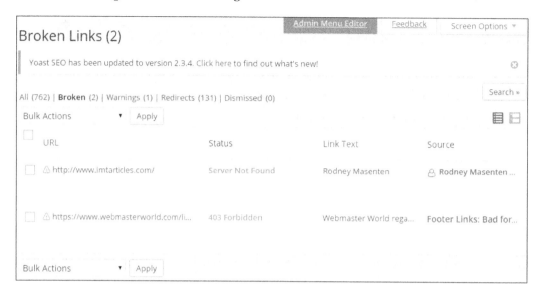

Broken links are listed and the plugin offers you several administration options for addressing any dead links that the plugin discovers.

If the plugin finds any links that are no longer working, you will see a number inside of a black circle next to **Broken Links**, in the left navigation bar of your admin panel. If you click on the link, you will be taken to a page that lists all of the links that were not working properly last time they were checked. The error status for each link is displayed, along with the amount of time the link has been broken. Underneath each link, you will have the option of editing the URL, unlinking it, or telling the plugin that it is not broken. The page on which the link appears is also provided. Below the page title, there are options to edit the article, put it in the trash, or view it.

This plugin is essential for nearly any site, especially large sites and sites that allow public commenting on posts. It would be overly burdensome to check all of the links on your WordPress website manually on a regular basis. Remember that search engines are all about the user experience: search engines reward sites that keep broken links to a minimum. You can change the options in Broken Link Checker, to tell the plugin how often you want your links to be checked, and it runs in the background so you never have to think about it unless a broken link is found. The Broken Link Checker plugin can be downloaded from `http://wordpress.org/ extend/plugins/broken-link-checker/`.

Google XML Sitemaps

Google XML Sitemaps is a plugin that creates an XML sitemap for your WordPress site, that serves as a road map for search engines so they can reliably and effectively crawl all the content on your site. The plugin is simple to use; all you have to do is install it and activate it. The plugin does the rest. You can download it from `http://wordpress.org/extend/plugins/google-sitemap-generator/`. After installing the plugin, you'll want to register your sitemap by logging in to Google Webmaster Tools at `http://www.google.com/webmasters/` and navigating to **Crawl** and then **Sitemaps**.

Akismet

Akismet ships with new installations of Wordpress. You'll find it already installed when you first set up your site. Akismet is a valuable anti-spam plugin that guards against the pervasive problem of comment spam. It is very effective at preventing spam that it blocks about 99 percent of all spam comments. You'll need to sign up at `http://akismet.com/` to get a free key to run the program. There are paid versions, but the basic functionality is available with the free offering.

Wordfence

WordPress security is an important consideration. It's a fair criticism of WordPress to say that the platform does allow, in some configurations, a hacker to gain access to your site. Generally, WordPress's security depends on the user keeping core files and plugin files updated.

Wordfence doesn't replace a user's responsibility to keep WordPress updated and secure, but offers additional layers of protection. It's very broadly featured, with dozens of available security settings, everything from scanning core files for changes, to blocking individual countries. The free version is certainly worthwhile, while the paid version adds additional layers of protection. There are a lot of settings here — and that's a good thing — but it will take some time to get it set up correctly.

WP Super Cache

The WP Super Cache plugin reduces the load on your server by storing static HTML files for the pages on your website and serving those, instead of running WordPress's PHP scripts every time a page is loaded. Google will penalize your site in the rankings if your pages take too long to load, and using a caching plugin such as WP Super Cache helps speed up the load time. It is especially helpful to use this type of plugin, if you have a lot of other plugins running on your website, because each plugin is another script that must be run each time your site loads and this slows down your load time. You can get the WP Super Cache plugin from `http://wordpress.org/extend/plugins/wp-super-cache/`. WP Super Cache is installed by default by some hosting companies. Remember to disable WP Super Cache when making design changes to your website, so you can see your design changes in real-time, rather than seeing a cached version of your pages.

WPtouch

The WPtouch plugin transforms your blog into a mobile-friendly theme, that can be displayed on the iPhone, Android, iPod Touch, Samsung Touch, Opera Mini, Palm Pre, and BlackBerry Storm/Touch. The plugin gives your blog a mobile option without changing your regular blog theme. Users have the option of switching between the regular theme and the mobile theme.

WPtouch is amazingly full-featured, but with those features comes a bit of complexity. With a little tweaking, you should be able to set up a mobile version of your blog in about 45 minutes. WPtouch is available in both, a free and paid version for about 40 dollars. The free version is remarkably full-featured. Keep in mind, though, that WPtouch is a less desirable alternative to a fully responsive design. But if your site is non-responsive and you don't have the resources for an immediate redesign, WPtouch can serve as a suitable alternative.

You can download WPtouch from `http://wordpress.org/extend/plugins/wptouch/`.

WooCommerce

If you're selling products or services online, you want your website to look like a store, not a blog. WooCommerce, from WooThemes, allows you to set up an online e-commerce site easily using WordPress. There are other e-commerce options for WordPress, but WooCommerce is the undisputed leader, and there is very little reason to use any other e-commerce solution.

WooCommerce is available in both free and paid versions, with several optional paid extensions, such as additional shipping modules and a fancy drag and drop shopping cart widget. The free version will allow you to set up a basic shopping cart within your WordPress installation and accept PayPal and credit card payments. However, WooCommerce will not serve as a substitute for a dedicated shopping cart such as Magento, which can painlessly handle tens of thousands of products, and manage thousands of transactions. WooCommerce is for smaller e-commerce stores with lower volume.

Download the plugin from `https://wordpress.org/plugins/woocommerce/`.

Yet Another Related Posts Plugin

As the title suggests, **Yet Another Related Posts Plugin (YARPP)** is one of the several related posts plugins available for WordPress. YARPP has emerged as the most effective and widely used of this family of plugins. YARPP analyzes the categories and tags of your Posts and automatically generates a list of related Posts at the end of each of your blog entries, once you have the plugin installed and set up. Including a set of related Posts tends to keep the visitors on your site longer and fully engaged with your content. But, before you install it, make sure your template does not have similar functionality already backed into your design.

You can set a threshold for the similarity level, so that the plugin will not display any Posts, unless you meet the minimum level of relatedness that you require. You can also set the plugin to ignore posts that are in certain categories, or those with specific tags when determining which posts to display. YARPP is available for download at `http://wordpress.org/extend/plugins/yet-another-related-posts-plugin/`.

FooBox HTML & Media Lightbox

FooBox HTML & Media Lightbox dresses up your image galleries and images within posts, with attractive and responsible lightbox features, and highly effective social sharing buttons. In the screenshot below, you can see how FooBox encourages the sharing of your images by bringing the focus of the image forward with a lightbox effect.

FooBox integrates seamlessly with all the major WordPress gallery plugins, with WooCommerce product images, and with Gravity Forms. FooBox is a paid plugin, with licenses starting at $27 per year.

B

Other SEO Resources

There are many SEO resources online that can help you learn the best practices for optimizing your websites. The algorithms used by the major search engines are constantly changing, so you can't expect to learn everything, set your site up according to the currently recommended SEO methods, and then forget about it. You need to keep up with the changes that are being made so that you can determine if and how you need to change your SEO strategy to adapt to the search algorithms as they are updated. Here are some resources, that can help you stay on top of the search engine optimization for your website.

Online forums

Nearly all readers will be familiar with the online forums. Online forums are topical discussion websites dedicated to a particular category or interest. There are online forums for every conceivable topic from sports, to hotel management, to search engine optimization. You can garner a lot of useful information from online forums dedicated to SEO, but you can also be led down the wrong path, if you're not careful. Some of the techniques you read about in online forums may be frowned upon by the search engines. We've learned about black hat techniques, and in online forums, you'll encounter both purveyors and advocates of these forbidden methods.

Every possible black hat technique ever conceived will be either described or offered in SEO forums: automated content, automated comment posting, link farms, and worse. We've learned, however, that all of the automated shortcuts you'll discover will qualify as black hat or gray hat, and are to be avoided.

When participating in online forums, consider the reputation of the speaker. Most online forums have some grading system and some even have a trading score, to monitor how trustworthy participants have been in business transactions with other forum members.

With that in mind, here are some forums where you can learn more about Internet marketing and SEO.

The Warrior Forum

The Warrior Forum is one of the largest Internet marketing forums on the Web. It is located at `http://www.warriorforum.com/`. The forum is divided into two sections: the free forum and the War Room. There is a one-time fee of $37 to join the War Room. Free members can read and post on the main forums, but you must be a War Room member to access the War Room forum, post a Warrior Special Offer, create a Warrior Forum blog, start a Warrior Forum group, or start a thread in the Warrior joint venture forum. War Room members can also send private messages to other members without restriction. Free members must make 50 posts before they can send private messages.

To give you an idea of how popular the Warrior Forum is, there are often around 8000 users viewing the main Internet marketing discussion forum at one time. This is the part of the forum where you will learn the most about Internet marketing. The Warrior Special Offers section is the section where the War Room members can post their own e-books and other products for sale at a special price for Warriors. The products offered in this section must be a better deal than what is offered to the general public. This can mean a lower price or extras that are not normally included with the product.

The Warrior Forum also has a section where Warriors can advertise their products and services, at their regular prices. This is the Warrior **Products & Services** section, and you can find complete websites for sale, classified ads for products, and service advertisements by Warriors who offer writing, programming, or other services. There are also sections in the forums to discuss ad networks, offline marketing, copywriting, AdSense, search engine optimization, and other Internet marketing topics.

The Digital Point forum

The Digital Point forum is located at `http://forums.digitalpoint.com/`. This is another popular forum for the SEO and Internet marketing community. There are boards for the major search engines: Google, Yahoo!, and Microsoft, where you can find information about the specific search engine you are trying to target. Some of the other boards on the forum include general marketing, search engine optimization, social networks, link development, pay per click advertising, and affiliate programs. You can also find information on running an e-commerce business, designing websites, and content management.

The most popular section of the Digital Point forum is the Buy, Sell, or Trade section. If you want to buy websites or domains, this is a good place to start looking. Be careful, though, because there have been some instances, where either the buyer or the seller has been ripped off. It's a good idea to use an escrow service when purchasing a domain or a website, especially if the price is high.

SEO Chat forums

The SEO Chat forums located at `http://forums.seochat.com/` have sections for discussion about each of the major search engines. There are also sections for search engine optimization, content management, affiliate marketing, keywords, e-commerce sites, and local search. Other topics include pay per click advertising, Google AdWords, HTML, SEO tools, analyzing website statistics, and testing SEO strategies. The SEO Chat forums are smaller and less vital to your education than Warrior Forum and Digital Point, but it's still worth checking out.

Google's tools for website owners

Google offers a range of tools that can help with search engine optimization. We've gone in depth with many of these resources, but here is a quick review of all of the tools Google offers; that you can use to improve your website's search engine optimization, as well as the tools you can use to monetize your site.

Google AdSense

Google AdSense is Google's advertising revenue sharing program for publishers. If you participate in this program, you can place Google text ads on your website and you will receive a share of the revenue from those ads when visitors click on them. You need to earn at least $100, before you can receive a payment.

Google AdWords

Google AdWords is Google's principal pay per click advertising program. Google's AdWords program allows you to place and purchase pay per click ads on the Google search engine results pages, as well as on Google Content Network, which consists of other people's websites. If you place ads through the Google Content Network through AdWords, they could appear on any of the websites that participate in the AdSense program.

Google Alerts

Google Alerts is a monitoring and notification system that alerts you whenever Google discovers new content, that includes a keyword, search term, or a phrase that you specify. These alerts can be sent to your e-mail address, or you can subscribe to them by RSS in any feed reader.

One way to use this service is for finding ideas to write about when you need new content for your website. Alternatively, you can use Google alerts to learn about new mentions of your company in links or on other websites. Let us take it a step further; you can set alerts for your competitor's business name, and discover where they are promoting or getting mentions. Alerts are based on query terms so get creative and broaden your thinking, about what sorts of alerts you would like to receive. Alerts can be particularly effective when trying to identify fresh content to share in social media.

The following screenshot shows a Google Alert that was triggered by new content that included the search term `tasty placement`. This specific alert advises of a newly-discovered Pinterest pin of content we produced:

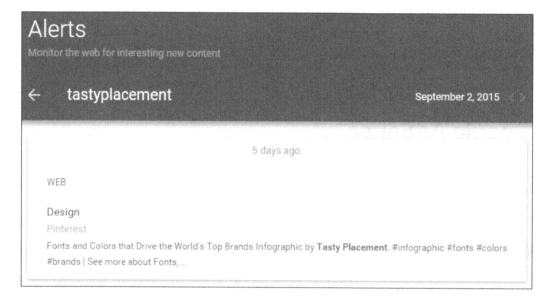

Google Merchant Center

Google Merchant Center is a Google service, where you can upload and manage product listings that you want to appear in Google Product Search, AdWords, and other Google properties. Google Merchant Center has been improved greatly in recent years. This service has gone through several invocations and name changes in its path to its current format. Previously, it bore the name Google Base.

If you sell tangible goods, Google Merchant Center is a mandatory additional channel, by which you can distribute your goods. Your products will appear in Google Product Search, and in some cases, alongside organic results in general Google searches. Google Merchant Center is more effective if you employ automatic data feeds to submit your products. The data feed system is well documented and can easily accommodate tens of thousands of products.

The following screenshot shows a product view from inside the Google Merchant Center. The analytics are helpful; you can see diagnostics and numbers of clicks for each of your products:

Other helpful SEO tools

Apart from the online forums and Google's robust offering, there are a range of specialized learning and diagnostic tools. What follows are a few tools that are especially helpful.

Copyscape

Copyscape is a free and paid online service that allows you to check an article, blog post or any piece of content, to make sure it doesn't contain content that has already been published somewhere on the Web. This is especially helpful if you are outsourcing the content writing for your website. Some writers may try to copy articles they find online and pass them off as their own. You can use Copyscape to make sure that the content you're buying is truly original. The free service is limited, but available and helpful for occasional use. The cost of the paid service is $0.05 per credit, and it consumes one credit for each article you check. You need to buy a minimum of 100 or 200 credits at a time, depending on your payment method. You can find the tool at `http://www.copyscape.com`.

The Pingdom Site Speed Checker

Pingdom offers a free tool that allows you to test the load time of any page on your website. The Pingdom Site Speed Checker is located at `http://tools.pingdom.com/`. Just type the URL of any web page in the box and click on Test Now. The test results will tell you how long the page takes to load completely, how many files make up the page, how many scripts and images are loaded, and more. With this tool, you can diagnose slow loading pages. If your pages take more than three to five seconds to load, you might consider reducing the file sizes of large image files. Pingdom will give you the load time per element, so you'll know which files are consuming the bulk of your load times.

In some cases, more significant problems can cause slow website loading times. Sadly, the cause is often poor performance of the web hosting server itself. This is a common problem on discounted shared hosting accounts. The hosting companies often sell hosting accounts on shared servers to hundreds of webmasters. Shared hosting means shared processing power, shared RAM, and shared bandwidth; all this can translate into slow loading times. Pingdom's Site Speed Checker can help you diagnose your web server's performance.

HubSpot's Website Grader

HubSpot is a purveyor of a reasonably effective do-it-yourself SEO solution for non-competitive markets. For a monthly fee, you get a host of online tools and access to consultants and webinars. The service is decent value for those willing to do the bulk of the work themselves. Among their free offerings (intended to introduce you to the HubSpot family of services) is HubSpot's Website Grader, located at `http://websitegrader.com`.

Just enter your website's URL and e-mail address, and the HubSpot Grader will deliver a report, which will be sent to you that analyzes your website for a group of optimization factors and determines a score from 1 to 100; if there is a blog on your site, it will receive a separate grade. And yes, you have to give your e-mail so expect some marketing pitches in your inbox.

The report also determines how many pages are indexed in Google and tells you the readability level of your site. Other information provided in the report includes the number of images on the page, the domain age, and the number of inbound links your site has. The report gives suggestions on how to improve your website's grade. The tool is a helpful one-stop glance at how effectively your optimization is progressing.

Flippa

Flippa is a marketplace where domains and existing websites are bought and sold. Flippa is a spin-off of the popular Sitepoint marketplace. Flippa is located at `https://flippa.com/`.

Flippa offers an auction format with a buy it now option. At any given time, Flippa will have about 1,000 listings. Websites from all niches are offered. Prices range from 50 dollars to hundreds of thousands of dollars for established sites with revenue. You can browse listings for free, but registration is required to send messages or bid on the websites for sale.

SEOmoz/Moz

Moz (formerly SEOmoz) offers SEO software tools for SEO professionals. Their plans start at $99 per month for the Pro package, which includes deep analysis for up to five campaigns, 250 keywords, 10,000 pages, two custom Q&As, and all of the Pro tools and guides. This software is not for the hobby blogger who is only making a few dollars per month. It is full-featured software that is highly respected within the industry.

The SEO Toolbar from Moz, on the other hand, is free, although somewhat restricted in features. This toolbar allows you to view information about the sites you visit, as you surf the Web. Metrics are given for Google, Yahoo!, and Bing. The toolbar also allows you to highlight nofollow links, so you can easily see whether the links on any given page pass link juice.

SEOmoz offers several other useful SEO tools. However, some of them require a Pro membership to be really useful. For example, the Open Site Explorer is a backlink checker that shows results for up to 1000 pages with a Pro membership, but free members can only see a few. The competitive link research tool helps you find sites your competitors are getting links from, and the juicy link finder tells you where other sites are getting links for your target keywords, but both of these tools are again available to Pro members only.

Other tools available through SEOmoz include a historical PageRank checker, which can give you a history of a website's PageRank, and the Linkscape Visualization and Comparison tool, which helps you compare the backlink profile of your website with that of a competitor. The Link Acquisition Assistant helps you find places where you might be able to get a high PR link for your website. You can find the site at `http://www.moz.com`.

Search Engine Journal

Search Engine Journal is a widely read, and widely respected search engine optimization blog and online magazine, that features articles by nine different writers (and guest authors) on a variety of topics related to search engines, especially Google. Topics covered recently include information that Google collects about its users, Google Places, and local search traffic. This website publishes new articles by SEO professionals on a regular basis.

You can find the Search Engine Journal at `http://www.searchenginejournal.com`.

Search Engine Roundtable

Another widely respected search engine optimization blog is an online magazine called; Search Engine Roundtable. The Search Engine Roundtable calls their site *the pulse of the search engine community*. The editors post regular articles about search engine news on a variety of topics. The Search Engine Roundtable has five editors and two writers who contribute content to the site. Find them at `http://www.seroundtable.com`.

ProBlogger

At ProBlogger (`http://www.problogger.com`), you'll find a variety of articles and videos about making money with your website. Examples of recent topics include how to run a contest on your blog, using a magazine to make your blog better, and finding ideas and inspiration. Darren Rowse makes a living from his blogs, which include TwiTip—Twitter Tips and Digital Photography School. His ProBlogger blog provides useful information about making affiliate sales, attracting subscribers, and monetization.

WebProNews

WebProNews publishes articles and educational information about search engines and e-commerce. Topics covered by this website include crafting good landing pages, remarketing to the customers who leave your site without buying anything, mobile web usage, marketing on social media sites, sales tax compliance, and more. You can find the site at `http://www.webpronews.com`.

David Mihm's Local Search Ranking Factors

David Mihm is a SEO professional with a focus on local search marketing. Each year, he publishes a definitive study on local search ranking factors. His study is more than a blog post; he interviews dozens of local search professionals, and invites them to contribute their assessment of specific ranking elements in local search. This annual post is the definitive analysis on the subject of local search factors. David Mihm no longer publishes the study on his own website, he now contributes the study to moz.com and you can find it at `https://moz.com/local-search-ranking-factors`.

Index

popularity patterns, spotting with Google Trends 55, 56

searching, with Google AdWords 72-74

keywords, prioritizing

about 68

accounting, for seasonal trends 69

competition, viewing 72

first tier keywords, building 68, 69

keywords, grouping into families 70, 71

negative keywords 69, 70

new keywords, searching 72

second tier keywords, building 68, 69

third tier keywords, building 68, 69

L

lettercount.com

URL 89

link anchor text

about 149

footer links 151

in HTML code 150, 151

repetitive links, from common IP addresses 151, 152

site-wide links 151

link bait

catchy title, using 169

controversial article, writing 168

creating, for building links 167

current events, writing 167

examples 169

expert, interviewing 168

give away, for attracting links 168

humorous story or article, sharing 167

information, developing 168

quizzes, creating 169

resource lists 167

testing 168

video content, creating 169

LinkedIn

used, for business promotion 177-181

links

about 19

creating 20

securing, through link directories 156

structure 13-15

links building

by commenting, on blogs 164

by commenting, on forums 164

through direct link requests 165

with article submission sites 159

with infographics 159

with mid-tier general directories 158

with niche directories 158

with regional directories 159

with super directories 156, 157

load speed

optimizing 13

local directory listings

categories, assigning 240

clicks, paying for 242

compelling business description, writing 242

fresh content, producing 243

ignoring 240

multiple entries, creating for multiple locations 242

optional fields, completing 241

pictures, uploading 241

reviews, obtaining 241

stray pages, leaving 243

local search

customers engagement 63

keyword list, honing 67

keyword list, tuning 67

local pages, building 65

long tail theory, applying 63, 64

people, following 65-67

Local Search Ranking Factors

about 279

URL 279

long tail keyword

Google Adwords Keyword Planner 52-55

keyword search volume, researching 51

search strategy, developing 51

user intent, examining 49, 50

versus short tail keyword 49

M

Majestic SEO

backlinks, monitoring 260, 261

URL 260

Thank you for buying
Wordpress Search Engine Optimization
Second Edition

About Packt Publishing

Packt, pronounced 'packed', published its first book, *Mastering phpMyAdmin for Effective MySQL Management*, in April 2004, and subsequently continued to specialize in publishing highly focused books on specific technologies and solutions.

Our books and publications share the experiences of your fellow IT professionals in adapting and customizing today's systems, applications, and frameworks. Our solution-based books give you the knowledge and power to customize the software and technologies you're using to get the job done. Packt books are more specific and less general than the IT books you have seen in the past. Our unique business model allows us to bring you more focused information, giving you more of what you need to know, and less of what you don't.

Packt is a modern yet unique publishing company that focuses on producing quality, cutting-edge books for communities of developers, administrators, and newbies alike. For more information, please visit our website at www.packtpub.com.

About Packt Open Source

In 2010, Packt launched two new brands, Packt Open Source and Packt Enterprise, in order to continue its focus on specialization. This book is part of the Packt Open Source brand, home to books published on software built around open source licenses, and offering information to anybody from advanced developers to budding web designers. The Open Source brand also runs Packt's Open Source Royalty Scheme, by which Packt gives a royalty to each open source project about whose software a book is sold.

Writing for Packt

We welcome all inquiries from people who are interested in authoring. Book proposals should be sent to author@packtpub.com. If your book idea is still at an early stage and you would like to discuss it first before writing a formal book proposal, then please contact us; one of our commissioning editors will get in touch with you.

We're not just looking for published authors; if you have strong technical skills but no writing experience, our experienced editors can help you develop a writing career, or simply get some additional reward for your expertise.

WordPress 3 Search Engine Optimization

ISBN: 978-1-84719-900-3   Paperback: 344 pages

Optimize your website for popularity with search engines

1. Discover everything you need to get your WordPress site to the top of the search engines.

2. Learn everything from keyword research and link building to customer conversions in this complete guide.

3. Packed with real-word examples to help get your site get noticed by the likes of Google, Yahoo, and Bing.

WordPress 3 Complete

ISBN: 978-1-84951-410-1   Paperback: 344 pages

Create your own complete website or blog from scratch with WordPress

1. Learn everything you need for creating your own feature-rich website or blog from scratch.

2. Clear and practical explanations of all aspects of WordPress.

3. In-depth coverage of installation, themes, plugins, and syndication.

4. Explore WordPress as a fully functional content management system.

Please check **www.PacktPub.com** for information on our titles

Made in the USA
Monee, IL
23 April 2020

27484187R00175